Leave Nothing on The Back Burner: My Happy Cooking Life

Leave Nothing on The Back Burner:
My Happy Cooking Life

Barbara Michelson

Opal Press
P.O. Box 1277
Cutchogue, NY 11935

ISBN 0-9754217-0-0

Library of Congress Control Number: 2004094282

Printed in the United States of America.

First Edition.

Dedication

This is my last will and cookbookament. It covers everything I would want everyone to know if I were suddenly struck by a bus and killed, including stories of many of the friends and family members who have nurtured my love of food—both preparing it and consuming it. Of course there are a few other people I have also loved. But since in their lifetimes they weren't able to produce one interesting, amusing or delicious dish, I'm sorry, they'll have to be in someone else's memoirs.

I dedicate this book to my grandchildren, as yet unborn and mostly undreamed of except by me. And to whichever of my daughters actually organizes a grandchild for me, I leave my thanks and all my money.

The Author

Contents

Growing Up on Pepperidge Farm

The Family

G.G.'s House

*T*he thing you need to know about my mother, G.G., is that she can do absolutely everything except sing, drive and withdraw money from a bank. And cook! So in life I have chosen to excel in all these categories, except that the singing thing did not work out.

At home we always had help to handle the cooking, and my mother finessed the weekends with restaurants, Sunday dinner at my grandparents' house, and her two specialties.

My father is a remarkably liberated man. He not only imagined that his wife and two daughters could reach the highest heights, but he expected us to. And G.G. did.

When my mother worked every other Saturday morning, he was in charge of us. And he did not park us in front of that great new invention, television, no. We did scintillating and educational things like go to the Museum of Natural History to compare my sister, Martha's, rock collection with specimens in the cases. On really grand outings—a treat we saved for my mother's at home Saturdays—we actually went out and collected rocks in state parks. Always the bright sider, I cheered myself with the thought "at least it's not raining so they're not doing Martha's stamp collection!" For me at least on Saturday afternoons there were tickling sessions and having my foot rubbed while watching baseball and then snoozing through golf on TV, compensations I considered completely satisfactory.

Anyway Horace was much too busy with us to cook, and his one product was not suitable for children or galley kitchens, so . . . weekends meant G.G.'s scrambled eggs and spaghetti with Del Monte sauce.

Being a two trick pony has its benefits. GG's scrambled eggs are the gold standard.

Scrambled Eggs
serves four

8 large eggs, thoroughly beaten with a wire whisk
1 T. butter

Heat butter in medium size non-stick skillet over medium heat. When butter melts, add eggs and stir often but not continuously with a wooden spoon. When eggs just lose their wet look, turn off heat and stir a second longer before serving immediately.

For a faithful historical recreation, it's important to use Mueller's spaghetti because other more realistic brands will not cook to a satisfactory gummy consistency in ten minutes or perhaps ever. Hard to believe, epicures, but I used to think this was manna, and when I got older and was sick or blue, this is what I craved. My parents and I have now reached the tacit understanding that the spiritual content of this experience has been transferred to De Cecco spaghetti cooked al dente and topped with a bit of homemade marinara sauce.

Mueller's Spaghetti with Del Monte Tomato Sauce
serves four

1 lb. Mueller's spaghetti
1 t. butter
1 small can Del Monte tomato sauce

Bring a large saucepan of water to boil with a dash of salt. Add spaghetti, broken into 3″ lengths. Stir right after adding and occasionally for the first few minutes. Cook ten minutes. Drain in colander. Return to pan. Over low heat, add butter and stir to coat spaghetti. Add sauce and cook until sauce bubbles, stirring once or twice.

People who didn't know me back when think that the signature snack at my parents' was chocolate chip cookies, but the original snack was carrot and celery sticks, a substantial vat of them on hand in the frig at all times.

The important detail here is the ratio of carrots to celery, few enough celery sticks that you actually did want one every ten or so pieces of carrot. And because you barely ate any celery you wanted those few bites to be stringy, so no peeling the celery. Lastly, while it isn't healthy to park those nutritious veggies in water since all the vitamins eventually climb into the water, it sure makes them taste sweet.

Carrots and Celery Sticks
snacks for a day or two

8 medium carrots, peeled and cut into 3″ sticks
1 large celery stalk, well washed and cut into 3″ sticks, leafy
  top included

Put cut vegetables in a large container of cold water. Chill in refrigerator until eaten.

Miss Brumm took care of Martha and me from when I was three until I was about seventeen. When we were teenagers she made these cookies practically daily. They were enormously popular with our friends. That and the fact that our bedroom was down a long hallway and seemed greatly removed from the adults (by NYC apartment standards) made hanging out at our apartment a great draw. Some time we'll discuss what we did back there.

Miss Brumm stayed with us until she was quite old. Lossie, who originally came to help with the heavy housework and the ironing (freshly washed and ironed sheets every Friday night!) eventually took on more and more of the responsibilities. Soon the chocolate chip cookie torch was passed on to Lossie, and when emotional transference was also complete, Miss Brumm retired to Mansfield, Ohio.

For the last decade and a half, Cheryl has been making the cookies. Perhaps when she completes her second decade, I'll be willing to call them Cheryl's chocolate chip cookies as my mother does. I personally cannot make them because I can't seem to bring myself to use margarine, which single ingrediently accounts for the desired crispness. The other secret is to bake these frequently to develop "the touch". That's actually the key to perfect pies, cakes, bread and every other baked product as well.

Something else you need to know about my mother is that while she will give you the cashmere coat off her back, she is not going to forgive you if you don't return the cookie tin. And everyone always wants some of these cookies "to go."

Lossie's Chocolate Chip Cookies
never makes enough

two 6 oz. packages Nestle's chocolate chips
ingredients as listed on wrapper for making "Toll House"
  cookies

Use margarine and have it at room temperature.

Follow all directions on package except double the chips. Make constantly.

Lossie's fried chicken is the best. Lossie's mother was born and raised in North Carolina and she let Lossie see how she did things as long as she didn't get under foot. Luckily Lossie always let me get in the way when she made this and everything else.

Lossie's Fried Chicken
serves six

2 small frying chickens, ideally 2½ lbs. each, cut in quarters
salt
flour
good grinding black pepper
Mazola corn oil

Soak chicken in heavily salted water for an hour or two. Drain and pat dry.

Dredge in flour. Season with salt and pepper.

Pour a ½″ deep layer of oil in a cast iron pan and heat until hot enough that a drop of water flicked into the oil sizzles immediately. Add as much chicken as fits comfortably in the pan, leaving plenty of room between pieces. Since the cold chicken cools the oil, raise the heat as you add it and turn it down when things get moving. Cook at a medium sizzle until dark golden brown, flip and cook the other side. Each side will take twelve minutes or so. Drain on paper towels. Finish cooking remaining pieces of chicken.

This is how I make fried chicken with a bit of Cajun spice.

Cajun Fried Chicken
serves six

2 small frying chickens, ideally 2½ lbs. each
milk to cover
2 c. flour
½ t. salt
¼ t. cayenne pepper
¼ t. white pepper
¼ t. freshly ground black pepper
¼ t. paprika
vegetable oil

Cut each chicken into ten small pieces. Put in a shallow container and cover with milk. Cover with plastic wrap and refrigerate for several hours. Put flour, salt, cayenne, white and black pepper and paprika in a paper bag and shake to mix well.

About a half hour before serving time, pour oil into a heavy skillet, preferably cast iron, to a depth of ½″. Heat until hot enough that a drop of water flicked into the oil sizzles immediately. While oil heats, take half the chicken pieces from the milk and put in the paper bag containing flour and spices. Shake bag to coat chicken with flour. Put chicken into hot oil with pieces close together but not touching. Flour and add more pieces of chicken if there is room now or later on as chicken cooks. Adjust heat to maintain sizzle. When chicken is light golden brown, use tongs to turn. Cook until golden brown on other side and turn again and cook until piece is deep brown in color. Turn again and brown other side. In total, each piece gets cooked twice on each side. Remove to plate covered with several thicknesses of paper towel. Finish cooking remaining pieces of chicken.

No one seems to remember exactly how we first were introduced to Olga Weissberg, a wonderfully talented Austrian who cooked the food for my Aunt Betty's holiday parties (using Aunt Betty's recipes, of course) and did occasional dinner parties for my mother. She was a stocky, white haired lady in her sixties and certainly no bigger that 4' 10." She learned everything there is to know about baking by attending Houtman's Pastry School on West Twenty-Seventh Street. When she retired she honored me, although I didn't know her that well, by passing along the complete lesson plans and recipes from this school as well as her own very small collection of personal recipes.

I'll always think of Olga who died several years ago, trundling home on the subway late at night after a successful party, her collection of cooking knives under her arm.

Olga made the best hors d'oeuvres, especially including phyllo triangles stuffed with mushrooms. I doubt she used a recipe, but I have created one for her. While on the subject, I include my recipe for spinach phyllos, also delicious. Olga always rolled isoceles triangles; mine are equilateral! Oh well.

Olga's Mushroom Phyllos
makes four dozen pieces

2 lb. well washed mushrooms, trimmed if necessary
1 stick butter
¼ c. minced shallot
¼ c. Marsala wine
salt
good grinding black pepper
freshly grated nutmeg
2 egg yolks

In large skillet melt half the butter over medium high heat. Chop half the mushrooms into very small pieces, but do not puree. Use the food processor only if you are very careful not to over chop and work in small batches. Add mushrooms to pan and cook until they release liquid. Add half of shallots. Cook stirring often until liquid evaporates and mushrooms begin to brown. Add half of Marsala. Cook until mushrooms are dry. Scrape contents into bowl and repeat with remaining butter, mushrooms, shallots and Marsala. Season mixture with salt, pepper and nutmeg. Cool and mix in egg yolks. Make phyllo triangles:

Assembling and Baking Phyllo Triangles
makes about eight dozen phyllo triangles

1 package phyllo leaves, thawed according to package
   directions
12 T. butter, melted
7 c. filling

Take the dough out of refrigerator an hour before assembling.
Work without stopping so that dough does not dry out. Take
a piece of dough and lay it on top of a cutting board with the
longer side running from left to right. Use a pastry brush to
spread a light layer of butter over phyllo dough. Lay a second
piece of dough on top and spread with a light layer of butter.
Use a sharp paring knife to cut dough vertically into seven
equal strips.

Put a tablespoon of filling at the bottom of each of the strips.
Begin to enfold filling in dough and continue to roll in dough
to form triangles. Fold ends of dough underneath so each
piece will have a smooth top. Put on baking sheet. Repeat
process until filling is used up. Brush tops of triangles with
butter. Cover tray with plastic wrap and freeze. Phyllos bake
best when put frozen into hot oven.

At baking time, preheat oven to 400 degrees. Unwrap frozen
phyllos and bake until puffed and golden, about forty minutes. Cool slightly before serving.

This hors d'oeuvres is one of my daughters' favorites. They can eat a dozen pieces each.

Spinach and Feta Phyllos
makes eight dozen pieces

2 lb. spinach leaves, washed and drained
6 T. butter
1½ c. finely chopped onion
½ t. salt
good grinding black pepper
2 eggs and 1 yolk, lightly beaten
12 oz. grated Feta cheese

Put spinach in large skillet, cover, and cook over low heat until wilted. Drain and refresh under cold running water. Squeeze dry and chop fine.

Put butter and onion in same large skillet and cook over medium heat until onion is golden brown. Add spinach and cook, stirring for about one minute to evaporate any liquid. Season with salt and pepper. Let cool. Add eggs, yolk, and feta and mix in well. Make phyllo triangles as described.

When Jim & I married, we certainly didn't want a wedding extravaganza, but we were more than willing to celebrate with Olga's chocolate mousse cake for dessert.

Olga's Chocolate Mousse Cake
serves twelve

2 dozen ladyfingers, bakery bought or homemade
½ c. water
¼ c. sugar
3 T. Kalua or Amaretto liqueur
12 oz. semi-sweet chocolate chips or semi-sweet chocolate,
   chopped in small pieces
1 oz. unsweetened chocolate, chopped in small pieces
1 t. instant espresso
2¼ c. heavy cream
6 eggs, separated
¾ c. sifted confectioner's sugar
pinch salt
¼ c. praline powder (following recipe)

Heat water and sugar to dissolve sugar. Cool. Add 1 T. liqueur. Dip ladyfingers to moisten on both sides with this syrup. Place upright ladyfingers around sides of 9″ spring form pan.

Make mousse:

Bring 1¼ c. of the cream to boil and add chocolate. Whisk together until chocolate is melted and smooth. Add egg yolks, remaining 2 T. liqueur and ½ c. confectioner's sugar. Beat until smooth. Set aside to cool.

When chocolate mixture is cool, beat egg whites with salt until they thicken. Add remaining ¼ c. confectioner's sugar and beat until stiff peaks form. Scoop a dollop of white into chocolate and beat in well. Pour chocolate mixture over remaining whites and fold gently with a rubber spatula.

(continued) ☞

Fill spring form pan with mousse. Refrigerate for several hours or overnight.

At serving time whip remaining 1 c. of cream until stiff. Put in a pastry bag. Trim ladyfingers so they rise ½″ above mousse. Use trimmings to cover top of cake. Remove rim from cake. Use pastry bag to cover top of cake with whipped cream. Sprinkle praline powder on top.

Praline Powder
makes three cups

1 c. sugar
3 c. slivered almonds

Preheat oven to 400 degrees.

Put sugar and 2 T. water in small heavy bottomed saucepan. Stir well over medium heat. Use a pastry brush dipped in water to wash down bits of sugar clinging to pan walls. When mixture boils, stop stirring. Cook until light brown. Turn off heat and stir in almonds. Pour praline out onto lightly greased baking sheet. Paying careful attention, bake until nuts are light golden brown, about ten minutes. Cool. Pulverize praline with rolling pin. Do not use a food processor because it will make powder too fine.

Extra praline can be stored in the freezer for several months.

On our birthdays, Martha and I had the special privilege of choosing the dinner menu. Martha wasn't much of an eater and used the occasion for an extra session of lamb chops (a dish we already ate faithfully once a week). I, on the other hand, had no problem filling up several courses with my favorites, all laden with cholesterol, a poison which fortunately hadn't yet been discovered. We had artichokes with drawn butter to start, roast prime rib of beef, corn pudding and some other vegetable I most likely doused with butter. When I got older, barley pilaf supplanted corn pudding, a slight health upgrade.

Since my birthday falls in late October, my birthday corn puddings were made with canned creamed corn. The corn pudding of my dreams, however, is this one taken from the cookbook of G.G.'s friend Gene Hovis, an outstanding cook and delightful person.

Corn Pudding (adapted from *Uptown Down Home Cooking*)
serves eight

1 T. melted butter
1 dozen ears of corn, husked
6 eggs
1½ c. heavy cream
½ c. milk
½ t. salt
¼ t. white pepper
good grating nutmeg

Butter a 10″ round baking dish or equivalent oval or square dish with sides at least 2″ high.

Preheat oven to 375 degrees.

Cut kernels off cobs and then use back of knife to scrape any remaining "milk" from cobs onto cut kernels.

Put half of kernels in a large food processor with eggs, cream, milk, salt, pepper and nutmeg. Puree until more or less smooth. Fold in remaining kernels. Put mixture in baking dish. Bake on middle rack of oven until puffed, set when tested by lightly shaking pan, and lightly browned. Serve right away.

Miss Brumm's Barley Pilaf

serves six

4 T. butter
10 oz. well washed mushrooms, trimmed if necessary, and
   sliced
¾ c. coarsely chopped onion
1¾ c. pearled barley
4 c. chicken broth
salt

Heat butter in medium skillet over high heat. When butter sizzles, add mushrooms. Cook until golden brown. Remove mushrooms with slotted spoon. Add onions, lower heat and cook until limp. Add barley and cook a few minutes, stirring often to brown slightly. Add cooked mushrooms, chicken broth and salt. Simmer covered until tender, about forty-five minutes. Adjust seasoning.

My version, with beef broth and stronger flavors.

Mushroom and Barley Pilaf with Cepes
serves six

½ c. dried cepes, otherwise called porcini mushrooms
3 T. butter
½ c. minced onion
10 oz. well washed mushrooms, trimmed if necessary, and
    sliced
1½ c. pearled barley
3 c. beef broth
½ t. salt
1 t. chopped dill

Soak cepes in 1½ c. hot water for thirty minutes. Lift cepes from water, squeeze dry and chop fine. Set aside. Filter soaking liquid through coffee filter or paper towel lined strainer. Reserve.

Over low heat in a medium size skillet, saute onion in butter until soft, stirring often, about five minutes. Turn heat medium high and add mushrooms. Cook until mushrooms are golden brown. Lower heat. Add barley and cook a few minutes, stirring often. Add cepes, their soaking liquid, broth and salt. Simmer covered until tender, about forty-five minutes. Remove from heat. Add dill, mixing and fluffing barley with a fork.

Now good lamb chops would seem pretty exciting especially dressed up for special occasions with paper frills covering the ends of the bones.

Frills for Lamb Chops
makes four

Cut a piece of plain white paper into four strips 8½″ × 3″. Fold each strip in half lengthwise. Make 1″ cuts at ⅛″ intervals starting with folded side and stopping well short of cut side.

Fold in opposite direction, so paper poofs out. Roll around an index finger and secure end with a minute bit of tape. Repeat with remaining pieces of paper.

A favorite respite from my mother's Sunday night spaghetti was dinner at the restaurant down the street, Villa Marbona. The cooking never deviated in the slightest from one month to the next. With a cocktail pianist and a waiter who called me "occhi forte" meaning "bright eyes" and the best eggplant ever on the hot antipasto plate, there was nothing more I could ask for. Well, except the recipe for the eggplant which I've never been able to recreate.

I used to feel the same about the chicken cacciatore, my regular meal, until I tasted Marcella Hazan's version in The Classic Italian Cookbook. *Probably it's the celery which I would never have thought of using that makes it so perfectly reminiscent. The restaurant used a very small chicken which added much elegance in my view.*

Chicken Cacciatore

serves six

2 small frying chickens, ideally about 2½ lbs. each
flour
vegetable oil
salt
good grinding black pepper
1⅓ c. white wine
⅔ c. thinly sliced onion
2 green peppers, cut into fine julienne
2 carrots, peeled and cut into fine julienne
1 stalk celery, cut in fine julienne
2 t. minced garlic
1⅓ c. canned tomato, coarsely chopped

Cut chickens into six pieces each: two breasts with wings attached but last wing joint removed, two thighs, and two legs. Dredge chicken in flour.

Heat a thin layer of oil in a large skillet over medium high heat until hot but not smoking. Slip in chicken pieces and cook quickly until golden brown on both sides. Remove to a plate and season with salt and pepper. Discard most of the fat in pan, add wine and cook, stirring and scraping over high heat until wine is reduced by about half. Lower heat, add onion and cook, stirring from time to time, for five minutes. Add

(continued) ☞

green pepper, carrot, celery, garlic and tomato. Put chicken on top. Cover skillet and simmer for ten minutes. Turn chicken and cook ten minutes longer. Put chicken on serving platter. Reduce sauce if necessary to a creamy consistency. Adjust seasoning and pour over chicken.

We celebrated really special occasions with dinner at the Coach House in the Village. The Coach House epitomized the type of cooking I admire, just the absolute best renditions of mainly American classic dishes. If they served something, you couldn't get it better elsewhere.

Years ago I clipped a lengthy article from a food magazine with a write up and numerous recipes from the restaurant. Making the steak au poivre is arduous since making the broth and then the demi glace takes about sixteen hours from start to finish, but it's the world's best and absolutely worth the trouble. Since the actual meat and pan sauce cooks in less than fifteen minutes, you'll then have the makings of unlimited quick, fabulous meals.

Coach House Steak au Poivre
served two at the restaurant but should feed four at home

two 18 oz. prime strip steaks
¼ c. peppercorns
salt
½ c. cognac
¾ c. red wine
½ c. demi glace (following recipe)

Preheat oven to 450 degrees.

Trim all but a ¼″ edge of fat from steaks. Put trimmed fat in a small heavy bottomed skillet with 1 T. water. Cook over medium low heat to melt. Discard any bits that don't liquefy.

Meanwhile, take a heavy pan and crush peppercorns coarsely. Press into steaks on both sides. Sprinkle generously with salt.

Heat rendered fat until very hot over medium high heat. Sear steaks until well browned, about a minute per side. Put meat on a baking sheet and put in oven to finish cooking, about eight minutes or so. Ideally, test for doneness by pressing steaks with finger. The more steaks resist, the more done they are. If you can't tell by touch, cut into a steak to take a look. (Cutting makes the steak lose some of the juice.)

Discard fat in skillet. Lower heat to medium. Add cognac and tip pan to ignite it in flames, or if you are working on an elec-

(continued) ☞

tric stove, light cognac with a match. Shake skillet for thirty seconds, add wine and demi glace. Cook, shaking from time to time, to reduce sauce slightly. Adjust seasoning.

Slice steaks. Pour sauce on top.

Demi Glace
makes several cups

5 lb. veal bones, sawed into 2″ or so pieces by the butcher
2 lb. chicken necks and backs
3 carrots, peeled and cut in 1″ pieces
2 large onions, unpeeled and cut in quarters
2 leek whites, well washed and cut in 1″ pieces
2 celery stalks, well washed and cut in 1″ pieces
3 unpeeled garlic cloves
2 bay leaves
2 t. salt
1 t. black peppercorns
a handful of parsley sprigs
two sprigs of fresh thyme
¾ c. flour
1 recipe beef broth (following recipe)
3 c. red wine
2 c. tomato puree

Preheat oven as hot as it gets. Combine veal and chicken bones, carrot, onion, leek, celery, garlic, bay leaves, salt, peppercorns, parsley and thyme in large roasting pan. Roast, stirring from time to time until very well browned, about an hour. Sprinkle flour over pan and mix in well. Roast fifteen minutes longer.

Put contents of pan in large soup pot. Add broth, wine and tomato puree to pot. Put two cups of water in roasting pan. Return pan to oven for ten minutes. Remove and stir and scrape up any browned bits clinging to pan. Add liquid to

(continued) ☞

soup pot. Simmer contents of soup pot uncovered, skimming frequently, for four hours. Strain. Cool, refrigerate until cold, and remove and discard fat.

Use as needed and freeze the rest in small containers or ice cube trays.

Beef Broth
makes ten cups

4 lb. beef bones, sawed into pieces by the butcher
4 lb. ham shank, sawed into pieces by the butcher
1 lb. meaty beef shinbone
1 t. black peppercorns
¼ t. celery seed
4 cloves

Put ingredients in soup pot with 18 c. cold water. Bring to boil. Reduce heat, simmer partially covered for eight hours, skimming off foam from time to time. Strain. Let cool before refrigerating.

After refrigerating, remove and discard layer of fat on top or reserve for another use.

The Coach House black bean soup was also remarkable—deep, winy and delicious.

Black Bean Soup
serves eight

1 lb. black beans
2 T. beef fat (reserved from beef broth)
1 c. finely chopped onion
½ c. finely chopped celery
1 t. minced garlic
7 c. beef broth (preceding recipe)
¼ c. sherry
salt
good grinding black pepper
2 lemons thinly sliced
2 T. minced parsley

Rinse and pick over beans, making sure there are no stones mixed in. Put in large bowl and add water to cover amply. Soak overnight. Drain.

In soup pot, cook beef fat, onion and celery over low heat for several minutes, stirring often. Add garlic and stir for a minute. Add broth and beans. Simmer until beans are extremely tender, about two hours, stirring occasionally. Add water if necessary to keep beans covered.

Cool slightly, then pass through food mill fitted with coarse screen. Add water if soup is too thick. Add salt and pepper to taste. Heat soup until piping hot. Add sherry.

Top each portion with lemon slices and sprinkling of parsley.

Horace's Family

*W*hen I was really little, my father's father was quite senile. Once he possessed a fearsome intellect and expected remarkable accomplishments from his four children. Family legend—Lee's—has it that when my Aunt Lee and Uncle Henry both made Phi Beta Kappa in the same year, she as a college senior and he as a junior, instead of offering congratulations, my grandfather inquired why Lee hadn't made it as a junior. (My father has a completely different recollection of the facts.) By his late eighties and early nineties Grandpa was the most gentle man, still beautiful to look at, with gorgeous hands and a legendary sweet tooth. He was my favorite, but when he died, I transferred my idolatry to my grandmother.

My grandmother, ten years younger than he but never a young grandmother for my purpose, was extremely undemonstrative. You could kiss her coming and going, but she was no cheek pincher or hugger. Her idea of a birthday gift for a grandchild of any age was a savings bond. If you stayed over at her house, however, she had plenty of time and energy to take you to the playground or bombard you with pillows at bedtime.

In old age, she was a great stoic, never complaining about aches and pains or the mounting losses as husband, sisters and friends all died before her. She had a gift for making new friends up until she died at age ninety-nine. Although I don't usually entertain beliefs of this sort, I am convinced she has been reincarnated as our horse Likely, the world's calmest and most stoical animal, with his steel grey coat, large ears, and friendly and curious nature.

Before her eyesight deteriorated, Grandma was an avid reader. She devoured a stack of library books on a weekly basis and regarded most things that interfered with her reading as a disturbance. Her kitchen motto was "whoever invented cooking should burn in hell" said with a strong Polish accent. Nonetheless when my family and various cousins visited practically every Sunday, she'd produce chopped liver, brisket, salad, various vegetables determined by the personal preferences of those on the guest list, two kinds of apple pie because Horace liked raisins and Martha didn't . . . . etc. Her cooking was remarkably consistent, since having arrived at versions that suited us, she had no artistic inclination to stray. She never measured anything, but these are her recipes regardless.

My grandmother and probably everyone else's always used a large circular bowl and half moon chopper or "lunette" for big time chopping projects like chopped liver. The only acceptable cracker to serve with her chopped liver is "Saltines," and if you drink a glass of tomato juice as well, you will be in quite a blissful situation.

Chopped Liver
makes three cups

½ lb. chicken livers
1 c. finely chopped onion
¼ c. rendered chicken fat
2 hard boiled eggs
¼ t. salt
good grinding black pepper

Use a paring knife to trim away any discolored bits and connective tissue from chicken livers. Discard trimmings. In medium skillet over low heat, cook onion in fat, stirring often until onion is golden brown. Remove onion with slotted spoon and reserve.

Raise heat to medium high. Cook livers in fat remaining in pan about two minutes on each side until nicely browned.

Remove from fat with slotted spoon, season well with salt and pepper and put on large cutting board with onions and eggs.

Chop with a large knife until finely chopped, well mixed and fluffy. Adjust seasoning.

Grandma made the filling ahead of time so it was always that unappealing blue grey color, but that never stopped anyone from eating plenty.

Celery Stuffed with Blue Cheese
serves six

10 pieces heart of celery
½ lb. blue cheese
3 T. soft butter
2 T. sour cream

Scrub, trim and peel celery. Cut into 2″ lengths. Mix blue cheese, butter and sour cream. Spoon (or pipe with a pastry bag) into celery.

My mother's favorite.

Stuffed Cabbage
serves six

1 large head of cabbage
1 small onion, finely chopped and 4 additional onions,
  peeled and quartered
1 t. rendered chicken fat
1½ lb. ground beef round
¾ c. cooked rice
salt
good grinding black pepper
1 heaping t. citric acid (sour salt)
¼ c. brown sugar
one 28 oz. can whole tomatoes

Bring a large pot of water to boil. Core cabbage as deeply as possible without cutting up leaves. Put cabbage in boiling water and boil for five minutes. Turn off heat, let stand until cabbage wilts, then drain.

In small saute pan over low heat, saute onion in chicken fat until soft. Cool.

Fluff beef with a fork and add onions, rice, salt and pepper. Start with the largest cabbage leaf and put 2 heaping tablespoons of beef mixture at the base. Fold in sides of cabbage to enclose snugly, then roll into a little packet. Set aside seam side down while you continue to stuff cabbage.

When meat is used up, chop remaining cabbage into 1" pieces and set at bottom of Dutch oven. Lay onion quarters on top. Then arrange cabbage rolls still seam sides down on top of onions.

Preheat oven to 350 degrees.

In small saucepan bring ¼ c. water to boil. Add citric acid and brown sugar and stir until dissolved.

(continued) ☞

Coarsely chop tomatoes. Mix tomato with citric acid mixture. Add salt and pepper. Pour over cabbage.

Cover tightly and bake for two hours.

When I got my driver's license I used to go visit my grandmother by myself. For lunch we'd share a huge bowl of salad with her vinegary dressing. The salad was completely to my liking with crisp lettuce like romaine and a bit of iceberg, lots of radishes and cucumbers. She made her dressing in a Good Seasons cruet but she never used that product as far as I know, just lots of apple cider vinegar, a bit of vegetable oil, salt, pepper, a dash of sugar and perhaps a pinch of oregano. When it was just the two of us she indulged our taste for salads so tart anyone else would have found them inedible. (Well, except for my daughter, Sarah, who douses her salad with straight vinegar!) I also inherited Grandma's taste for limp left-over salad which my mother tells me is a Polish taste.

You couldn't visit without getting homemade apple pie, no matter how little notice you provided. Vegetable shortening gives the flaky texture that we all liked.

Apple Pie with and without Raisins
makes one ten inch pie

2 c. plus 1 T. flour
¾ t. salt
½ c. vegetable shortening
8 large tart apples
¼ c. sugar
2 T. yellow raisins, optional
1 T. flour
¼ t. cinnamon

In food processor fitted with metal blade, or by hand in a bowl, combine 2 c. flour and salt. Cut in vegetable shortening thoroughly until mixture is the consistency of cornmeal. Add ½ c. cold water mixing as little as possible to incorporate. Form dough into two balls, one about a third larger than the other. Flatten balls, wrap in plastic wrap and refrigerate while you prepare apples.

Peel, core and slice apples into thin pieces. Combine with sugar, raisins if using, remaining 1 T. flour and cinnamon and mix well.

(continued) ☞

Preheat oven to 375 degrees.

Roll dough into a 14″ and a 10″ circle. Put larger circle into 10″ pie pan. Put apple mixture inside. Moisten edge of dough with water. Put remaining circle on top and press edges together. Trim away excess dough and discard. Crimp edge by pressing outward with left index finger while pinching with right thumb and index finger. Cut a slit in center of pie with paring knife so steam can escape.

Bake until golden brown, about forty-five minutes.

My grandmother's oldest sister was Helena Rubenstein, who founded from scratch what turned out to be a huge cosmetics empire. When she died, I believe she was the world's richest self-made woman. Three of my grandmother's sisters who survived the Holocaust (there were originally eight girls in the family), were pillars of her business, running affairs in France, England and the United States. They were petite, dynamic and enormously glamorous women. I knew Manka who lived in New York best as I used to drive my grandmother to her apartment on upper Fifth Avenue to visit her. Even when she was ancient (in her 90's) she had the most stunning legs. I knew Ceska, my London aunt, rather well and Stella, my dad's favorite, very little.

Helena, "Hella" to family, invited the whole clan once a year to her Park Avenue triplex for a pre-Christmas party. She had her Christmas tree decorated by a bona fide fashion designer at least three decades before that was a common notion. The tree I remember was done all in pink with huge pink bows. Hella collected miniatures and had illuminated cases filling what seemed to be a vast area of her apartment's lowest level. These went to the museum in Tel Aviv when she died; God only knows what the museum did with them. For dinner her Chinese butler served egg drop soup as we sat at a long table that must have accommodated twelve to a side. Thankfully, I was only old enough to attend two of these functions before she died. The whole experience was a bit overwhelming.

In all my memories and photos these aunts are turned out in classic haute couture and rings with huge rubies or emeralds, depending on the color scheme. Manka used to pass along her outmoded Hermes pocketbooks to my grandmother who lived completely out of the fast lane in Bound Brook, New Jersey.

My grandfather, a Socialist intellectual, ran a hardware store when he could look up from his studies. Customers were a great inconvenience, and he was fortunate there weren't many of them. As much as my grandmother adored her sisters, she always seemed content in her very humble life.

Anyway, this sandwich is my father's idea of comfort food. I like to think it sums up the dichotomy of my grandmother trotting around Bound Brook with her probably empty "Grace Kelly" bag. A bit of Wonder bread from the corner store, the finest Belgian chocolate the sisters could bring from their travels. Serve with a side of puffed rice and milk for double the comfort. It's not clear who you'll be able to serve this to except Horace.

Chocolate Sandwich
serves one Horace

2 slices Wonder Bread
butter, at room temperature
very thin bar of top quality dark chocolate, preferably
    Suchard

Generously butter bread. Put chocolate between slices.

In World War II Horace served in the infantry in the South Pacific. He was an officer who received the purple heart, the bronze star, the silver star, and a sniper's bullet through the neck, but he returned to see more action. During these years he developed his love—I'm not speaking facetiously—of institutional food. If you are ever stuck with a can of Spam or Vienna sausages, he is the one person in a developed country you may be able to serve them to.

In the field he learned to prepare his only specialty.

Coffee Made in an Undershirt
serves a full company

several pounds of ground coffee
egg shells, optional

Boil a vat of water. Fill undershirt (preferably clean) with coffee. Tie in a knot. Put in boiling water with egg shells, if using. Let stand. Remove shirt, clean and save for another use.

Working around egg shells, serve coffee with powdered or condensed milk.

An intellectual like his father, Horace is notoriously impossible to please with a gift. But if you offer him crouton rounds for a special occasion, he will accept them graciously.

Crouton Rounds
about fifty pieces

1 loaf slightly stale French bread, preferably homemade
olive oil

Preheat oven to 350 degrees.

Use a serrated bread knife to slice bread into ⅓" rounds. Use pastry brush to spread a light coating of olive oil on one or two baking sheets. Lay bread rounds flat on sheet. Dab tops of bread with a light coating of olive oil.

Bake until golden brown, about twenty minutes, rotating pans during baking to ensure even browning.

This fruitcake was developed by Lorette Patzwald, a friend who worked in our business, Local Talent, and developed some of our favorite recipes before moving to California and on to better things. I've included it in the family section in homage to Aunt Lee, Horace's sister who dutifully baked fruitcakes every Christmas for all the family.

Dutifully may be the operating word. If memory serves, Lee inherited my grandmother's lack of enthusiasm for the kitchen and created a life filled with other endeavors she found more fulfilling.

Lee was one of the early career women—a government agricultural economist during the depression and a UN food specialist afterward—original resident and active volunteer in Reston, Virginia, a planned community outside DC, and adventurous world traveler.

Lee's fruitcake was on the maraschino cherry side of the spectrum, so I am attempting to graft her memory onto this preferred cake.

Fruitcake
makes six 7" tube cakes or eight 8" × 5" loaves

1 lb. dried apricots, in small dice
1 lb. pitted dates, in small dice
1 lb. yellow raisins
12 oz. dried cherries
3½ c. rum
2¼ c. flour
¼ c. cocoa
1 T. baking powder
1 T. salt
½ t. ground cloves
4 c. toasted hazelnuts, skins rubbed off
4 c. walnuts
2 c. pecans
1¼ c. unsweetened coconut
1¼ c. chopped candied orange rind
3 T. finely chopped candied ginger
2 T. grated lemon rind
12 eggs
1 c. sugar
1 c. packed brown sugar
1 c. orange juice

(continued) ☞

Soak apricots, dates, raisins and cherries in 1½ c. rum for several days.

Sift flour, cocoa, baking powder, salt, and cloves together.

Combine hazelnuts, walnuts, pecans, coconut, candied orange rind, candied ginger and lemon rind, mix well, and set aside.

Butter and flour six 7″ tube pans or eight 8″ × 5″ loaf pans.

Preheat oven to 300 degrees.

Beat eggs in a large bowl. Add sugar and brown sugar and beat for five minutes. Beat in orange juice.

Add soaked fruit and mix in well. Fold in flour mixture. Fold in nut mixture.

Divide batter in pans.

Bake for approximately one hour and 45 minutes until set and light brown.

Let cool in pans on cake racks for 15 minutes. Take out of pans.

Soak several dishcloths in remaining 2 c. rum. Wrap warm cakes in cloths. Put cakes in plastic bags. (Unscented garbage bags will work well.) Let macerate in refrigerator for at least two weeks, checking every few days to be sure dishcloths have not dried out. If necessary, sprinkle cloths with additional rum.

Lee's husband, Munie, was one of my father's favorite relatives, and we used to make the trip to the DC area from time to time to visit. Before they moved to Reston and long before malls Tyson 1 and Tyson 2, Tyson's Corner, Virginia was a rural spot where my aunt and uncle had an old farmhouse on seven acres of land. Mall shopping on the spot where Martha and I used to hide under the huge pine trees does not console me.

I don't think we ever went for Thanksgiving, but Lee would make a turkey and let me help with the pan gravy.

Roast Turkey with Pan Gravy
allow one pound of turkey per person which will cover you for leftovers

1 turkey
two onions
1 carrot
1 stalk celery
melted butter
2 T. flour
salt and white pepper to taste

Preheat oven to 325 degrees.

Chop the vegetables into 2″ pieces. Put in a metal roasting pan with the turkey neck and giblets but not the liver. (If you do this, you will never be among the thousands of people who mistakenly roast the bird with the giblet package inside!) Salt and pepper the bird inside and out. Stuff, truss, and brush it with melted butter.

Roast turkey until golden brown and cooked through, basting often with the pan juices. Allow 18 minutes per lb. for a bird that weighs less than 20 lbs. and about 15 minutes per lb. for a larger one. In the last 40 minutes, pour as much of the accumulated juice as possible into a heat proof cup, preferably the type with a low spout designed for separating fat. Let juice stand while turkey finishes.

When turkey is done, clear liquid will flow from the thigh joint when it's pierced with a fork. Turn off the oven. Remove

(continued) ☞

finished turkey to a shallow pan or heat proof serving platter and keep warm in the oven. (I realize this is easier said than done, so wear shoes.)

Add any additional juice to that which you have already set aside. Put the roasting pan on the stove over low heat to get all the bits clinging to the pan slightly browner and to render the fat. Add the flour and mix in well. Remove layer of fat from pan juices. If you don't have a separator, use a ladle. Discard the fat. Pour the defatted juices into the roasting pan slowly, stirring and scraping as you add. Simmer for several minutes. Strain. Season with salt and pepper. Remove stuffing from turkey, carve, and serve gravy in a gravy boat.

My Aunt Dusty was the wife of my father's brother, Henry, and mother of my older, much admired cousins, Janet and Bobby. She was a softie with a great love for stray dogs and mutts, good at growing things, a seemingly effortless entertainer and a great Italian cook. From her I learned that there was a world of pasta outside of Mueller's spaghetti when she made marinara sauce with me and turned it into pasta fazul.

Marinara Sauce
makes six cups

3 cans whole tomatoes
⅓ c. olive oil
1½ c. thinly sliced onions
¾ c. peeled carrots, thinly sliced
1 heaping T. minced garlic
1½ t. dried oregano
1½ t. dried basil
½ t. salt
good grinding black pepper

Pass tomatoes through the coarse blade of a food mill.

In shallow casserole, heat oil, onion and carrot over medium heat until onion begins to brown, stirring often. Add garlic and cook a minute or so longer, stirring.

Add tomatoes, bring to simmer and cook over medium low heat for fifteen minutes, stirring occasionally.

Pass sauce through fine blade of food mill. Add oregano, basil, salt and pepper. Return to pan and simmer over medium low heat for fifteen minutes longer, stirring occasionally.

Sauce can be frozen for several months.

Dusty's Pasta Fazul

serves six

½ c. dried chick peas
1 lb. linguine noodles
2 c. marinara sauce (preceding recipe)
2 T. shredded basil leaves
salt
good grinding black pepper
2 T. minced parsley
freshly grated Parmesan cheese

Soak chick peas in ample amount of water overnight. Drain, put in saucepan with ample water to cover. Bring to boil, lower heat, and simmer until very tender. Drain and reserve.

Bring a large pot of well salted water to boil. Add linguine and cook until al dente.

While linguine cooks, heat marinara. Fold in about two thirds of chick peas and heat.

Drain pasta, return to pot and mix with sauce, basil and salt and pepper to taste. Put in warm serving dish and garnish with remaining third of the chick peas and minced parley.

Serve grated cheese at the table.

Aunt Gertrude was the sibling closest in age to my father, a mere five years older. Although she was the underachiever in a family of achievers, my father thought she was the smartest of them all. My grandfather had his own opinion: when Gertrude didn't make Phi Beta Kappa as either a junior or senior, he inferred the expense of an education was being wasted and suggested removing her from college, but he didn't prevail.

Gertrude was the keeper of the family flame, and I wish I had asked for more stories while she was alive. She also kept the family food traditions going. Her daughter, Peggy, passed these recipes along.

Sweet and Sour Cabbage
serves eight

1 red cabbage
1 c. coarsely chopped onion
1 apple, cored and cut in ¼″ dice
¼ c. vegetable oil
1 t. sour salt
1½ t. salt
½ t. sugar
large pinch white pepper

Quarter and core cabbage and soak in cold water for about an hour. Drain and slice thin.

Put onion and apple in large pot with oil. Cook over medium low heat stirring often for about ten minutes. Add cabbage and cook, stirring from time to time, for fifteen minutes.

Dissolve sour salt in ⅓ c. water. Add to cabbage along with salt, sugar and white pepper. Stir well. Cover and cook for about thirty minutes, until cabbage is limp, stirring once or twice. Adjust seasoning.

Pre-peeled baby carrots weren't in the store during my grandmother's cooking day, but she would surely have approved a short cut that was delicious and got her back to her reading as quickly as possible.

Grandma's Carrots
serves eight

2 lb. baby carrots
1 t. soft butter
1 t. flour
½ t. sugar
¾ t. salt
pinch white pepper

Cook baby carrots until almost tender. Drain reserving a bit of the cooking liquid. Mash butter and flour together with a fork. Add a bit of reserved cooking liquid to flour mixture. Put carrots back in pan with flour mixture, sugar, salt and pepper. Cook over low heat for ten minutes, stirring often. Adjust seasoning.

Clan Fare

*M*y mother's father, Thomas Rosen, was one of seven siblings all of whom lived at one time in the upstate area of Jamestown, New York. Because G.G.'s mother Celia was diagnosed with tuberculosis months after my mother's birth, the extended clan was particularly important to G.G. Tom's parents took care of G.G. as a young child while her parents, sister Mildred and brother Joseph travelled the U.S. looking for a climate that might improve Celia's health. Aunt Betty was still living with her parents then, and she and G.G. formed close ties which they maintained throughout Betty's lifetime by means of the nightly phone call.

At age three G.G joined her family in their travels, living various places in the southwest and for a short time with her siblings in an orphanage, a place G.G. actually remembers rather brightly. Celia died when G.G. was eleven and the family settled back upstate.

My mother has never outgrown her fondness for her extended family, and feelings are strong even where the relationship is something like third cousin-ship at best. This makes family gatherings somewhat over-sized for the Manhattan apartments where they're usually held. If you take things as seriously as G.G. does, then you may never go a month without attending a wedding, bar mitzvah or funeral. Most of my generation is not as zealous. Still when we do gather, we adhere faithfully to tradition, making all the old dishes though generally dividing up the duties that any one of the old matriarchs would have managed by herself.

Six Ways of Looking at a Beef Brisket

With acknowledgement of Wallace Steven's "Thirteen Ways of Looking at a Blackbird," a poem I learned from my friend Matthew, I present everyone's brisket submission. For in canvassing my relatives I have determined that while I may speak evil of the dead, under no circumstances can I omit anyone's recipe for brisket.

The parents of my Aunt Sadie (sister of my grandfather, Tom) and Uncle Morrie met while taking the waters in upstate New York and came up with the idea of uniting the families. By the time Betty and Julius, the respective younger siblings of the newlyweds, met, fell in love and wanted to marry after dating for three years, the families were no longer so enamored, so Betty and Julie eloped. That made all my Lipsett cousins into double cousins and explains why I only have to attend family occasions half as often!

When they set up housekeeping, neither Sadie nor Betty's kitchen practices were sufficiently orthodox for their mother, so she did not help them when they learned to cook. Instead they relied on less observant friends, Mrs. Aronson and Mrs. Israel.

Sadie became famous for her brisket both because it was good and because it was the thing you were going to be served if you were invited for dinner. This is her recipe according to her daughter, Marcia (Lipsett) Warner.

Sadie's Brisket According to Marcia
serves twelve

5 lb. first cut beef brisket
crushed whole garlic
crushed fresh ginger
4 carrots, peeled and cut into 1″ pieces
4 thinly sliced onions
lots of pickling spice
salt

The night before cooking, rub brisket with garlic and ginger and return to refrigerator.

Next day, preheat oven to 450 degrees. Put brisket in Dutch oven and bake uncovered until nicely browned. Remove and lower oven temperature to 325 degrees.

Add carrots to brisket. Smother it with onions and season with pickling spice and salt. Cover and bake until tender,

(continued) ☞

basting every twenty minutes, for a total of about two and a half hours. Test for tenderness by piercing with a cake tester. If it slides in without resistance, meat is done.

Cool. Remove meat and carrots, and put in refrigerator overnight. Pass gravy through food mill fitted with fine screen to remove pickling spices while blending in onions. Refrigerate gravy overnight in separate container.

At serving time, scrape fat off top of gravy and discard. Slice meat. Heat meat, carrots and gravy together until piping hot.

When Judy Lipsett, wife of Sadie's son Allen Lipsett, gave me Sadie's recipe, it was something else altogether.

Sadie's Brisket West Coast Style
serves twelve

5 lb. first cut beef brisket
1 heaping T. minced garlic
1 t. paprika
good grinding black pepper
2 bay leaves, broken into several large pieces
pinch red pepper flakes
10 cloves
6 thinly sliced onions
4 carrots, peeled and cut in ½″ pieces
1 stalk celery, cut in ½″ pieces
salt

Combine garlic, paprika, pepper, bay leaves, and pepper flakes and rub into meat on both sides. Pierce meat with five cloves per side, evenly spaced. Cover and refrigerate overnight.

A few hours before cooking, bring meat to room temperature. Remove bay leaves and reserve.

Preheat oven to 350 degrees.

Over medium heat in Dutch oven, brown meat on both sides. Add onions, carrots, celery, reserved bay leaves, salt and 1 c. hot water to meat. Cover, bring to simmer, put in oven and bake until tender, about two and a half hours, turning meat halfway through. Test for tenderness by piercing with a cake tester. If it slides in without resistance, meat is done.

Cool. Remove meat and carrots, and refrigerate overnight. Strain gravy and refrigerate.

Next day, scrape off fat on top of gravy and discard. Slice meat, discarding cloves. Heat meat, carrots and gravy together until piping hot.

Although Aunt Betty didn't ever keep kosher, she knew the best meat came from the kosher butcher. When she lived in Jamestown the closest such butcher was in Erie, Pennsylvania. Once a week he'd pull up on his motorcycle with a sidecar filled with the meat delivery. Later when Betty and Julie moved to NYC the meat had to come from the kosher butcher in Riverdale. Betty always sent a weekly package to Audrey. At 6:00 A.M. the call would come on the house phone "Meat delivery for Dr. Goldberg." The butcher persisted in believing that Betty's daughter would never be married to anyone less than a doctor, although actually Ralph was a mere lawyer!

Kosher meat was the best, but when Sadie's children, Marcia and Allen, were small the notion was that bacon was "good for the children". Not one to deprive her children of anything beneficial, but with a kosher-style home to consider, Sadie resolved her dilemma by sending them over to Betty's house for a few rashers. Betty's brisket, however, plays by the rules.

Betty's (and now Audrey's) Brisket
serves twelve

5 lb. first cut beef brisket
salt
good grinding black pepper
paprika
4 medium onions, thinly sliced
¼ c. water
5 medium carrots

Rinse brisket with cold water and pat dry. Mix salt, pepper and paprika and rub on the brisket.

Brown the meat quickly on each side in the pot you'll be roasting in. There's no need to use any oil. Remove the meat. Lower heat and add onions. Cook until soft. Put meat in pot and arrange onions on top of meat. Add ¼ c. water. Cook slowly, tightly covered on top of stove. As meat begins to cook, prepare carrots by peeling and cutting into 2″ chunks. Add carrots to meat. Cook for several hours until meat is tender, turning meat and scraping pan bottom several times. Test for tenderness by piercing with a cake tester. If it slides in without resistance, meat is done.

Make a day ahead to develop flavors. Fat will congeal. Spoon it off and discard it.

Betty's daughter-in-law, Susan, agrees the most important factor is the quality of the meat but without regard to its religious status. She requires an untrimmed brisket covered in fat from a good butcher. According to her, if you make the brisket a day ahead so you can skim all the fat from the gravy, and trim the fat from the meat as well, the end product won't be a bit fattier than if you used lean meat, but it will be much more succulent.

Also Aunt Sadie told Susan Lipsett thirty-seven years ago that the secret to good gravy is adding boiling water (not regular tap) to the pot when everything's set to go, a tip you'll notice that does not appear in Marcia's or Judy's Aunt Sadie's briskets. I asked Susan why this would be, but it didn't seem like the sort of thing she could ask. So now "just do it!"

Susan's (and mother, Hilda Sind's) Brisket
serves twelve

5 lb. first cut beef brisket, with all the fat left on
minced garlic
paprika
salt
good grinding black pepper
3–4 large yellow onions, thinly sliced
8 carrots, peeled and cut in 1″ hunks
1 lb. small new potatoes, well scrubbed
¼ c. ketchup
1 t. Worchestershire sauce
1 c. canned tomatoes, chopped
½ c. sun dried tomatoes, cut in quarters
½ c. dried cherries or dried cranberries
1 bay leaf

Rub garlic, paprika, salt and pepper into brisket. Sear meat on both sides under broiler or in frying pan.

Cover bottom of large Dutch oven with sliced onions and carrots. Put brisket on top. Surround with potatoes, and add boiling water to just cover potatoes. Top brisket with all other ingredients.

(continued) ☞

Cover pot and bake at 325 degrees until tender, about three or four hours. Test for tenderness by piercing with a cake tester. If it slides in without resistance, meat is done.

Remove from oven, take off lid and cool. Wrap brisket and refrigerate. Put gravy in separate container.

When ready to serve, cut all fat from brisket and slice. Skim fat from gravy and bring to boil.

Put sliced meat in Dutch oven and pour hot gravy on top. Cover pot. Heat in 350 degree oven for forty-five minutes.

This is one (from my husband's side) I refuse to try, so the recipe enters this book untested. My children and Jim tell me it's great, but I feel the need for a few principles in this life, and not cooking with Coca Cola is one of them. In the same vein, I've never forbidden my children to visit McDonald's, but I certainly haven't taken them there either.

I changed this recipe a bit to make it more presentable. If I did venture to try it, I'd get asked lots of questions in the grocery store when caught buying "dry spaghetti sauce mix" and it wouldn't help to explain, "I use it when I make my mother-in-law's brisket with Coke." By the way, in spite of this recipe, Stella Heffron is an outstanding cook, and some of the best recipes in this book are hers!

Stella's Brisket with Coca Cola
serves eight

5 lb. beef brisket
2 T. vegetable oil
1 c. minced onion
1 c. minced celery
1 t. minced garlic
1 T. paprika
salt
good grinding black pepper
1½ c. marinara sauce (p. 39) or "dry spaghetti sauce mix"
   equivalent
1 T. onion soup mix
1 c. Coca Cola
2 c. baby carrots
2 c. small new potatoes

Preheat oven to 350 degrees. Brush meat with oil. Combine onion, celery, garlic, paprika, salt and pepper and rub into meat. Put meat in large Dutch oven.

Mix marinara sauce, onion soup mix and Coca Cola. Pour over meat. Cover tightly and bake for three hours, turning meat every half hour or so.

Halfway through cooking add carrots and potatoes to bottom of pan. Finish cooking.

(continued) ☞

Take cooked meat from pan and let stand thirty minutes before cutting into thin slices.

Lower oven to 300 degrees.

Put sliced meat on top of vegetables. Ladle some gravy over meat. Cover pot and cook twenty minutes longer.

My grandmother's brisket with its inordinate amount of onions is the inspiration for my own. If my grandmother were alive, she would be perfectly content for me to compile these recipes and leave her recipe out, but hopefully she would be quite happy to know that each and every time I make my version, I can imagine being with her, which is better than any brisket I ever ate.

My Brisket Pot au Feu
serves ten

2 T. vegetable oil
5 lb. beef brisket
12 c. thinly sliced onion
1 T. flour
1 t. salt
½ t. paprika
good grinding black pepper
2 c. baby carrots
5 c. pearl onions
5 c. sweet potatoes, peeled and cut in 1″ chunks
6 c. potatoes, peeled and cut in 1″ chunks

In a large Dutch oven, heat oil over medium heat. Put in brisket and cook until well browned, about ten minutes. Using tongs, turn meat and brown second side well. Remove meat and set aside on a plate. Discard almost all the fat in the pan. Add the onion and stir well, scraping up any particles clinging to the bottom of the pan. Cook covered for five minutes. Uncover, stir and let onions cook until limp, stirring frequently. Add flour, salt, paprika and pepper. Stir in well. Add 3 c. water, meat and accumulated meat juices. Cover and cook over low heat until tender, turning with tongs and scraping bottom of pan every half hour or so. Test for tenderness by piercing with a cake tester. If it slides in without resistance, meat is done. Remove meat, let cool and wrap in plastic wrap.

While meat cooks, prepare vegetables. Steam carrots until just tender. Refresh under cold running water and drain. Peel

(continued) ☞

and cook pearl onions. Drain. Put both kinds of potatoes together in a large pot with enough cold water to cover. Bring to a boil over medium high heat, turn heat to low and cook until tender. Drain. Put vegetables in pot with gravy. Cook for twenty minutes over low heat, stirring occasionally. Cool, refrigerate overnight. Scrape fat off gravy and discard. Slice meat into ⅓" slices. Heat meat over gravy and vegetables in pot or in microwave.

While I've allowed all-comers in the brisket category, Susan's matzoh balls are the best and we won't be hearing from the runners-up. Unfortunately the definitive matzoh ball requires a pinch of baking powder which is not permitted for Passover. So on Passover, when the youngest asks, "Why is this night different from all other nights?" one of the answers has to be "On this night the matzoh balls are not quite as perfect."

Susan's mother, Hilda Sind, taught Susan to compensate for chickens that "aren't as tasty as they used to be" with the addition of the G. Washington's seasoning mix. This is great soup!

Susan's Matzoh Ball Soup
serves eight

2 carrots, peeled
1 parsnip, peeled
1 stalk celery, cut in 1" pieces
2 leeks, very well washed inside and out, cut in 1" pieces
few sprigs parsley
few sprigs dill
G. Washington's Seasoning
salt
good grinding black pepper
large pinch white pepper
4 lb. chicken — a whole stewing hen or any chicken parts,
   bones, necks or giblets, but no livers
1 recipe matzoh balls (following recipe)

In large pot, put vegetables, parsley, dill, some G. Washington's Seasoning, salt and black and white pepper. Put chicken on top. Cover amply with water. Bring to simmer, skimming foam off top as much as possible. Cover partially and simmer for close to two hours until chicken is falling apart. Strain, reserving carrots and parsnips. Line a fine sieve with two thicknesses of cheesecloth and strain again.

Cut carrot and parsnip into fine dice and put in pot with strained broth. Add matzoh balls and heat over low heat until piping hot.

Matzoh Balls
makes eight

2 eggs
½ c. matzoh meal
½ t. baking powder (except during Passover)
salt
1 T. or so chicken fat
1 T. or so hot chicken soup

Beat eggs and then add other ingredients. Refrigerate for an hour or more.

Half fill a large pot with water, salt it well, and bring to a boil.

Roll matzoh balls the size of walnuts and add to water. Cover and cook over medium heat for a half hour. Remove balls with slotted spoon and place in simmering chicken soup.

I learned to make this at my Aunt Betty's side, more to be able to pass her recipe along than to assure myself a lifetime supply of gefilte fish. I can't help but regard gefilte fish as an exercise in diminishing marginal returns or much ado about nothing. At the end of the day, it's the horseradish on the side that's really of interest.

For as long as I can remember my aunt had her housekeepers Joanie, then Rosalie, make this fish, and later on Olga, the caterer, followed her recipe. It's a great recipe, and I recommend delegation.

Aunt Betty's Gefilte Fish

serves at least sixteen since a good six will decline

2½ lb. whitefish
2½ lb. pike
1 lb. carp
4 stalks celery
4 peeled medium onions
3 peeled carrots
1 T. and 2 t. salt
½ t. sugar
½ t. white pepper
¼ t. paprika
sprinkling matzoh meal
3 eggs

Have the fish market bone fish reserving remnants, and have them grind the fish twice. Add one stalk celery and one onion and grind again. (Aunt Betty could get the fishmonger to do this too, but she had a way about her!)

Put fish bones in large pot with plenty of cold water. Coarsely chop remaining three onions and three stalks celery, cut carrots into chunks, and add with 1 T. salt, ¼ t. sugar, ¼ t. white pepper and paprika. Cover pot and bring to simmer. Cook for an hour or so. Strain stock, reserving carrots and discarding the rest. Slice carrots into thin rounds.

To chopped fish mixture, add matzoh meal, eggs, remaining 2 t. salt, ¼ t. white pepper and ¼ t. sugar. Beat in cold water

(continued) ☞

as needed, about one cup. Firm up balls by adding a bit more matzoh meal if needed. Roll into balls and wrap each ball with a thin piece of fish skin.

In clean large pot, put gefilte fish. Pour hot stock on top and cook until done, about one hour.

Remove fish, cool, chill, and serve one piece per person on a leaf of iceberg lettuce with a bit of the jelled fish stock and a few slices of the cooked carrots.

Pass bowls of freshly grated red and white horseradish.

Stella's friend Doris Haskel is the source of this great recipe for challah.

Challah
makes two braided loaves

2 packages dry yeast
⅔ c. sugar
7 c. flour
2 t. salt
pinch cinnamon (optional)
⅔ c. vegetable oil
3 eggs, plus additional yolk
1 t. poppy seeds per loaf (optional)

Dissolve yeast in ½ c. warm water with 1 T. of the sugar. Let stand five minutes. Combine remaining sugar, flour, salt and cinnamon (if using) in bowl of large mixer fitted with dough hook. Add yeast mixture, oil, 3 whole eggs and up to 1½ c. additional water to form moist but not sticky dough. Knead for ten minutes.

Put dough in oiled bowl, cover with dishcloth and let rise until doubled, about two hours in a warm kitchen.

Punch down, hand knead for a minute to remove air pockets, return to bowl, cover and let double a second time.

When risen, punch down and divide into eight equal pieces. Roll pieces into balls and rest five minutes. Rolls balls into strips about twelve inches long. Put four together and braid. Repeat with remaining four.

Set each bread on a greased baking sheet. Let rise covered with cloth until very light looking, about an hour.

Before dough has risen fully, preheat oven to 325 degrees.

Beat remaining egg yolk with 1 T. water and brush tops of loaves gently all over. Sprinkle one or both with poppy seeds if using. Put in oven and bake until golden brown, about forty-five minutes.

Aunt Sadie's Potato Kugel

serves six

4 large potatoes
¼ c. chicken fat
4 eggs, well beaten
2 heaping T. matzoh meal
1 t. baking powder
½ t. salt

Preheat oven to 400 degrees.

Peel and coarsely grate potatoes. Drain liquid that runs out of potatoes.

Melt chicken fat in large cast iron skillet. Cool and pour into bowl with eggs, matzoh meal, baking powder and salt. Mix well. Mix in potatoes.

Brush skillet all over with bit of fat that remains in it.

Add potato mixture to skillet and bake for one hour and fifteen minutes until golden brown. Cut into wedges.

When Phoebe started school in the homogeneous hamlet of Cutchogue, she was practically the first brunette. I explained to her kindergarten teacher that Phoebe didn't celebrate Christmas and that instead she celebrated Chanukah. Her teacher responded, "How nice! I think that's so broadening."

These potato pancakes became part of my annual cultural awareness road show. Every December for years I called to borrow Marcia and Jerry Brown's electric skillet and made these great latkes with a classroom full of kids.

Potato Pancakes with Fruit Sauce
fifty small pieces

5 lb. all purpose potatoes, peeled
2 medium onions, peeled
3 eggs
⅓ c. flour
2 t. salt
½ t. white pepper
vegetable oil as needed
salt to taste
1 recipe fruit sauce (following recipe)

Use coarse side of a grater or food processor with coarse grating blade to grate potatoes and onions. Dump onto a large dishcloth or apron. Wrap up cloth and wring out as much water as possible. Beat remaining ingredients together in large bowl and mix in potato and onion shreds.

Pour oil into a large skillet, preferably cast iron, to a depth of about ¼". Heat until hot enough that a drop of water put into the pan will immediately sizzle. Use a slotted spoon to form pancakes about 1" in diameter. Press on each one to remove additional water and to firm. Fill the pan quite full with pancakes. As the edges turn golden brown, flip with a spatula. When second side is brown, remove to a plate covered with several thicknesses of paper towel. Sprinkle with salt and serve at once with fruit sauce and sour cream.

Fruit Sauce
makes about two cups

4 large red skinned apples, well washed
4 large ripe pears, preferably with red skins, well washed
2 T. raspberries, fresh or frozen
1 T. sugar, or more or less to taste
¼ t. cinnamon

Quarter, core and coarsely chop apples and pears. Put in a heavy bottomed saucepan, and cover and cook over low heat until limp.

Add raspberries, sugar and cinnamon to hot apples and pears. Mix in well. Pass through the fine screen of a food mill. Serve warm or at room temperature.

Betty's Passover Lemon Cake
serves twelve

9 eggs, separated
1½ c. sugar
¾ c. cake meal
¼ c. potato starch
finely grated rind of 1 lemon
2 T. lemon juice
pinch salt

Preheat oven to 325 degrees. Lightly oil a 10″ tube pan with removable sides.

Beat yolks with ¼ c. sugar at medium speed for five minutes, until light yellow in color. Beat in rind and juice.

Mix cake meal and potato starch. Add to yolks, just mixing to combine.

In clean bowl with clean beaters, beat egg whites with salt until soft peaks form. Gradually add remaining ¾ c. sugar and beat until peaks are stiff. Add a large scoop of whites to yolk mixture and beat in. Pour yolk mixture over remaining whites, and gently fold until well combined.

Pour into prepared pan, level and bake until golden brown, about an hour. Cool slightly before removing cake rim to finish cooling.

Here's an apple cake containing no dairy, so suitable for serving after holiday meat meals. Another of Susan Lipsett's specialties, she apologizes for its appearance, but says the taste is "incredible." I agree.

Susan's Apple Cake
serves twelve

3 c. flour
1 T. cinnamon
1 t. baking soda
1 t. salt
1½ c. vegetable oil
2 c. sugar
3 eggs
1 t. vanilla extract
3 c. peeled, cored and thickly sliced Delicious apples
1 c. coarsely chopped walnuts

Preheat oven to 350 degrees. Oil and flour a 9″ tube pan.

Sift together flour, cinnamon, baking soda and salt.

Beat oil and sugar together well, preferably in an electric mixer. Add eggs and vanilla and beat until creamy.

Add flour mixture and mix at low speed until almost mixed in. Add apples and walnuts and beat until they are mixed in, but no longer. Put batter in pan and bake until done, about one hour. Cake will just start to come away from edge of pan and will test dry when stuck with a cake tester. Cool in pan on top of wire rack. Turn out.

During my mother's working Saturdays, Aunt Betty often took me for a day on the town. A day on the town meant lunch at Schrafft's and the show and a movie at Radio City Hall. These expeditions were a little rough around the edges with Aunt Betty invariably snoringly asleep during the film, but she did me every kindness. We usually had to dash into "Glad Rags" for a small gift for me at the end of the visit.

By the time I came along, Aunt Betty had already passed down her recipes for the household help to execute. One anonymous source told me Betty's daughter Audrey's kitchen talents extend to a knack for ordering Chinese food, and since niece G.G. had equally little plan to carry the torch, I like to think somewhere the descendants of housekeepers, Joanie and Rosalie, are blissfully eating perfect pink applesauce and light as air matzoh balls. These are among the few of Betty's recipes we have.

From her Jamestown era, a popular dish for the ladies luncheon set. This is of more archival than gastronomic interest.

Golden Glow Salad

serves six

1 package lemon jello
3 carrots, coarsely grated
shredded lettuce

Make the Jello according to package directions. Fold in the carrots. Chill in a mold.

At serving time, dip mold in hot water for a few seconds. Wipe dry. Put a plate on top. Invert. Garnish with shredded lettuce.

Betty's Noodle Pudding
serves six

one 8 oz. package medium wide noodles
3 eggs, beaten
½ lb. cottage cheese
1 c. sour cream
½ c. white raisins
3 T. sugar
2 T. lemon juice
¾ t. salt
6 T. melted butter
½ c. crushed corn flakes
½ c. sliced almonds, lightly chopped

Preheat oven to 375 degrees. Generously butter a small baking dish.

Cook noodles according to package directions. Drain.

Combine eggs, cottage cheese, sour cream, raisins, sugar, lemon juice and salt. Fold in noodles.

Put noodle mixture in baking dish. Combine remaining butter, corn flakes and almonds. Sprinkle over noodles. Bake until golden brown, about one hour.

Betty's Baked Beans
serves twelve

1 lb navy beans
1 t. baking soda
1 medium onion, coarsely chopped
6 T. butter
¾ c. lightly packed brown sugar
1 t. salt

Soak beans overnight in cold water to cover amply. Drain. Put beans in pot with baking soda and cold water to just cover. Bring to boil, drain and rinse.

Wash out pot. Put beans back in pot with cold water to cover amply and onion. Cook slowly until partially cooked, about forty minutes. Drain reserving some of the cooking liquid.

Preheat oven to 375 degrees.

Put beans and two cups of cooking liquid in casserole with butter and brown sugar. Mix well. Bake covered until tender, about one and a half hours, adding additional cooking liquid if necessary. Uncover, add salt, and bake twenty minutes longer.

According to Marcia Warner, Sadie's daughter, Sadie's entertaining style was lavish and featured generous portions and the best of everything. Her soup reflects that with succulent meat and bones enough to make soup for twenty in most other households. Very rich and delicious.

Sadie's Lentil Soup

serves six

1 lb. flanken or short ribs of beef
one beef marrow bone, cut into 2″ pieces
1 heaping cup lentils
1 c. coarsely chopped onion
1 c. coarsely chopped carrot
½ c. coarsely chopped celery
2 bay leaves
salt
good grinding black pepper

Put meat and bones in soup pot with 10 c. cold water. Bring to boil, lower heat and simmer for one hour, skimming off scum from time to time.

Rinse and pick over lentils, making sure there are no stones mixed in with them. Add lentils to pot with onion, carrot and celery. Cook half an hour. Add bay leaves, salt and pepper to taste and cook until lentils are tender. Remove meat, bones and bay leaves from soup. Refrigerate several hours so fat has time to harden. Remove and discard fat.

Heat until piping hot.

One of Susan Lipsett's secular specialties. Herbes de Provence is a blend of rosemary, thyme and other good things, and if it's not on your shelf, you can fake it with your own mix.

Grilled Provençal Chicken
serves six

4 chicken breasts on the bone, split or 24 chicken wings, cut
    at the joint
1 c. olive oil
½ c. Dijon mustard
¼ c. balsamic vinegar
¼ c. lemon juice
2 T. minced garlic
2 T. Herbes de Provence
salt
good grinding black pepper

Put chicken in a non-reactive container or heavy duty plastic bag. Mix olive oil, mustard, vinegar, lemon juice, garlic and Herbes de Provence. Pour over chicken and marinate for four hours in the refrigerator.

Bring chicken to room temperature. Heat grill to medium. Season chicken with salt and pepper and grill on both sides until done, approximately fifteen minutes per side for breasts, less than ten per side for wings.

Serve hot or at room temperature.

Judy Lipsett sent me this recipe with a note that it was Allen's favorite salmon recipe. The San Francisco Lipsetts are easily the most food obsessed people I've met in my long life as a food professional. Judy's email address says it all: "FoodieJudy." So . . .

Allen's Favorite Salmon

serves six

2½ lb. boneless filet of salmon, center cut
2 T. Dijon mustard
1 T. lemon juice
1 T. grated orange rind
1 t. ground cumin
¼ t. mustard seeds
salt
pinch red pepper flakes
2 T. oil
2 T. white wine

Line a small flat baking dish with foil. Put in salmon.

Combine mustard, lemon juice, orange rind, cumin, mustard seeds, salt and pepper flakes. Whisk while adding oil in a thin stream. Spread over fish. Let stand for 30 minutes or so.

Preheat oven to 350 degrees.

Pour wine around salmon. Put in oven and bake until fish is almost done.

Heat broiler and broil a minute or so to brown topping.

Marcia Warner attributes this delicious pie to her friend Billie Tisch.

Pumpkin Chiffon Pie
serves eight

1½ c. graham cracker crumbs
4 T. melted butter
3 eggs, separated
1 c. sugar
1¼ c. pumpkin puree
½ c. milk
½ t. salt
½ t. ginger
½ t. cinnamon
½ t. nutmeg
1 package gelatin

Preheat oven to 375 degrees.

Mix graham crackers and butter and use to line a 10″ pie pan. Bake shell ten minutes. Cool.

Put yolks and ½ c. sugar in large bowl set over simmering water. Beat constantly until thick. Add pumpkin, milk, salt and spices and beat a few minutes longer.

Soften gelatin in ½ c. cold water and add to hot pumpkin mixture, beating until well dissolved. Cool.

Beat egg whites until soft peaks form. Gradually add remaining ½ c. sugar and beat until stiff peak stage. Add a large scoop of whites to pumpkin mixture and beat well. Pour pumpkin mixture over remaining egg whites and fold gently to combine. Pour mixture into pie shell. Refrigerate until set.

Marcia always puts on great summer parties in the backyard. This is one of her favorite finales. Great if you like meringue. (I don't!)

Blueberry Meringue Pie
serves eight

2 pints blueberries
1¼ c. flour
½ c. and 2 T. sugar
¼ t. freshly grated nutmeg
pinch salt
3 T. cold butter, cut in ¼" cubes
2 T. vegetable shortening
2 egg yolks
½ c. sugar
3 T. quick cooking tapioca
finely grated rind of 2 lemons
2 T. lemon juice
½ t. cinnamon
pinch cream of tartar
⅓ c. confectioner's sugar

Rinse, drain and pick over blueberries, discarding any that are under ripe or shriveled and picking out the stems.

Mix flour, 2 T. sugar, nutmeg and salt in food processor or large bowl. Cut in butter and shortening until mixture resembles cornmeal. Mix yolks with 3 T. ice water. Add to dough and combine with a few pulses or a minimum of mixing. Form into a ball and refrigerate for a half hour.

On lightly floured counter, roll dough into 12" circle. Gently place in 9" pie pan, trim away excess dough and flute edges. Refrigerate for another half hour or more, or make ahead and store in freezer until baking time.

Mash 1 c. of the blueberries with a masher or in the food processor and combine with remaining ½ c. sugar, tapioca, lemon rind, lemon juice and cinnamon. Fold in remaining blueberries. Let stand for an hour.

(continued) ☞

Preheat oven to 375 degrees.

Line cold pie shell with aluminum foil and fill with dry rice or beans. (I use the same beans over and over again for baking empty pie shells, a procedure that is called "baking blind.")

Bake until dough is set, about ten minutes. Remove foil and beans and bake empty shell two minutes longer, piercing any bubbles that form with a fork. Do not brown shell.

Pour berry mixture into shell. Bake loosely covered with foil for thirty-five minutes.

Remove from oven and reduce heat to 325 degrees.

Beat the egg whites with cream of tartar until soft peaks form. Add confectioner's sugar and continue beating until stiff peaks form. Use a metal spreading spatula to distribute egg white mixture over entire surface of pie. Swirl with dinner knife to make little peaks all over.

Bake until golden brown, about fifteen minutes. Cool slightly before serving.

Jimmy Warner gets his cooking talent from both the Rosen and Lipsett sides of his family, but his love of grilling is pure Warner.

The infused butter makes an equally delicious marinade for sea scallops.

Grilled Swordfish à la Paulie
serves six

1 stick butter
1 can flat anchovy filets
6 individual swordfish steaks, about 10 oz. each

In small skillet, melt butter over low heat. Add anchovies leaving oil behind. Stir and crush with fork until anchovies are dissolved. Cool butter.

Coat both sides of swordfish steaks with butter and marinate for five minutes.

Cook quickly on both sides over hot coals until just done.

From the Terr Table

GG's father, Tom Rosen, was the oldest child. He came over from Russia as the first from his family when he was sixteen years old, bringing over his siblings and parents later on. Since he was big and tough looking, one of his numerous positions was police officer on the lower east side, uniform complete with bobby hat.

GG's grandfather had been a cooper in the old country. In the U.S. he took to driving a horse and buggy and collecting rags and paper for resale. That was the origin of the family scrap business which Tom operated. The husbands of his sisters, Betty and Sadie, raised scrapping to new heights when they became demolition experts in New York City. Their firm Lipsett Brothers took down the old Penn Station (although I hope they didn't come up with the idea!)

Celia Cohn, soon Celia Rosen, had been Tom's neighbor in Russia, and she didn't like him much there. When she emigrated with her brother as a young woman, she met up with Tom in New York City and fell in love. GG's siblings, Mildred and Joseph, were born seven and five years before her. The family was based in western New York state, but became peripatetic after GG's birth when Celia was diagnosed with TB. Celia died eleven years later.

Siblings Joseph and Mildred settled in Northern Michigan. Eventually Aunt Mildred and her husband, Terry, moved to Las Vegas, New Mexico (yes there is another Las Vegas) and raised a family of five kids, all of whom now live in that area.

Mildred was a great beauty and enjoyed a brief career as a successful fashion model in NYC. Neither motherhood nor the harsh southwestern sun ever spoiled her looks, and even in her eighties she is stunning with cornflower blue eyes. A talker, listener and story teller, she's a great companion and also a fine cook.

Family legend has it that my grandfather Tom, would return from his travels describing some great thing he had eaten and my aunt would recreate it from the description. Mildred is the Rosen repository of family stories and guardian of recipes.

This recipe comes from Aunt Mildred's mother in law, "Grandma Terr." The Terr family serves this loaf with soup.

Kasha Babka
serves sixteen

½ recipe for challah made without cinnamon (p. 58)
½ lb. or more of chicken livers
2 c. onions, finely chopped
¼ c. chicken fat
salt
good grinding black pepper
3 c. cooked kasha, made according to instructions on the
  box

Make dough and let rise once.

While dough rises, trim any bits of membrane away from chicken livers. Dry livers well on paper towels.

In large saute pan over medium heat, cook onions in chicken fat until onions are limp, stirring often. Raise heat to high, add chicken livers and cook quickly until browned on both sides. Season generously with salt and pepper. Cool. Chop coarsely. Mix with kasha. Adjust seasoning.

Roll risen dough out as for a jelly roll to about 12 × 18 inches. Spread liver mixture over dough. Roll dough from longest side into a cylinder. Place in oiled tube pan. Let rise until double in bulk.

Preheat oven to 375 degrees. Bake for forty minutes, until brown. Cool and slice.

Lima Bean and Barley Soup
serves twelve

1 c. dried lima beans
1 lb. chuck or flanken
2 T. vegetable oil
¼ c. dried cepes, otherwise called porcini mushrooms
1 c. coarsely chopped onion
1 c. diced carrot
1 c. diced celery
½ c. barley
salt
good grinding black pepper

Soak lima beans overnight in water to cover amply. Drain.

In soup pot over medium high heat, brown meat on both sides in oil. Pour off fat. Add three quarts water and lima beans and cook for one hour.

Soak cepes in 1 c. hot water for thirty minutes. Lift from water and chop coarsely. Filter soaking liquid through coffee filter or strainer lined with paper towel to remove sand. Add liquid to soup along with chopped cepes and remaining ingredients and cook forty minutes longer, until barley is tender. Adjust seasoning. Cut up meat. Return 1 c. of meat to pot. Reserve rest for another use.

Cran-Apple Compote
serves eight or more as a relish

1¾ c. sugar
4 Winesap apples
1 lb. fresh cranberries

Put sugar with 1¾ c. water in large saucepan. Bring to boil over high heat stirring often. When syrup boils, turn heat to medium low and simmer for five minutes.

Peel, core and cut apples into eighths. Add to simmering syrup and cook for five minutes. Rinse and pick over cranberries discarding under ripe and shrivelled berries. Add cranberries to syrup and cook ten minutes longer. Cool to room temperature.

I've made this cake literally hundreds of times and given the recipe away many times too, and it always travels as "Mildred's Chocolate Cake." My aunt, however, claims no relationship and has the temerity to say she makes a different cake altogether. So if you bake it, feel free to name it after yourself.

Mildred's Chocolate Cake

serves sixteen to twenty

2⅔ c. sifted cake flour
1 t. salt
2 c. sugar
⅔ c. sifted cocoa
2 sticks butter, melted
2 eggs
2 t. vanilla
2 c. buttermilk
2 t. baking soda

Preheat oven to 400 degrees.

Grease two 10″ cake pans, line bottoms with a circle of wax paper or parchment and grease paper. Sprinkle pans with cocoa, shake to distribute all over bottom and sides and dump out excess or line 24 cupcake pans with paper holders.

Sift flour with salt.

Mix sugar, cocoa and butter together well. Beat in eggs and vanilla. Mix buttermilk and soda together in a bowl large enough to accommodate some expansion. Let stand five minutes but not longer.

Alternately add flour and buttermilk by thirds to cocoa mixture, incorporating each addition thoroughly. Immediately put batter in pans. Tap the pans to level and to remove air pockets. Bake for approximately thirty minutes. Center of cake will spring back when gently pressed, and cake will just start to shrink from sides of pan when it is done.

Cool on wire rack for five minutes. Turn out cakes and remove paper. Let cool completely before icing.

Lewis is the second oldest of my Terr cousins and he became my childhood hero the night he saved Emily. Emily was one of my "familiars" that I took to bed every night. I slept with so many that when my mother came to kiss me in the dark, she had a hard time identifying me and probably often gave Froggie the intended send-off. But Emily was especially important to me because the ladies at my mother's dressmaking shop made her for me.

I'm not sure what incited G.G. to have custom made clothes since she's always had some ideal model size figure, but on many Saturdays she used to take me with her to the West Village for fittings. All this labor ultimately resulted in a memorable green dress that had one of the panels sewn in inside out. I spent my time productively picking up the many pins on the floor of the shop, which I used to refer to as "Ye Olde Pin Town." For this work the ladies made me a little frog with bright black button eyes and tiny beans inside.

On a visit with the Terrs at their home in New Mexico, Martha and one of my cousins engaged in a tug of war over Emily which caused her to split down the middle and "spill the beans" all over the living room. The adults were out, and I was inconsolable. Lewis, then called "Butch," spent the entire evening sewing Emily and putting the beans back in. You have to love a teenage boy who does that. Forever.

Since then, while I don't seen him that often, every time I do, he adds a new reason for being a favorite. Whether spray bleaching the shingles of our house to get the mold off or chasing the guys who broke into his car down the NYC streets, Lewis is never a dull guest.

This is Lewis' recipe for black eyed peas (inspired by Emily perhaps) with kale. His proud brother Jim sent this unsolicited, insisting it's "one of those magic, synergistic recipes where the result adds up to much more than the sum of its parts." If everyone else sent their recipes with the lead-in written, this book would have been a whole lot easier to do!

Black-Eyed Peas and Kale
serves twelve

1 lb. black-eyed peas
1 bunch kale, well washed and cut in small pieces
1 large onion, coarsely chopped
½ lb. bacon ends
2 t. minced garlic
good grinding black pepper
salt
lemon juice

Soak black-eyed peas overnight in water to cover amply. Drain.

Put in a soup pot with water to cover amply and add kale, onion, and bacon ends. Bring to boil then simmer for about four hours, adding garlic and pepper toward the end. When everything is very soft, add salt and lemon juice to taste.

Although we see her rarely, Dana Terr Konno is also a special guest, one we will drop everything to receive. But actually it's completely unnecessary to drop anything. When she comes, she participates fully in the life of our household, deciding all the females need pedicures or taking over the kitchen to cook southwestern fare.

On one of Dana's visits, she got up early to fix a special breakfast for the girls before they went to school. This sacrifice made both Dana and her potatoes immortal.

Dana's Fried Potatoes

serves four

3 T. vegetable oil
4 potatoes, peeled, cooked and cut in large dice
1 medium onion, coarsely chopped
1 T. mild green chile, if available
salt
good grinding black pepper

Put oil in large cast iron pan. Heat until hot. Add potatoes and onions. Cook over medium high heat until well browned, stirring from time to time. Add chile during last few minutes of cooking. Season with salt and pepper.

Only New Mexicans can eat the full amount of green chile in this recipe.

Dana's Calabacitas
serves four

3 medium zucchini, scrubbed
½ c. coarsely chopped onion
3 T. corn oil
2 c. cooked corn
2 T. to ½ c. chopped green chile
1 t. minced garlic
salt
good grinding black pepper
1 c. grated mild Cheddar cheese

Cut zucchini into medium dice. Put in large skillet with onion and oil and cook over medium heat until tender, stirring often. Add corn, green chile and garlic and cook until piping hot. Season with salt and pepper.

Cook for several minutes until heated through, stirring occasionally. Top with cheese. Cook without stirring until cheese melts. Serve with warm tortillas.

Family Friends

*I*n spite of their demanding professional lives, my parents always found the time to nurture friendships. The children of many of their friends are special friends of my own family's now even though we often rely on the older generation to bring us together. Recipes from these good friends always remind me of happy family gatherings over the years.

Edna cooked for one of my mother's closest friends, Joan Sperling, her husband Don, and brood of four. I used to think we were visiting the estate of a country squire with Don's bird dogs romping freely about the place in Chappaqua, NY. Now I know it was the suburbs. Playing outside with the dogs made me starving for one of Edna's many rich and creamy specialties.

Chicken Tetrazinni
serves eight

6 whole chicken breasts, boned and split
flour
salt
good grinding black pepper
1 stick butter
¼ c. vegetable oil
½ c. minced shallot
1 c. chicken broth
½ c. white wine
1 t. tarragon
½ t. marjoram
¼ t. thyme
1 lb. fresh fettucine noodles
½ c. grated Parmesan cheese
¼ c. minced parsley
⅔ c. sour cream

Season flour with salt and pepper and dredge chicken breasts. In a large skillet over medium high heat, heat 4 T. butter and the vegetable oil until sizzling. Add chicken and lightly brown on both sides. Set chicken aside on plate.

(continued) ☞

Pour almost all the fat from the pan. Add shallot and stir to loosen browned bits clinging to pan. Add 2 T. of the dredging flour. Mix in well. Slowly add chicken broth and wine, whisking as you add. Add tarragon, marjoram and thyme. Simmer for five minutes.

Return chicken to pan, cover and cook for about eight minutes, turning once.

While chicken cooks, bring a large pot of heavily salted water to boil. Cook pasta a few minutes until al dente. Drain and mix noodles with remaining 4 T. butter, cheese and parsley. Put on large platter. Arrange chicken on top. Whisk sour cream into sauce and heat until piping hot but not boiling. Adjust seasoning and pour over chicken.

This is one of my favorite desserts after a large meal. It always feels right and is beautiful to behold. Making it brings back special memories of Trudy and Joe Rosen, two of my parents' dearest friends, cooking together in the womb-like kitchen of their otherwise grand Tudor style home in Great Neck.

Joe was an invalid for many of the years I knew him but was always willing to do the painstaking knife work for this dish, always turned out in a natty black and white striped apron. Joe was a great listener in a house full of talkers, and an avid newspaper reader. I can still picture him reading in "the studio" wearing his white gloves so he didn't get ink stains on his hands (back when newspapers used to bleed.) He was a one man clipping service, and to this day whenever I cut things out of the paper, I think of him and know he would approve. Two splendid memories in black and white.

A permitted substitution is one or two pink grapefruits filling in for several oranges.

Trudy and Joe's Marinated Citrus
serves eight

8 large navel oranges
1 c. sugar
⅓ c. honey
1⅓ c. orange juice, preferably freshly squeezed
⅔ c. brandy
⅓ c. Grand Marnier

Use a vegetable peeler and a light touch to remove the colored zest from two oranges. Be sure not to cut into the bitter white pith that lies beneath the zest. Lay a few strips of peel on top of each other on a cutting board and use a sharp knife to cut at an angle into thin julienne strips. Put the strips of zest in a saucepan, add cold water to cover amply and bring to a boil. Boil for two minutes, drain, wash out pan and repeat the procedure. This blanching process removes the bitter taste from the zest.

Put the sugar, 1 c. cold water and honey in a small saucepan. Bring to a boil, stirring occasionally. Before the mixture boils, dip a clean pastry brush in cold water and brush down any

(continued) ☞

sugar residue on inner edge of pan. When syrup begins to boil turn heat down to medium low, put in a candy thermometer and let cook without stirring until thermometer registers 230 degrees. Turn off heat and add blanched zest immediately. Let sit for at least thirty minutes.

While syrup cooks, "supreme" the oranges. Cut off ends and outer peel with a sharp knife. The membranes are now visible. Working over a bowl, use a sharp paring knife to cut fruit sections right next to the membranes. Let sections fall into the bowl and as each orange is done squeeze membrane over bowl to extract juice. Discard membranes.

Add orange juice, brandy and Grand Marnier to fruit sections. Add the syrup and peel. Mix well and let macerate overnight.

Serve chilled.

Trudy taught me how to live it up! When I was little, she took me to Rum-pelmeyer's in the St. Moritz Hotel on Central Park South. Not only was that the most glamorous lunch place a small girl could imagine, but the turkey sandwich lives on in memory. She also introduced me to Rafetto's, the Italian pasta maker on Houston Street. She never walked into a store or restaurant either, sailing in was and remains her style!

Trudy has raised food procurement to the highest art, going to one place for one thing and another, possibly in another state, because it makes the best something else. So when we are invited for a meal at her huge round table with the three foot lazy Susan in the middle, we know we are going to eat fab-ulously well. But what we really are hoping for is one of her soups. We'll take the carrot soup, vicchysoise or cold borscht over the best of the food shops everyday!

Trudy makes no apologies for using chicken cubes as her base in all her soups. She uses a bit more than one per cup and finds she rarely needs to add salt. If you make your own broth, so much the better, although you won't be able to improve on the taste.

Carrot Soup
serves six

4 T. butter
1 c. coarsely chopped onions
2 lb. peeled carrots or baby carrots
9 c. chicken broth
1 t. powdered ginger
salt

In soup pot, saute onions in butter over medium heat, stirring often. When onions are soft, add carrots, broth and ginger. Simmer thirty minutes until carrots are tender. Cool slightly and puree in batches in a blender. Strain to remove lumps. Add salt if necessary.

Serve piping hot.

Summer Carrot Soup
serves eight

1 recipe carrot soup (preceding recipe)
1 small can frozen orange juice concentrate

Add undefrosted orange juice and two cups cold water to cold soup. Puree in blender.

Joe was Trudy's "soup partner," cheerfully doing all the prep work. He loved this served hot with no milk added, as a hearty winter soup.

Leek and Potato Soup
serves eight to twelve

1 stick butter
4 large leeks
4 medium onions, coarsely chopped
6 medium potatoes, peeled and cut into 1″ chunks
6 c. strong chicken broth
2 c. milk
salt
1 c. heavy cream (for cold soup only)
3 T. snipped chives

Trim away most of green leek top, leaving on an inch or so. Save greens for flavoring broths or stews. Split leeks lengthwise and wash well, separating layers to get out sand and grit. Drain. Cut into 1″ pieces.

In soup pot saute leeks and onions in butter over medium heat, stirring often. When they're soft, add potatoes and broth. Simmer a half hour until potatoes are tender. Cool slightly and puree in batches in a blender. Add salt to taste.

If serving hot, put back over medium low heat, add milk and simmer until piping hot. Top with chives.

For cold soup, chill puree and add milk and heavy cream at serving time whisking in well. Top with chives. Serve small portions as the soup is rich.

Cold Borscht
serves eight to twelve

2 large bunches of beets
10 c. chicken broth
1 c. coarsely chopped onion
4 medium potatoes, peeled and cut into 1" chunks
¼ c. lemon juice
1 c. sour cream

Scrub, peel, and coarsely chop beets. Put in soup pot with chicken broth, onion and potato. Simmer until beets are tender.

Cool. Add lemon juice and sour cream. Blend and chill. At serving time add salt as needed. Top each portion with chopped garnishes like cucumber, scallion, or hard boiled egg and a dollop of additional sour cream. Or slip in a few freshly cooked small new potatoes.

Dana, Trudy & Joe's daughter, is the second generation friend to us all. She lives in a beautiful town in the South of France. When she made this dish for me, it instantly became a personal favorite.

Endives Mornay
serves four

10 medium endives
1 t. butter
juice of half a lemon
¼ t. salt
dash white pepper
1 recipe Mornay sauce (following recipe)
10 thin slices Black Forest ham
2 T. coarsely grated Gruyere cheese

Set rack high in the oven and preheat to 400 degrees. Butter bottom and sides of a 9″ × 12″ or similar size nonreactive baking dish. Trim bottoms of endives if discolored and cut in halves lengthwise. Put cut sides down in dish. Mix 1 c. cold water, lemon juice, salt and pepper. Pour over endives. Cover dish with foil and bake until endives are tender, about forty minutes, turning the endives a couple of times during cooking. Drain well.

Pour one third of the Mornay sauce into the baking dish used for braising endives, making sure first that the dish is quite dry. Take two endive halves and wrap together in a piece of ham. Set in dish. Repeat for all endives. Cover with remaining sauce. Sprinkle cheese on top. Cover dish with foil and bake for twenty minutes. Uncover and bake until piping hot and golden brown, about twenty-five minutes more.

Mornay Sauce
makes two cups

2 T. butter
2 T. flour
1½ c. milk
¼ t. Dijon mustard
¼ t. Worcestershire sauce
½ t. salt
pinch cayenne pepper
pinch white pepper
1 c. grated Gruyere cheese

In medium saucepan over medium heat, melt butter. Whisk in flour. Add milk in several additions whisking well after each. Add mustard, Worcestershire sauce, salt and cayenne and white pepper. Cook over low heat for five minutes whisking frequently. Turn off heat. Whisk in cheese.

This regional specialty of Dana's makes a fabulous gift.

Preserved Cherries (Griottes à l'Eau de Vie)
makes two quarts

2½ lb. sour cherries
2 c. sugar
1½ c. eau de vie (such as Kirsch)

Sterilize jar, lid and a large spoon by boiling for several minutes. Drain and cool.

Wash and dry cherries. Cut stems off, half-way. Add sugar and eau de vie to jar. Stir well with sterile spoon to dissolve sugar. Add cherries. Seal hermetically. Hold in dark place for at least two months, inverting jar every week or so.

Fred Fisher was my mother's friend and boss at Macy's for a number of years. According to GG, he was an enormously self-confident person who "could give tremendous responsibility and recognition." When Fred came to Macy's from Douglas Aircraft, all the top brass obsequiously called Jack Strauss, scion of the founding family, "Mr. Jack." Fred quickly pronounced, "I can call you Jack or Mr. Strauss, but not Mr. Jack."

Fred and Nina Fischer were already retired to Peconic, NY when Jim and I moved to the North Fork. We actually spent our "honeymoon" with them and Nina's elderly parents while our rental house was being renovated and while Jim started his new law job. They were great first friends, frequently inviting us for dinner and introducing us to many of their circle of friends. Fred was an avid jam maker and baker. You were very lucky if he gave you a gift of calamondin jam. Although I have his recipe I have been completely unable to source calamondins, so Fred's lace cookie recipe will have to be his memorial.

Fred's Lace Cookies
makes about four dozen

2¼ c. oatmeal
2¼ c. lightly packed light brown sugar
3 T. flour
1 t. salt
2 sticks butter, melted
1 egg, lightly beaten
1 t. vanilla

Preheat oven to 375 degrees.

Mix oatmeal, sugar, flour and salt. Stir in butter. Add egg and vanilla. Mix well. Drop by teaspoonsful at least 2″ apart on cookie sheets covered with baker's parchment or wax paper. Bake until light brown, about seven minutes, reversing pans midway through baking. When cookies are cool, remove with spatula to wire rack.

Fred's Gateau Riche

1 recipe lace cookie batter (preceding recipe)
vanilla ice cream
1 recipe chocolate sauce (p. 126)

Make large lace cookies by baking on the backs of cake pans covered with parchment or wax paper, leaving room for expansion. Cool.

Spread soft ice cream and make sandwiches. Cut wedges. Serve with chocolate sauce.

Jean and Charlie Segal are so warm and gracious that whatever they offer tastes fantastic. The sea air blowing into their magnificent beach house contributes to a good appetite too. This explains why when our daughter Phoebe was really little she would sit with Jean and gobble down broiled bluefish she wouldn't have come near at home.

Even though it's completely unnecessary under the circumstances, Jean is a wonderful cook. I could live on her eggplant caviar.

Eggplant Caviar
makes two cups

2 medium eggplants
1 green pepper
1 small onion, finely chopped
1 t. minced garlic
1 T. extra virgin olive oil
1 T. & 1 t. lemon juice
½ t. salt
good grinding black pepper

On charcoal grill or under broiler, blacken eggplants on all sides. Continue to cook at low heat either on grill or in 300 degree oven until limp. Cool in colander so liquid can drain away. Discard tops and skin and chop flesh very fine.

Char green pepper at same time as eggplants, but do not continue to cook after charring; it will be better if left slightly crisp. Cool in colander. Peel, discard top and seeds and chop flesh medium fine.

Put eggplant and pepper in a bowl with onion and garlic. Beat in oil. Add lemon juice, salt and pepper. Adjust seasoning.

Serve on wedges of toasted pita.

This is the rice pudding my mother has so thoroughly adopted she dares to call it Cheryl's rice pudding!

Jean Segal's Rice Pudding

serves six

½ c. rice
4 c. milk
4 T. butter
3 eggs
½ c. sugar
½ c. raisins, optional
½ t. vanilla
dash of cinnamon

In a large pot with a tight-fitting lid, bring 1 c. cold water to boil. Add rice, stir, cover and cook over low heat for seven minutes. Add milk and butter. Stir. Cook uncovered for forty-five minutes. Beat eggs with sugar and raisins. Pour a ladleful of rice mixture into eggs and beat well. Pour egg mixture into pot. Stir vigorously with wooden spoon until mixture just begins to thicken. Remove from heat. Add vanilla. Pour into serving dishes and sprinkle with cinnamon.

Cherie and Ken Mason live in paradise in the coastal area of Sunset, Maine. Not only do they have unlimited sea urchins attaching themselves to the dock, they have access to all the fresh picked crab meat a person could want, and Cherie knows how to make the most of it.

Cherie's Crab Frittata
serves six to eight

1 lb. Maine crab meat
½ lb. mushrooms, thinly sliced
2 T. butter
1 t. lemon juice
4 eggs
1 c. sour cream
1 c. small curd cottage cheese
4 T. flour
½ c. finely chopped scallions
¼ t. salt
6 drops Tabasco sauce
2 c. grated Gruyere cheese

Preheat oven to 350 degrees.

Gently pick over crab meat to remove any bits of shell or cartilage, being careful not to break up crab meat.

In small skillet over high heat, saute mushrooms in butter and lemon juice for a few minutes. Drain.

In food processor or blender, combine eggs, sour cream, cottage cheese, flour, scallions, salt, and Tabasco sauce. Pour into large bowl. Add crab meat, mushrooms and cheese. Gently mix. Pour into a 10" quiche dish.

Bake until golden brown, about fifty minutes. Let rest five minutes before serving.

Raising Myself to be a Chef

*A*s the foundation for his interest in food, the typical chef looks back either on a childhood filled with a rich tradition of foraged and farm raised foods prepared by his fun loving Italian (or French or Polish family) or, alternatively, one of complete sensory deprivation in the average American home. My vocation springs from neither source.

My family sat down at 6:30 P.M. sharp to a dinner of correctly cooked simple foods, prepared and served butler style by Miss Brumm, and eaten with our best table manners (no talking with mouth full, no using bread as a "pusher!") While everything was nutritionally and culinarily correct, we did frequently find ourselves eating an all white dinner—chicken breast, rice and cauliflower—on our all white dinner plates. To Miss Brumm's credit in fourteen years of cooking for us, I don't believe she ever burned, ruined or allowed any food to spoil in the refrigerator, a remarkable accomplishment.

As the never married eldest child in a large German family, Miss Brumm was extremely orderly and tidy. Because she was the cornerstone of our smooth existence as a rare and possibly controversial family with a working mother, and most importantly, because we loved her, we were not allowed to make her life too miserable by bringing home unexpected dinner guests and getting underfoot in our minute apartment kitchen.

Since "don't" and "can't" were—and continue to be—two words that really make me jump out of my chair, I decided early on that the kitchen was the place for me and that on weekends when Miss Brumm was away and my parents out, the way I wanted to misbehave was by throwing dinner parties.

By the end of high school, I was deeply into a vegetarian mode which enabled me to skip polite family dinners in favor of bedroom snacks of peanut butter on cracked wheat bread chased with a glass of chocolate milk (no recipe included.) The elaborate vegetable curry from Alan Hooker's Vegetarian Gourmet Cookery was my typical dinner party offering of the era. Later in a move to disavow my hippie past I purged this really nice book from my collection and was so happy to reacquire it when family friend, Nina Fischer, offered me Fred Fischer's cookbooks when he died.

To make the curry you have to chase around for ten kinds of spices that you will never use again until you remake this recipe. You need to drill open a whole coconut, smash it with a hammer, use a chisel to pry the meat from the shell, peel it and then grate it. My father used to walk in and see my bleeding knuckles and intone "grate until red." This dish is just the thing to make when the kitchen is really clean and you are not supposed to be there.

Vegetable Curry
serves ten

1 T. whole coriander seeds
3 small dried red chilis
1 T. ground turmeric
1 small stick cinnamon
1 t. fenugreek seeds
1 t. whole mustard seeds
1 t. whole cumin seeds
1 t. whole black peppercorns
4 cloves
2 cardamom seeds
2 T. butter
2 c. finely chopped onion
1 heaping T. minced garlic
1 T. minced ginger
3 c. coconut milk (following recipe)
8 c. par-cooked vegetables (pearl onions, carrots,
    cauliflower, Brussels sprouts, zucchini, lima beans, green
    beans)
2 red peppers
1 c. frozen peas
3 T. lemon juice
2 T. lime juice
¼ c. high quality orange marmalade
salt

Put all the spices in the blender and blend to a powder.

Put butter, onion, garlic and ginger in a medium skillet and cook over medium low heat, stirring often, until onions are limp. Add spices and cook over very low heat, stirring often, for thirty minutes. Stir in coconut milk and simmer for five minutes.

Put cooked vegetables in a large heavy bottomed pan, add liquid and simmer for fifteen minutes.

(continued) ☞

Meanwhile, char peppers on all sides under broiler. Cool slightly, peel, remove and discard tops and seeds, cut in ½" dice.

Add to stew with frozen peas, lemon and lime juice, marmalade and salt. Simmer for five minutes. Adjust seasoning.

Serve curry with basmati rice and bowls of garnishes like raisins, unsalted peanuts or cashews, freshly grated coconut and mango chutney.

Coconut Milk
makes three cups

1 c. fresh coconut, peeled and cut in ¾" cubes or 1 c. dry
   shredded, unsweetened coconut
3 c. boiling water

Combine coconut and water in blender for a minute or so. Let stand five minutes. Strain, pressing on bits of coconut to capture all the milk.

My first formal cooking training came in sixth grade in a class for kids at the Jewish Y on 14th Street. We learned to make butter cookies which I practiced constantly. I don't know what became of all those cookies since I don't remember liking to eat them, just to make them.

Later I realized that Lois Cowan, a dear family friend, had a better recipe, and I converted. She also introduced me to the cookie press which did not reduce my fixation.

Lois Cowan's Butter Cookies
makes at least eight dozen

4 sticks soft butter
1 c. sugar
4 c. flour
1 egg

Preheat oven to 375 degrees.

Cream butter. Add sugar and cream well. Mix in 2 c. of the flour. Add egg. Mix in remaining 2 c. flour.

Put dough in cookie press. Press out shapes onto ungreased cookie sheet. Bake until just slightly brown. Cool a minute, then remove with spatula to wire rack. Cool cookie sheet before shaping more cookies.

Another of my early specialties from a recipe of Miss Brumm's. I did like to eat this.

Banana Nut Bread
makes one loaf and one dozen mini-muffins

2⅔ c. sifted flour
1 T. baking powder
1 t. salt
¼ t. baking soda
2 sticks soft butter
¾ c. sugar
3 eggs
2 very ripe medium bananas, mashed
¾ c. finely chopped pecans
1 t. grated orange rind

Preheat oven to 325 degrees. Oil a 9" × 5" loaf pan, line with wax paper and oil paper. Grease mini muffin tin or use paper cupcake holders.

Sift together flour, baking powder, salt and baking soda.

Cream butter and sugar together until fluffy. Add eggs one at a time, beating well after each addition.

Stir in flour mixture in two parts, alternating with bananas. Add nuts and orange rind.

Fill muffin cups two-thirds full. Pour remaining batter into loaf pan, level with spatula and tap gently on counter once or twice to remove air pockets.

Bake until light brown and dry when tested with a cake tester, about twenty-five minutes for muffins and one hour and five minutes for loaf.

Marina Kalem is one of my oldest friends and my first cooking partner. We used to walk over to her house every day after school and make something from the old Joy of Cooking. *We did every baking project imaginable, even ambitious things like yeast raised doughnuts. We probably made an awful mess although we attempted to clean-up, but Marina's mother, Helen, encouraged us anyway. The only rule was we had to bake "from scratch."*

Helen was also one of the charter devotees of health food, making frequent shopping excursions to Brownie's, the nearby and first health food store I ever knew about in NYC. The products like turbinado sugar she kept in her pantry were an early inspiration.

I must have stayed for dinner often, but the only dish I remember is fossilakia, possibly because it was so far removed from he plain cooking served at home that I dreaded it. Now I love practically anything Greek.

The Kalem version I remember included meat, but I could not get Marina to dredge up a recipe. This meatless version is delicious.

Fossilakia
serves eight

2 lbs. string beans
½ c. olive oil
2 c. sliced onion
2 t. minced garlic
3 c. fresh tomatoes, peeled, seeded and coarsely chopped
½ t. salt
good grinding pepper

Wash string beans, remove stem end and break into 2″ pieces.

Put olive oil and onion in shallow pot and cook over medium low heat, stirring often, until onion is limp. Stir in garlic and cook a minute or so more. Add remaining ingredients, mix well, cover and cook over low heat about half an hour until beans are tender. Stir from time to time. Adjust seasoning.

My sister died when she was nineteen and I was seventeen, and that is why she disappears from this book without even leaving a recipe. She was living off-campus in a rented house with two other college students from Goddard in Vermont. One very cold night the house caught fire from the wood burning stove and burned down. From Martha, my daughters, Phoebe, Sarah and Claude inherited their love of horses.

At that sad time, Matthew Atkinson was my high school boyfriend and his mother, Elizabeth, my very close friend. They took all kinds of care of me. Elizabeth was working as school nurse at Friends Seminary where I went to school and living in Stuyvesant Town with Matthew and his brother, Leeds. She always made something delicious and comforting for dinner and no matter who dropped in from her large circle of friends, there was always plenty of food. I remember her dinners as being in the pot roast family, but Matthew says his mother's specialty was shrimp creole. No matter the offering, she was always there to dish up support and comfort. Elizabeth taught me the why of cooking.

Elizabeth never came near a recipe that I noticed, and since she died several years ago after being ill for years, I've had to imagine this one.

Shrimp Creole
serves six

2 lb. large shrimp
3 T. vegetable oil
2 c. finely chopped onion
1 c. finely chopped celery
1 c. finely chopped green pepper
2 t. minced garlic
½ c. white wine
4 c. chopped canned tomatoes with their juice or 4 c. fresh
    ripe tomatoes, peeled, seeded & chopped
1 t. chopped fresh oregano
1 t. chopped fresh basil
salt
good grinding black pepper
1 T. minced parsley

Peel and devein shrimp.

(continued) ☞

Put oil, onion, celery and pepper in large skillet. Cook over low heat for ten minutes, stirring often. Stir in garlic and cook a minute or so longer. Add wine, tomatoes, oregano, basil, salt and pepper to taste. Cook for fifteen minutes. Add shrimp and cook a minute or so longer until shrimp curl. Garnish with parsley. Serve with plain rice.

Matthew came from a family of Quakers for many generations. As I attended Quaker school from kindergarten through high school, my indoctrination with Quaker values was pretty strong. But not so strong that I couldn't be amazed by seeing them put into practice.

When we were high school seniors, Matthew's interview for admission to Columbia University slipped his mind, and he missed it entirely. That afternoon he called up, and forgoing the little white lie admissions officers expect and deserve, he said, "I'm sorry, but I completely forgot." I was even more shocked when the school admitted him!

After college, Matthew lived for a number of years in the Southwest. It shows in his cooking as he makes the purest and best enchiladas. Gathering to eat them at his family place in Laurel is a real treat, but following his recipe is next best.

Matthew's Enchiladas
serves eight or more

18 dried poblano chiles
1 T. vegetable oil, plus oil for toasting tortillas
1 T. minced garlic
large pinch cumin
salt
1 lb. sharp Cheddar cheese, coarsely grated
1 lb. Monterey Jack cheese, coarsely grated
1 c. coarsely chopped onion
2 dozen corn tortillas

Rinse chiles. Put in large saucepan, cover with water and simmer over low heat until flesh is rehydrated and the skin is loose, about half an hour. Drain.

Remove tops, skins and seeds from flesh by passing through food mill fitted with fine screen.

In saucepan put oil, garlic and cumin. Cook over low heat a minute or so until fragrant, stirring often. Stir in chile puree and cook a minute or so longer. Add one quart water and salt to taste. Simmer for thirty minutes.

(continued) ☞

Coat a large baking dish with sauce. Pour some of the rest of sauce into a shallow bowl, replenishing as needed.

Mix two cheeses and onion.

Over medium low heat in a cast iron pan, toast each tortilla lightly on both sides, brushing pan with a light coating of oil before you add each tortilla.

Using tongs, dip toasted tortillas in sauce in shallow bowl, lightly coating both sides.

Set tortilla on a plate. Sprinkle with cheese and onion mixture. Roll. Set seam side down in baking dish. Repeat until all but 1 c. of cheese mixture is gone.

Top enchiladas with remaining sauce and remaining cheese mixture.

Cover dish with foil.

Set rack in top third of oven and preheat oven to 350 degrees.

Bake enchiladas for twenty minutes. Remove foil and bake until cheese topping bubbles, about ten minutes more.

Serve with bowls of homemade salsa, guacamole, and refried beans as well as sour cream, chopped red onion and shredded crisp lettuce.

When it was time to pick a college, Herb Ernest, father of my good high school friend Lisa, and earliest and greatest supporter and mentor for my cooking career, told me "If you love to cook, you should go to Cornell." He never told me he meant the hotel school.

So I gave the vetting of colleges my usual five minutes of attention, observed that the boys at Cornell were very cute, and enrolled in the school of Art and Sciences. Therefore cooking was never on the academic menu, and I had to squeeze my academic life into a very small space to make time for my cooking experiments. The Agriculture School at Cornell ran a butcher shop, a dairy and an orchard, so I could round up top ingredients merely by riding the campus bus, a very agreeable arrangement.

An indication of my devotion (to cooking) was a typical choice to make steak au poivre for my momentary boyfriend, involving making stock, then demi glace and finally the sauce, somewhat extreme for dinner for two. At the time I didn't have the Coach House restaurant's recipe for the definitive steak au poivre, but my labors were equivalent.

Sue Rohr, a friend and apartment mate, shared my interest in cooking. I believe she's the one who taught me how to make tarragon chicken, to this day a staple of my repertoire.

Tarragon Chicken
serves four

3 whole chicken breasts, boned and halved
flour
3 T. butter
3 T. oil
salt
good grinding black pepper
3 T. minced shallot
¼ c. white wine
1 t. tomato paste
2 T. fresh tarragon leaves or 2 t. dried tarragon
¾ c. chicken broth
¼ c. sour cream

Dredge chicken breasts lightly in flour. In heavy skillet over medium high heat, heat butter and oil until sizzling. Slip in chicken and cook quickly until golden brown on both sides. Remove to plate. Season with salt and pepper.

(continued) ☞

Lower heat. Discard almost all of the fat in pan. Add shallot and stir for a minute, scraping up the browned bits on bottom of pan. Add wine, 2 T. of the dredging flour, tomato paste and tarragon. Stir until smooth. Add chicken broth, stir until smooth. Return chicken and any juices to pan, cover and cook over low heat for fifteen minutes, turning chicken midway through cooking. Remove chicken to warm serving platter. Whisk sour cream into sauce. Heat until piping hot but not boiling. Adjust seasoning and pour over chicken.

During my Cornell era, I began my quest for the perfect quiche. Here's the recipe I ended up with.

Broccoli (or anything else) Quiche
serves six to eight

1 recipe basic pie dough, amount for 10″ shell (following recipe)
2 c. broccoli florets
2 c. grated Gruyere cheese
2 c. heavy cream
4 eggs
salt
good grinding black pepper
good grating nutmeg

Roll dough into 12″ round. Fill 10″ pie pan. Flute edges. Prick dough all over with fork. Put shell in freezer for one hour.

Preheat oven to 400 degrees. Take pie shell from freezer. Cover with aluminum foil and weigh down with beans or rice. (Beans or rice can be reused many times.) Bake about fifteen minutes until dough begins to get dry. Remove foil and weights. Bake three minutes longer, piercing any bubbles that form.

Steam broccoli until just tender, refresh under cold water. Drain well. Put broccoli and cheese in half-baked shell.

Beat cream, eggs, salt, pepper and nutmeg together well. Pour into shell and bake until puffed and set, about forty minutes.

Basic Pie Dough
one 10″ shell

1 c. and 3 T. flour
scant ½ t. salt
pinch baking powder
7 T. butter, cut in ¼″ cubes

In food processor fitted with metal blade, combine flour, salt and baking powder. Cut in butter until mixture has the consistency of cornmeal. Add 4 T. cold water mixing as little as possible to incorporate. Form dough inxto ball, flatten, wrap in plastic and refrigerate an hour or more.

one 9″ shell

1 c. flour
¼ t. salt
pinch baking powder
6 T. butter, cut in ¼″ cubes

Follow directions above. Use 3 T. cold water.

Years later I learned this creamless quiche variation (adapted from a cook-book by Simone Beck, Simca's Cuisine*) which I also love.*

Eggplant Tart
serves eight

1 recipe basic pie dough, amount for 9″ shell (preceding
   recipe)
1 T. Dijon mustard
2 T. grated Gruyere cheese
1½ lb. eggplant, peeled and cut in ½″ cubes
1 t. salt
2 T. olive oil
¼ lb. thickly sliced bacon
1½ lb. ripe tomatoes, peeled seeded and chopped
3 eggs
2 T. shredded basil leaves
2 T. minced parsley
good grinding black pepper

Partially bake shell as above. After removing weights, brush with mustard and sprinkle with cheese. Return to oven until very lightly brown, piercing any bubbles that form with a fork or skewer.

Mix eggplant with salt. Put in colander over bowl or in sink to discharge liquid for several hours, mixing from time to time.

Preheat oven to 375 degrees.

Rinse eggplant under cold running water, drain and squeeze dry a handful or so at a time in a clean dish cloth. Toss egg-plant with oil. Bake on foil lined baking tray stirring from time to time until light brown, about thirty minutes.

Meanwhile in small skillet over low heat, cook bacon until crisp, drain and chop into very small pieces.

(continued) ☞

Puree tomatoes in food processor. Add eggs, basil, parsley and pepper and mix well.

Put cooked eggplant into pie shell. Pour filling on top. Bake until puffed and set about thirty minutes.

Serve hot or at room temperature.

Blue Collar Work in a White Collar Shirt

Cooking School

It scares me to reflect that whenever I've come to a fork in the road I haven't even done something structured like eeny meeny miny mo. I've just forged ahead on one of the paths pulled by some irresistible force. After college, I thought I planned to go to Appalachia with my then boyfriend as he started his career in health planning with United Mine Workers. Although going to the Cordon Bleu was a lifelong fantasy and I had once sent for literature, imagine my surprise when instead of driving to West Virginia, I found myself on a cheap flight to Luxembourg and thence by train to Paris.

The Cordon Bleu then had no entrance requirements, and I confess no real exit requirements either, but there was a year long waiting list. It was completely by chance that on the day I materialized, someone had cancelled. I enrolled in the six week course.

The six week course teaches you that while you thought you were pretty good, you don't know anything, and the few things you had learned were incorrect. I watched the graduating "grande diplome" students do their end of course demonstrations and I knew I had to stay until I got that good! Later I learned that these stars were the merest beginners and that the track ahead was years long.

When I asked to continue, luck was with me again and an opening for the whole program developed. I was permitted to subsidize my tuition by working as dishwasher and occasional chef's assistant which created still more learning opportunities.

Dish washing at a cooking school is an education in itself. You really learn how to get the burned stuff from the bottoms of copper pots! My co-worker at the sink, a long suffering one eyed Algerian man, used to grumble in his halting baritone, "Jamais les couteaux a la plonge" whenever one of the students was foolish enough to approach the deep soapy water to drop in a sharp knife. For God's sake, wash your knife by hand and put it aside!

My work life was humble, but my living quarters deluxe. My cousin Giza in Paris called on my Aunt Manka in New York to allow me to live in her apartment on Rue de Faubourg St. Honore. Manka had maintained this apartment over the decades so she could have a place to stay when she came to Paris for the haute couture showings twice a year, but in her nineties she was no longer making the trip and the apartment was empty. Two blocks from the Elysees Palace and near all the grandest stores like Ungaro and Hermes, I lived in splendor amid the Limoges china and my five Picassos. The merchants had to tolerate the sight of the hippie denizen in American uniform of denim skirt and Frye boots!

Manka died in early spring; the appraiser descended and I moved into my cooking school friend, Sturgess Spanos' place on Rue Monge. It's been downhill ever since, but the low spots suit me more.

Many students were dissatisfied with the Cordon Bleu. After all, they had their own lifelong fantasies to contend with. For me it was like the womb. The professors were enormously talented and warm even when critical and for the first time ever the task at hand was just what I most felt like doing.

It's inexcusable that I don't have a single recipe to sum up Mr. Simon the head chef, but I have one indelible memory. With my Texas friend Joy, I whipped up a huge pot of south of the border spaghetti sauce which we brought in to share with the group. In the seventies, spicy ethnic cuisines had made no inroads in France, and the French could not tolerate any form of heat, certainly not the four alarm stuff Joy liked to produce. Mr. Simon took one bite, fanned his mouth and gasped for five minutes before pulling himself together to pronounce "pas assez de sel." Not enough salt!

The French think béarnaise sauce is zippy, and truly it is one of my favorites, so this recipe will be from Mr. Simon who taught us all this and so much more with abundant patience and good humor. Be sure to check for salt.

Béarnaise Sauce
makes two cups

1¾ c. melted butter
2 T. white wine
2 T. tarragon vinegar
⅓ c. minced shallot
2 T. minced fresh tarragon
4 egg yolks
1 t. minced fresh chervil, if available
salt
pinch white pepper

Several hours before making sauce, refrigerate melted butter. When it solidifies, scrape off and discard any white solids on top. Then lift off the yellow butter leaving the watery waste behind. Remelt butter and cool slightly.

In small shallow pan cook wine, vinegar, shallot and 1 T. of the tarragon over low heat until practically all the liquid has evaporated, stirring from time to time. Beat in egg yolks and 2 T. cold water and whisk constantly until yolks thicken enough to show the path of the whisk. Remove from heat and whisk a minute longer. Add melted butter in a thin stream whisking vigorously as you add. Add remaining 1 T. fresh tarragon, chervil, salt and pepper to taste.

This is the official Cordon Bleu onion soup recipe, more or less. Onion soup was one of the menu items at the student demonstration that inspired me to stay for the full year course.

Onion Soup Gratiné
serves six

8 c. thinly sliced onions
3 T. butter
2 t. salt
¼ t. white pepper
¼ t. sugar
3 T. flour
4 c. chicken broth
4 c. beef broth
¼ c. sherry
2 T. brandy
18 slices of French bread, well dried in a moderate oven
1½ c. Gruyere cheese

Put the onions with the butter in a heavy bottomed pot of medium size. Cook covered over low heat for fifteen minutes, stirring once or twice. Remove cover and raise heat to medium. Add salt, pepper and sugar, and cook for another half hour, stirring frequently and mixing in browned bits from bottom of pan. When the onions are a deep golden brown, sprinkle in flour and mix in well. Add about one cup of broth, mixing it in well. When it simmers, repeat with another cup of broth, then add all remaining broth and the sherry. Simmer for thirty minutes. Taste and adjust seasoning.

Preheat broiler. Add brandy to soup and pour into oven proof tureen. Cover soup with bread slices and sprinkle cheese over bread. Put under broiler until cheese is melted and golden brown. Serve immediately.

Monsieur Tric came to teach at the Cordon Bleu after a long career making Provencale specialties in his native south of France. He brought with him a love of garlic that in the land of classic cooking bordered on the subversive and a boyish enthusiasm for practical jokes. He immediately picked up on the fact that commencing with a whole chicken or duck and proceeding to behead, disembowel, remove pin feathers, feet, and tendons was not especially my favorite way to start the day. On more than one occasion he snuck the head of the duck into my pocketbook. If he didn't get to hear my shriek at the Metro station when I reached in for my subway pass, he could at least imagine it!

I learned to roast duck this way from a recipe of Marcella Hazan's. It's a true pain, but nothing else seems to work as well for getting out all the fat. The sauce formula is pure Cordon Bleu and shows classic cooking at its best. A perfect brown sauce is married to the sweet fruit with a complex liaison of caramel deglazed with vinegar. The diffuse elements don't just co-exist in the sauce; they're knitted together, and the difference is unmistakable. If the end product weren't way above restaurant renditions, I'd never come near this recipe.

Duck à l'Orange
serves four

4½ lb. duckling
salt
good grinding black pepper

Remove neck and gizzards from duck along with any bits of fat from inside or outside that can be pulled away. Reserve neck and gizzards for sauce and fat and liver for another use such as in pâté.

Boil a large pot of water. Put in the duck and simmer for three minutes. Drain and pat completely dry inside and out with paper towels. Use a blow dryer set on high heat to "dry" open the pores in the duck's skin by blow drying the duck all around for about ten minutes. Salt and pepper well inside and out and truss tightly.

Cook on a rotisserie until beautifully browned on all sides and done within, about an hour and a half. When done, clear juice will flow from the thick part of the leg when it is pierced with

(continued) ☞

a cake skewer. You may have to pour off the fat that accumulates in the drip pan below the duck several times. Save the fat for some future unhealthy but delicious frying project.

If you don't have a rotisserie, preheat oven to 400 degrees. Set duck on rack and roast until done, pouring off fat several times.

Make sauce while duck cooks. Let duck stand before quartering with poultry shears.

Orange Sauce
2 medium oranges
2 T. sugar
1 T. white wine vinegar
1½ c. demi glace (p. 21)
salt
¼ t. white pepper

Cut a few strips of peel from oranges using peeler and a light touch. With sharp knife, cut at angle into 1½″ long fine julienne. Put in a small pot of cold water and bring to a boil. Simmer three minutes, drain. Wash out pot and repeat.

Cut rest of peel from oranges, removing white pith. Over bowl, cut orange flesh from between membranes, dropping sections into bowl as you cut. Over bowl, hand squeeze remaining membrane to extract all juice, then discard membrane. Repeat with second orange.

Put sugar and 2 T. cold water in small saucepan. Stir well. Moisten pastry brush with additional water and wash away any bits of sugar clinging to sides of pan. Cook over medium heat without stirring until mixture turns deep brown. Lean back as you add vinegar. Boil a few seconds before adding demi glace, salt and pepper. Cook stirring occasionally until the caramel is dissolved.

Fold orange peels, sections and juice into sauce. Heat until piping hot and serve underneath or along side duck.

Chocolate truffles looked so easy when the chef did them in demonstration. When Joy and I tried to recreate them at home, we learned that they're yet another one of those touch endeavors where everything has to be at the right consistency and temperature, at which point things will indeed work perfectly. Truffle making taught me to beware recipes bearing few ingredients! For those who won't or can't make the effort to master chocolate, thankfully, there's always la Maison du Chocolate right near Place Madeleine and now one in New York!

Chocolate Truffles
makes about 30 pieces

9 oz. excellent quality semi sweet chocolate, chopped fine
1 c. cream
6 oz. covering chocolate*
3 T. best quality cocoa, sifted

Melt semi sweet chocolate and cream together over low heat. Stir until smooth. Let cool then chill slightly in the refrigerator until firm enough to scoop. Scoop into 1" balls with a melon baller or small scoop.

Melt covering chocolate over low heat or in microwave, stirring until smooth.

Roll balls in melted chocolate, place on wax paper until chocolate sets.

Roll balls in cocoa powder.

*Covering chocolate or "couverture" is chocolate with a cocoa mass of 70% or higher, but it should contain some sugar as well.

Before Joy Lukacs, now Lokey, morphed into a (seemingly) well-behaved matron, she was one wild Texas girl. I was willingly pulled into her vortex on many occasions, not the least of which was when after cooking school, she recruited me and my then boyfriend to work with her as chefs/butlers in an American family's chateau in Switzerland. The unexpurgated story will have to await my unauthorized biography, but suffice it to say, a mere few months after our escape from this caper, Joy talked me into doing a department store cooking demonstration with her.

This seemed innocuous enough until she selected as our subject "choux" pastry, the base of profiteroles and eclairs. When we got together to practice our routine, on neither of two occasions would the dough do anything remotely resembling puffing up. Unfortunately we had to head for the store without further rehearsal. It was one of those exciting life moments when I got to open the oven door in front of fifty people and see—yes!—the dough did rise. After decades of success with this truly easy dough, I still approach cream puff dough with trepidation.

Cream Puff Dough or Choux Pastry
makes two dozen puffs

1 stick butter
¼ t. salt
1¼ c. flour
4 eggs, plus 1 yolk

Preheat oven to 375 degrees.

In a large saucepan over medium heat, bring 1 c. cold water, butter, and salt to boil. When butter is melted, dump in flour and stir well over low heat. Dough should come together in a ball. Turn off heat and add 4 whole eggs one at a time until each egg is completely incorporated, or better yet, after beating in flour, transfer dough to bowl of an electric mixer and beat with paddle after each addition.

Drop the dough by the tablespoonful onto ungreased baking sheets leaving plenty of room between pieces. Beat the yolk with 1 T. water and brush over each puff. Bake until dough is puffed and golden, about half an hour. Pierce each puff with a cake tester to allow steam to escape. Turn off oven and put puffs back in for twelve minutes to dry out interiors.

(continued) ☞

NOTE: For eclairs, follow instructions exactly but use a pastry bag with a large circular tip to pipe out 4″ fingers of dough.

Cream puffs gained importance when my daughters made Shun Lee, a fancy New York Chinese restaurant, their favorite special occasion spot. Not only does Shun Lee make elegant Chinese food using perfect ingredients, but it follows up with fabulous western desserts.

Someone made a big mistake when he took off the menu the cream puffs filled with hazelnut cream served in a pool of chocolate sauce and adorned with a few choice berries and a fresh litchi. Thankfully, when the cream puffs rise, I can make a decent reproduction.

Hazelnut Pastry Cream
makes four cups, enough to fill one recipe of cream puffs

2 c. milk
6 egg yolks
¾ c. sugar
¼ c. cornstarch
3 T. hazelnut paste
1 T. Frangelico (hazelnut liqueur)
2 T. soft butter

In large heavy bottomed sauce pan over low heat, bring milk to the verge of boiling. While it heats, beat yolks and sugar until light yellow using an electric mixer if possible. Beat the cornstarch in well. Add half the hot milk, beat in well, then return egg mixture to saucepan. Whisk constantly over low heat until mixture bubbles and thickens. Cook for a minute or so, whisking hard. Off heat, whisk in hazelnut paste, Frangelico, and butter.

Cool, fill pastry bag and use to pipe hazelnut cream into choux which have been cut open near the tops. Replace pastry lids.

Chocolate Sauce
makes one and a half cups

1 c. cream
8 oz. semi sweet chocolate, chopped fine
2 T. Frangelico (hazelnut liqueur)

In small saucepan heat cream over low heat until it is almost boiling. Turn off heat and add chocolate. Stir until smooth. Cool, add Frangelico.

I actually prefer choux as a savory, either as small puffs or made in a large ring and called "gougere." It's certainly not French, but my husband, Jim, likes it best when I tuck in some New Mexican green chilis for a great hors d'oeuvres.

Choux au Fromage
makes four dozen

1 c. chicken broth or water
1 stick butter
½ t. salt
¼ t. grated nutmeg
pinch cayenne pepper
1 c. flour
4 eggs, plus 1 yolk
1 heaping c. grated Gruyere cheese
2 T. or more finely chopped green chile, flesh only (optional)

Preheat oven to 375 degrees.

In a large saucepan over medium heat, bring broth or water, butter, salt, nutmeg and cayenne to boil. When butter is melted, dump in flour and stir well over low heat. Dough should come together in a ball. Turn off heat and add whole eggs one at a time until each egg is completely incorporated, or better yet, after beating in flour, transfer dough to bowl of an electric mixer and beat with paddle after each addition. Add cheese, reserving a tiny bit, and add chile if using. Beat in well.

Drop the dough by the tablespoonful onto ungreased baking sheets leaving plenty of room between pieces. Beat the yolk with 1 T. water and brush over each puff. Place a few shreds of cheese on each puff. Bake until dough is puffed and golden, about 25 minutes Pierce each puff with a cake tester to allow

(continued) ☞

steam to escape. Turn off oven and put puffs back in for twelve minutes to dry out interiors.

Gougère
one ring

Make exactly as above, but form into a large 10″ ring. Baking time will be a bit longer. Pierce in several places and dry out for fifteen minutes. Cut into wedges.

Since school Joy and her husband, Carey Lokey, have created a wonderful country business called "L'Esprit de Campagne," growing and drying tomatoes and all manner of fruits on their Virginia farm. This savory cheesecake is the perfect showcase for their tomatoes. For a smaller group, cut recipe in half and bake for a bit less time in a 7" spring form pan.

Chèvre Cheesecake
serves twenty or more as an hors d'oeuvres

11 T. melted butter
8 oz. sesame bread sticks
½ t. salt
2 lb. goat cheese, at room temperature
1 lb. cream cheese, at room temperature
3 eggs
1 T. minced fresh rosemary
1–2 eight oz. jars L'Esprit de Campagne minced dried
   tomatoes

Brush 1 T. butter all over inside of 9" spring form pan. Put bread sticks and salt in food processor fitted with metal blade. Process into crumbs. Add all remaining butter and pulse to combine well. Put all but 2 T. of crumb mixture in pan and press into bottom and sides in an even layer. Refrigerate for an hour or so.

Preheat oven to 350 degrees.

Beat cheeses until perfectly smooth. Add eggs and rosemary. Pour into crust. Level with spatula. Sprinkle reserved crumbs over top. Put in oven and reduce heat to 325 degrees. Bake until puffed, set and lightly browned, about forty minutes. Turn off oven and leave chevre cheesecake in oven for twenty minutes longer. Remove and let cool.

Drain tomatoes well. Spread over top of cheese cake.

Serve with crackers and French bread.

Joy contributed this recipe which has been in her family for generations. It's great served with fresh berries and unsweetened whipped cream.

Chess Pie
serves ten

1 recipe pie dough, amount for 9″ shell (p. 112)
2 c. sugar
4 eggs
6 T. melted butter, cooled
1 t. vanilla
2 T. flour
1 t. cornmeal
¾ c. milk

Roll dough into 11″ round. Fill 9″ pie pan. Flute edges. Prick dough all over with fork. Put shell in freezer for one hour.

Preheat oven to 425 degrees. Take pie shell out of freezer.

Combine all ingredients except milk. Beat well. Beat in milk.

Pour mixture into pie shell. Bake ten minutes, then lower heat to 300 degrees. Bake for forty-five minutes longer. Cover with foil during last fifteen minutes of baking if pie appears to be getting too brown.

This is the first thing I made in cooking school. My assigned partner was Sturgess Spanos who later became my good friend and even inadvertently introduced me to Jim. He did not give me a friendly look, but I still have the happiest thoughts when I make this because as I've said already, I just loved le Cordon Bleu.

Chocolate Mousse le Cordon Bleu
serves at least six

8 oz. semi-sweet chocolate chips, ⅔ of a 12 oz. bag
7 T. butter
4 eggs, separated
pinch salt

Melt chocolate and butter in double boiler, stirring often. Take off heat and beat in yolks. Cool slightly. Whip whites with a pinch of salt until they make stiff peaks when you lift the beater. Mix one large scoop of whites into chocolate mixture. Pour chocolate mixture over remaining whites and fold gently until no traces of egg white remain. Pour into clean bowl, cover and refrigerate for a few hours. Serve with whipped cream.

Sturgess' grandmother, Marigoula Spanos, makes the best Greek baked goods imaginable, but she's a recipe hoarder, not a sharer. Sturgess, among his family members, was the privileged recipient of her secrets. Once while teaching him a treasured formula, she got up and closed the kitchen door, causing her daughter to howl from the other room, "Why are you shutting that door?" Now that she's one hundred, I hope she'll be happy to know her baklava and feenikia will live on.

Baklava
serves twenty

2 c. finely chopped walnuts
6 crushed zwieback cookies
2⅓ c. sugar
1 t. cinnamon
2 sticks butter, melted
1 lb. phyllo leaves
1⅔ c. sugar
1 t. lemon juice
½ t. vanilla extract

Butter a 10 × 13 baking pan.

Preheat oven to 350 degrees.

Mix walnuts, zwieback crumbs, ⅓ c. sugar and cinnamon.

Place full sheet of dough on counter. Using pastry brush, butter lightly. Place second sheet on top. Butter lightly. Sprinkle lightly with nut mixture. Top with a third sheet of dough. Butter lightly. Sprinkle lightly with nut mixture. Fold short edge over 1″. Butter lightly and roll from this edge to within 2″ of end. Fold edge in half. Butter lightly remaining 1″. Finish rolling and set in pan seam side down. Repeat with remaining leaves and nut mixture to form seven rolls. Add them to the pan as you make them, fitting them in tightly so there's room for all. Butter tops lightly. Cut through rolls at an angle to form diamond shapes. Pour remaining butter over all.

(continued) ☞

Bake for twenty to thirty minutes until brown, reversing pan after fifteen minutes to ensure even browning.

When baklava is almost done, make syrup by boiling 2 c. water, remaining 1⅓ c. sugar, lemon juice and vanilla over medium heat for ten minutes. Take baklava from oven and immediately pour piping hot syrup over all. Let cool uncovered.

Feenikia
makes five dozen

6 c. flour, plus additional as needed
4 c. plus 2 T. sugar
1 T. baking powder
½ t. baking soda
1 c. orange juice
1 c. corn oil
2 sticks melted butter, cooled
⅓ c. whiskey
grated zest of 1 orange
2 t. cinnamon
20 oz. dried dates without pits
2 T. lemon juice
½ t. vanilla extract
3 c. finely chopped walnuts

Put oven rack in center of oven and preheat oven to 375 degrees.

In food processor fitted with metal blade or in large bowl, mix flour, 1 c. sugar, baking powder, and baking soda.

In small bowl, beat together orange juice, corn oil, butter, whiskey, orange zest, and 1 t. cinnamon. Add liquid to flour mixture and pulse or stir to form a slightly greasy dough. Test consistency by trying to form an "egg" with a piece of dough. Mix in flour as needed in small additions until the dough just holds together. It may be necessary to add as much as a cup more.

Scoop dough by the tablespoonful, then form into flat eggs, about 1¼" long, laying a date atop each egg and enfolding with dough. Place creased side down on ungreased cookie sheets, leaving a bit of space between each piece.

Bake until golden and firm, about half an hour. Bottoms burn easily so it's best to make these one rack at a time in center of oven.

(continued) ☞

While cookies bake, prepare syrup by combining 3 c. cold water, 3 c. sugar, lemon juice, and vanilla in saucepan and simmering for several minutes over low heat, stirring from time to time.

As you take cookies from oven, pierce them all the way through with a skewer in a couple of places. Dunk four or five cookies at a time in the simmering syrup, removing after eight seconds with a slotted spoon. Set on a piece of wax paper with a bit of space between cookies. Repeat baking and dunking process until all cookies are done. Cover remaining syrup and save.

Allow cookies to cool and set for about six to eight hours. Pick cookies up after the first hour to make sure they are not sticking to paper.

Make topping by combining chopped walnuts, remaining 2 T. sugar and remaining 1 t. cinnamon.

Return reserved syrup to simmer. Dunk cookies in syrup just to moisten, set on clean wax paper and roll in nut mixture. Cool.

Sturgess contributed this to one of my family Thanksgivings and it's become the stuff of legend. Serve with whipped cream.

Chocolate Walnut Pie
serves six to eight

1 recipe Joseph's pie dough (p. 163)
4 oz. unsweetened chocolate
4 T. butter
6 eggs
⅔ c. lightly packed light brown sugar
1½ c. light corn syrup
2 c. walnut halves

Roll pie dough out to fill 10″ pie pan. Trim and flute edges. Hold in freezer until ready to bake.

Preheat oven to 400 degrees. Take pie shell from freezer. Cover with aluminum foil and weigh down with beans or rice. (Beans or rice can be reused many times.) Bake about fifteen minutes until dough begins to get dry. Remove and cool.

Turn oven down to 350 degrees. Melt chocolate and butter together in double boiler, stirring often. Off heat, stir until smooth. Beat eggs well. Add sugar and corn syrup and beat until well combined. Add nuts and chocolate mixture and combine well.

Pour filling into partially baked pie shell and bake until set, about one hour, turning pan about midway through baking for even browning.

In the seventies, Chef Paul Bocuse towered above every other working chef in France. With his television appearances, books and international restaurant and cooking empire, he created the category of celebrity chef. Inevitably when a group of underfunded cooking students decided to make their one excursion to a three Michelin star shrine (generously treated by my parents,) it could only be to Bocuse's place in Lyons.

For the journey Sturgess drove a carload of us in his aged Renault Quatre. Unfortunately the ancient car picked that inopportune day to lose its muffler completely, so we traveled the auto route hanging out of the windows gasping for air and halted in the restaurant parking lot with a volley of backfires. We're here!

In spite of our shabby appearance which we were able to maintain in the dining room as well as in the parking lot, we were treated to the meal of a lifetime, sampling the legendary Soupe aux Truffes and the Poulet Bresse in Demi Deuil, two of Bocuse's great specialties. Anyone who thinks a great meal is not worth the price is not taking into account memories that last forever. And those who travel around France eating at two places like this a day, well, I don't understand them either.

What a rich experience! For cooking students it was a revelation. Service so perfect we didn't even notice we were being served and a dining room so commodious that we felt like the only people in it. Although we didn't over drink—who could afford to?—that night we were all overcome by thirst. Finally we got Mr. Simone's message about using enough salt. The food had been salted to the quintessential degree, bringing every element into focus, but without one superfluous grain.

Joe and Norma Walsh, friends of Ralph and Audrey Goldberg, lived in Paris while I was in cooking school. They took me under their wings and introduced me to several of the fine restaurants of Paris including Chiberta and Le Grand Vefour. One meal at a place like Grand Vefour could illuminate my cooking school experience for weeks. After I tried the "feuilleté des asperges," asparagus in puff pastry, I realized what I was trying to accomplish by making puff pastry dough week after week and also how far I had to go.

When we all were back in New York, they took me out to a tiny Greenwich Village place, Mon Petit Robert, and introduced me to Sauternes wine and this great and easy dessert which I believe Robert learned from a Gourmet magazine or perhaps the magazine learned it from him.

Ginger Pots de Crème Mon Petit Robert

serves eight

1 quart heavy cream
12 egg yolks
¾ c. sugar
1 T. powdered ginger

Preheat oven to 325 degrees.

In heavy pot over low heat, bring cream to simmer. Meanwhile beat yolks and sugar together well. Add ginger and beat in well.

Slowly pour hot cream into egg mixture while beating vigorously. Return mixture to pot and cook over low heat while stirring continuously with a wooden spoon, being sure to get spoon into angles of pot. When mixture thickens enough to coat spoon, strain into bowl.

Neatly fill eight custard cups (pouring out of a Pyrex measuring cup works well) and set them in a baking pan with sides approximately 1½″ high. Pour in boiling water to a depth of ¾″ and bake until custards set, about twenty-five minutes. Cool, wrap with plastic wrap and refrigerate. Serve cold.

Work Fare

After cooking school my friend, Carol Pomerance, helped me get a job at One Fifth on Eighth Street where she was working as a waitress. I doubt I'd have had the moxie to walk into such an "in" restaurant on my own. The first night I started work serving up the cold dishes was the night of the NYC blackout of 1977. We worked for several hours in the dark imagining the power might come on at any time. The next day, the restaurant opened its doors and gave all the food away so it wouldn't spoil.

Since I could do my first assignment in the dark, I spoke up when there was an opening on "the line." The real cooking jocks worked the line, and at a happening restaurant with many seats, the line was pretty intense. I worked there for a couple of weeks, more or less mastering the ten or so dishes that came from my station in large number, although not long enough to figure out how the One Fifth omelet differed from the ones I was turning out.

At twenty-two, I was a skinny thing, and the temperature on the meat thermometer in my shirt pocket registered 105 degrees during service. I used to lose ten pounds every night then spend the next day loading up on food and water to regain them. Incidentally, I also worked until one o'clock in the morning, a fact that will be greeted with universal disbelief among those who know me now. I have witnesses.

Both because they were great and because they bring back happy memories, I still like to make dishes like the ones on the restaurant menu.

Steak à l'Amoreuse
serves two

2 pieces of beef filet, about 10 oz. each
salt
good grinding black pepper
piece of beef fat
3 T. cognac
2 T. minced shallot
2 t. Dijon mustard
1 scant T. green peppercorns, the kind in brine
½ c. demi glaze (p. 21)
¼ c. cream
1 t. dried tarragon
1 T. minced fresh chives

Preheat oven to 400 degrees.

Tie a piece of butcher's twine around each piece of meat to maintain the shape, or get the butcher to do it. Generously season meat with salt and pepper.

Render the beef fat over medium high heat in a medium size skillet and discard the bit of solid fat that remains. Brown the meat on both sides in the hot fat, then transfer the meat to a "sizzler" platter or baking sheet and put in oven to finish cooking while you make the sauce, just a minute or so longer. Test doneness by pressing on the meat with your forefinger. The more it resists, the more it's cooked. You can sure get a feel for this sort of thing in a short time in a restaurant job, especially since, if you get it wrong, that meat will be coming back to you post haste!

(continued) ☞

Pour off grease in skillet. Part of the fun at One Fifth was we used to pour that grease right inside the stove. I'm not sure where it went. Pour in cognac and ignite by tilting pan so flames reach the cognac. With an electric stove, you'll need to use a match. To flaming pan, add shallot, mustard, pepper-corns, demi glaze, cream, and tarragon, shaking to mix and to keep the flames going awhile. Reduce to a sauce-like consistency.

Take meat from oven, cut away strings and put on two plates. Divide sauce over meat. Sprinkle chives on top.

At One Fifth the handsomest man from Fukien Province in China whose unpronounceable name I no longer carry with me (we called him Wongo) used to spend twelve hours a day, six days a week in the restaurant basement doing one thing only, peeling shrimp. Although he could have done all the more glamorous, higher paying (but not well-paying!) jobs upstairs, we could never have done his, so there he remained. At least One Fifth was an equal opportunity after hours social club. We shared little language but you could always share a snifter of Remy Martin or Martell with the guys from Fukien.

Shrimp Scampi
serves two

14 large shrimp (16/20 count)
3 T. oil
1 T. butter, plus 1 t. butter cut into bits and frozen
2 T. minced shallots
1 T. minced garlic
salt
good grinding black pepper
¼ c. white wine
2 T. parsley

Peel and devein shrimp.

Heat oil and 1 T. butter in large skillet over high heat. When oil is piping hot, add shrimp and toss or stir for about twenty seconds until shrimp are bright pink and starting to curl. Add shallot, garlic, salt, pepper and wine. Cook flipping or stirring to mix for thirty seconds longer. Off heat, add frozen butter and parsley. Frozen butter will thicken the sauce slightly. Serve with rice pilaf and sauteed spinach.

This ridiculously easy dish wows everyone!

Shrimp with Dill
serves two

14 large shrimp (16/20 count)
3 T. vegetable oil
1 T. butter
2 T. minced shallot
salt
pinch white pepper
⅓ c. white wine
½ c. cream
2 T. minced fresh dill

Peel and devein shrimp.

Heat oil and butter in large skillet over high heat. When oil is piping hot, add shrimp and toss for about twenty seconds until shrimp are bright pink and starting to curl. Add shallot, salt, white pepper, wine, cream and dill. Cook stirring or flipping to mix for thirty seconds longer. Remove shrimp to plates, reduce sauce a bit and pour over shrimp. Serve with the same side dishes as for scampi.

I think of this as one of the dishes from my saute station, although I'm not certain that's where it actually originated. Now I only use the local scallops from Peconic Bay.

Peconic Bay Scallops Scampi Style
serves two

14 oz. bay scallops
¼ c. flour
3 T. olive oil
2 T. butter, plus 2 t. butter, cut into bits and frozen
salt
good grinding black pepper
2 T. minced shallot
1 t. minced garlic
¼ c. sherry
2 T. minced parsley

Dry scallops by spreading on paper towels. Heat oil and 2 T. butter in large skillet over medium high heat until sizzling. Lightly flour scallops and slip into oil. Cook until golden brown on all sides, turning by flipping pan or stirring. Remove from pan with slotted spoon. Season with salt and pepper.

Discard practically all the grease in the pan.

Add shallot and garlic and cook over low heat, stirring and scraping up browned bits in pan. Add sherry. Cook a minute. Add parsley. Turn off heat and add frozen butter, shaking pan to mix in. Return scallops to pan, toss in sauce and serve right away.

Sauteed Spinach

serves one

1 very large handful of clean, drained spinach leaves
1 T. olive oil
1 t. minced garlic
salt
good grinding black pepper

In medium skillet over high heat, get oil very hot. Add spinach and toss for a few seconds. Add garlic and salt and pepper. As soon as leaves are limp, put with pan juices onto plate.

Rice pilaf is a restaurant work horse, always holding up in the steam table and harmonizing with everything in the fish and chicken family, at least. I'm sure at One Fifth, pilaf was produced in vast quantities, but this recipe is family scale. For a different treat altogether, substitute coarse bulgur wheat for the rice.

Rice Pilaf

serves six

¾ c. minced onion
3 T. butter
1⅔ c. rice
3 c. chicken broth
1 bay leaf
salt

In saucepan over medium heat, cook onion in butter until soft, stirring from time to time. Add rice and cook, stirring often, a few minutes longer. Add broth, bay leaf and salt. Bring to boil, lower heat and simmer covered for eighteen minutes. Remove bay leaf and fluff with fork.

Beef dishes were often accompanied by these zippy potatoes.

Horseradish Mashed Potatoes
serves eight to ten

4 lb. Yukon Gold potatoes
salt as needed
3 T. butter
1¼ c. milk
large pinch white pepper
good grinding nutmeg
freshly grated horseradish to taste

Peel potatoes and cut into large chunks. Put in a large saucepan and cover with cold water. Add a generous amount of salt. Cook over medium low heat until tender when pierced with a cake tester. Drain, return to pot and cook over low heat a minute or so to evaporate excess moisture. Mash with a potato masher or put through a food mill, depending on whether you favor lumpy or smooth mashed potatoes. (I like both.) Heat butter and milk in cooking pot. Beat in potatoes, white pepper and nutmeg. Add salt to taste. Beat in horse-radish as you finish seasoning potatoes. Potatoes should be quite zesty.

When the position of chef garde manger opened up, I took it. Not studly, but a day job. The highlight was making gallons of cucumber borscht in a gigantic stainless steel blender which iced up from the cold ingredients in a most gratifying way. Earlier in this book, I include Trudy Rosen's recipe for a similar, fantastic cold borscht.

Tim McGrath, a co-worker gave me this pâté recipe which I'm pretty sure came from the Culinary Institute of America where he had been a student. This comes out great for anyone willing to go to the trouble and mess. It's worthwhile to make it on this epic scale and share it with friends.

Pâté de Campagne
makes four pates

4 lbs. pork butt
4 lb. veal
1 large carrot peeled
2 large stalks celery
1 medium onion
1 bunch parsley, well washed and dried but intact
1 lb. pork liver
1 lb. duck liver
1 c. brandy
1 c. Madeira
2 T. minced shallot
2 T. minced garlic
¼ c. salt
1 T. freshly ground black pepper
2 crushed bay leaves
2 t. dried thyme
1 heaping t. dried marjoram
1 heaping t. dried basil
1 heaping t. dried tarragon
1 heaping t. dried chervil
¼ t. white pepper
¼ t. ground ginger
¼ t. freshly grated nutmeg

(continued) ☞

¼ t. ground cloves

8 eggs

1 lb. pork caul fat

Through meat grinder with medium blade, put pork, veal, carrot, celery, onion and parsley twice and set aside overnight in refrigerator.

Marinate livers overnight in remaining ingredients except eggs and caul fat. Next day, puree livers in food processor and add with eggs to ground meat, mixing well.

Line four 9″ × 5″ loaf pans with caul fat. Fill with pate, then cover with caul fat. Wrap each pan in aluminum foil.

Preheat oven to 325 degrees and boil a pot of water. Put pates in two baking pans with two inch sides and pour in 1½″ boiling water. Bake for 2½ hours. Remove pates and weigh down while hot with something heavy like a clean brick wrapped in foil. Refrigerate when cool, still with weights. Serve the next day.

Eventually, in one of millions of staff moves, the owner hired a new head chef. The day the chef threw the quiches I made the day before into the garbage proclaiming "we make fresh quiche every day" was the day I left in the middle of lunch service. Oh well, I met my future catering partner, Barry Wildman there, and was related by past servitude with practically all the American cooks working in downtown kitchens. Not bad for a few weeks' work.

I met Barry Wildman when he was sous chef at One Fifth and I was the lowly garde manger. When I left the restaurant (in a huff), we started a catering business, "Michelson & Wildman." Barry was long on confidence, so he didn't allow our complete lack of experience to prevent the launch.

Lois Cowan got us our first catering job. Nothing like starting at the top. She had lovely and very successful friends, the Edersheims, who entertained frequently in elegant style in their apartment overlooking Central Park. I still don't know if she told them we knew what we were doing or that we were just starting out and needed a break. The Edersheims were just nice enough to take us on that basis, but I fear Lois had built us up.

We planned a beautiful menu for a sit down dinner party for ten. Just "off the boat" from France, I was very enthusiastic about a first course of poached turbot in a light cream sauce. I had no idea there wasn't a turbot swimming within a thousand miles of New York City, and at that time, no one was air lifting ingredients from place to place. To my great relief, Slavin, one of the big fish wholesalers, had a turbot for me. Ecstatic, I walked to Chelsea on the afternoon of the party to pick it up only to discover my turbot was a huge frozen slab almost three feet in diameter. With tears streaming down my face, I walked the half mile home carrying it in front of me like a tray. Barry and I got the thing thawed out by giving it a two hour cold shower.

So much for omens! And it didn't get better with the next course, rack of lamb "en couronne." Most of the success of a rack of lamb is determined at the butcher shop. Racks vary widely in size and quality. For the Edersheims' party, we purchased meat of impeccable quality from Jefferson Market and had several racks joined together in a crown roast. In the center we piled a lovely meat laced filling of spinach and herbs.

I was already plenty inexperienced in cooking a top cut of meat—the frugal proprietress of the Cordon Bleu had us taught hundreds of dishes with the cheaper cuts but not so many with the better ones. The variability of size and quality of the meat makes it difficult for even the experienced to gauge cooking times for a rack. In fact in my recipe I give no set time. Putting the racks together as a crown roast and then putting filling inside added the final element of uncertainty to the timing process

Suffice it to say, when the roast looked absolutely beautiful on the outside we presented it proudly to the guests and then took in to the kitchen to carve. At that point we discovered it was completely raw. After presentation, a delay of ten minutes would probably be the most that could possibly be deemed

(continued) ☞

acceptable, but this roast looked to have thirty minutes of cooking to go. Well, we made the best of a bad situation and got that dinner on the plates within the deadline. Dealing with disaster is truly what catering is about.

In spite of that fiasco, I still adore rack of lamb—when it's good—and it's one of my favorite things to order in a restaurant. But then it's such a simple dish to make it home if you are content to serve the plain pan juice instead of a sauce.

Rack of Lamb
serves four or more

2 single racks of lamb
1 T. vegetable oil
salt
good grinding black pepper
¼ c. fresh bread crumbs
3 T. olive oil
2 T. minced parsley
1 t. minced garlic
½ t. minced fresh rosemary

Have butcher trim away all but a thin layer of fat from on top of meat and completely clean up bottoms of bones.

Preheat broiler. Rub racks with oil and season generously with salt and pepper. Broil racks fat side up quite close to heat until golden brown, about five minutes. Turn and brown bone side a few minutes. Remove and preheat oven to 450 degrees.

Mix bread crumbs, oil, parsley, garlic, and rosemary. Season crumb mixture with salt and pepper. Pack on top of browned meat. Put racks in oven and bake until done, about five minutes or so for really small racks. Test with an instant reading meat thermometer which should read 125 degrees when racks are done. Let meat stand a few minutes before you slice into individual chops. Save the juice which collects on the cutting board and and add to platter with any juices in roasting pan.

Not only did the Edersheims have us back, but we eventually came to know what we were doing, although continuing to have disasters all the while. When Paula Wolfert did a pull-out spread for New York Magazine *on "The Best Caterers in Town" she attended one of our parties and wrote us up as among the best "itinerant chefs." That led to an avalanche of business.*

At the time of the review, I was in my second semester at Columbia Law School, a place to which I saw fit to apply when I broke my foot crossing Canal Street. The day I hobbled home to my walk-up apartment and found the phone disconnected for non-payment was the day blue collar work no longer seemed so glamorous. I continued to cater while in law school, however, since I had already discovered as an undergraduate that the secret to academic survival is paying your tuition bill on time.

When the review broke and we had our choice of jobs, I realized how little I wanted a life spent in panty hose or a chair, so my law career ended when the semester did. I slightly redeemed myself a few years later when I married Jim, and G.G. had an announcement put in the New York Times. The headline read: (at least) "Ms. Michelson Weds Lawyer." My law school friends found it hilarious and featured the clipping on the refrigerator for years.

One of Barry's creations, better than turbot!

Barry's Seafood Salad

serves sixteen to twenty as part of a buffet

1 recipe court bouillon (following recipe)
2 lbs. large shrimp (16/20 count)
1¼ lb. bay scallops
one 3 lb. lobster
⅔ c. minced red onion
½ c. thinly sliced scallion
⅓ c. peeled and finely chopped celery
1 roasted red pepper, cut in ¼" dice
¼ c. minced parsley
1 heaping t. minced garlic
⅔ c. safflower oil
⅓ c. lime juice
⅓ c. lemon juice
1 T. sherry
salt
¼ t. white pepper

(continued) ☞

Make court bouillon, return to large pot and bring to boil.

Meanwhile peel and devein shrimp.

Put shrimp in court bouillon and cook until they just begin to curl, stirring once or twice. Drain, reserving bouillon. Let shrimp cool. Return court bouillon to pot, and when it simmers, add scallops. Cook for seconds until scallops are opaque. Drain, reserving court bouillon. Let scallops cool. Return court bouillon to pot, and when it simmers, add lobster. Cook about 10 minutes to the pound or 26 minutes for a three pounder. Turn off heat and let stand for fifteen minutes. Drain. Cool.

Remove lobster from shell and cut meat into 1″ pieces.

Mix seafood with remaining ingredients. Let stand for half an hour. Adjust seasoning.

Court Bouillon
makes one gallon

1 c. sherry
1 onion, quartered
1 large celery stalk
10 parsley stems
2 bay leaves
several sprigs fresh thyme, if available
1 T. whole white peppercorns
2 t. salt

Simmer 20 c. water, sherry, onion, celery, parsley stems, bay leaves, thyme, peppercorns and salt in large pot for half an hour. Strain, reserving liquid.

My only cushy job ever was as chef in the private dining room of L.F. Roth-schild, Unterberg, and Towbin, an investment banking firm at 55 Water Street in NYC. I had the run of a huge, immaculate kitchen maintained by a clean-ing service, had no budget concerns and an amiable and ample staff to pre-pare breakfast and lunch for the partners. There was even a separate man-ager who handled details like ordering and staffing.

By my best assessment I cook like Rod Carew batted, able to pound out unlimited hits, without being much of a home run threat. The best part of the Rothschild job was having a captive audience to feed and nurture day after day. If today wasn't perfect, there was always tomorrow. The low pressure atmosphere was ideal for developing skills and recipes.

Of course, for good or ill, I had to work with what came before. My predeces-sor left behind his delicious formula for the house salad dressing and the absurd moniker it's never been able to shake:

Sexy Salad Dressing
makes three and a half cups

½ c. Dijon mustard
½ c. Hellman's mayonnaise
1 T. lemon juice
1 t. sugar
½ t. salt
large pinch white pepper
1 c. extra virgin olive oil
1 c. safflower oil
⅓ c. white wine vinegar
1 T. dried thyme leaves
1 T. dried tarragon
1 T. dried basil
2 T. minced parsley
1 t. minced garlic

Have all ingredients at room temperature.

In blender combine mustard, mayonnaise, 1 T. hot water, lemon juice, sugar, salt and pepper. Blend and slowly add both oils through the top of blender and then add the vinegar. Put in large jar and add herbs and garlic. Shake to combine.

This dressing finds its absolute best use coating fresh beets served on a bed of pungent arugula.

Beet Salad
serves eight

1 large bunch arugula
3 lb. beets, tops discarded or used in another dish
¾ c. coarsely chopped red onion
¼ c. minced parsley
salt
good grinding black pepper
1 c. sexy salad dressing (preceding recipe)

Wash and dry arugula thoroughly.

Wash beets, put in large pot with water to cover amply and boil until tender when pierced with a cake tester. Drain, rinse under cold water, and slip off skins while beets are still warm. Cool beets and cut into ½″ dice. Add onion, parsley, salt and pepper to beets. Mix well. Pour dressing over beets and let stand a half hour or so. Pile beets on a platter and surround with arugula.

Every day there was soup on the menu, often a clear soup with lots of "stuff" in it, always an agreeable notion. Edie, the German waitress, trained me to save the vegetable parings for the compost heap in her backyard garden in Queens which she hauled home by subway and bus. She repaid with home-grown tomatoes and other treats for this delicious, not authentic gumbo.

Chicken Gumbo
serves eight

2 T. butter
2 c. coarsely chopped onion
1 c. peeled celery, cut in ¼" pieces
1 c. mixed green and red pepper, cut in ¼" pieces
2 tomatoes, peeled, seeded and cut in ¼" pieces
10 c. chicken broth
2 bay leaves
salt
good grinding black pepper
large pinch cayenne pepper
⅓ c. rice
1 c. small okra pods, tops removed and discarded, sliced ⅓" thick, or frozen okra treated the same
2 c. cooked chicken meat, cut in ½" pieces
1 c. uncooked corn, cut off the cob or 1 c. drained canned corn

In soup pot, put butter, onion, celery and peppers. Cook over medium low heat for several minutes until vegetables soften, stirring occasionally. Add tomatoes. Cook a minute longer. Add broth, bay leaves, salt, pepper and cayenne pepper. Bring soup to a simmer and cook about ten minutes. Add rice and okra. Cook for ten minutes. Add chicken and corn. Return to simmer. Turn off heat. Remove and discard bay leaves. Adjust seasoning.

Toby, a waiter from Ecuador, had his own specialty. Between salmonella and e coli fears, I doubt anyone would now come near this, but in the good old days when food was not out to get you, this was great!

Steak Tartare
serves two

14 oz. freshly chopped, highest quality lean beef
2 egg yolks
a little chopped anchovy
a little minced onion
a little Pommery mustard
a little Worcestershire sauce
a few capers
salt
good grinding black pepper

Mix everything together in a bowl. Serve with Melba toast.

Joe, the security guard, used to make the sweep of the kitchen around lunch time. We always had a plate of food for him and he often had his wife's calzone for us.

Joe's Wife's Calzone
serves twelve

1 recipe focaccia, dough only (p. 346)
1½ lb. ricotta cheese
¼ c. freshly grated Romano cheese
½ lb. mozzarella cheese, cut in ¼″ pieces
½ lb. thinly sliced sopressato or other dry Italian sausage,
   cut into ¼″ pieces
¼ lb. thinly sliced prosciutto, cut into ¼″ pieces
2 eggs
good grinding black pepper

Make dough for focaccia and let rise two times. Meanwhile make filling for calzone by mixing cheeses, sopressato, prosciutto, eggs and pepper.

Preheat oven to 425 degrees.

Divide dough into four pieces. Roll or stretch into thin rounds, about 12″ in diameter. Put a quarter of the filling on half of each piece of dough, leaving 1″ edge. Moisten edge with water. Fold and crimp to seal. Pierce dough with paring knife in several places. Let rest ten minutes.

Bake until golden brown, about twenty-five minutes, reversing baking sheets midway through baking.

Cool. Cut each calzone into pieces.

Alida, the manager I originally worked with, was from Holland. Her specialty was a fritter made from shredded beef. If she ever parted with the recipe, I no longer have it. I remember it was a great deal of work, but she took pleasure in bringing it in for her co-workers.

Joseph Viggiani, replaced her when she retired. He was a fabulous baker who had trained with Nick Malgieri and had his own baking business in Greenwich Village. Joseph gave me several recipes which became family favorites. When our friends, Rob Horwitz and Cathy Redlich, married at home in New Jersey, I recommended Joseph as caterer. He baked his usual amazing creation for their wedding cake, but it melted utterly when the car overheated in a Holland Tunnel traffic jam. Since Cathy would rather tell a great story than eat a good dessert, over time the cake has given total satisfaction. And Joseph's name is often spoken!

Here are a few of his recipes.

Melon Soup
serves four

½ of a ripe cantaloupe, peeled, seeded and cut in chunks
2 c. orange juice
⅓ c. lime juice
1 T. honey or slightly more to taste

Puree all but 1 c. melon and all other ingredients in blender. Chill. Cut remaining melon into fine dice and use as garnish.

Field Green Salad with Walnut Dressing

serves four or more

1 small head Boston lettuce or two heads Bibb lettuce
1 small bunch young dandelion leaves
1 small bunch arugula
2 cups wild greens like lambs quarters, orach, mustard
    greens or 2 c. mesclun
¼ c. snipped chives, basil or other salad herbs and edible
    flowers
1 recipe walnut dressing (following recipe)

Wash and dry lettuce, dandelion, arugula and other greens thoroughly. Put in large salad bowl and top with herbs and flowers. Toss greens with a moderate amount of walnut dressing at table side. There will be extra dressing.

Walnut Dressing

makes one cup

1 T. walnuts
1 T. blanched almonds
1 clove garlic
½ slice fresh bread, crumbled
salt
good grinding black pepper
1 T. white wine or sherry vinegar
juice of ½ lemon
2 T. heavy cream
⅔ c. extra virgin olive oil

Blend all ingredients with a dash of water until smooth.

Swedish Apple Cake
makes one 10″ cake

1 recipe Joseph's pie dough (following recipe)
14 Granny Smith apples
½ c. walnut halves, slightly crushed
⅔ c. yellow raisins
½ c. lemon juice
½ c. sugar
1 T. cinnamon
2 t. ground coriander seed
2 T. melted butter

Roll dough out to cover bottom and sides of 10″ spring form pan. Set aside in refrigerator while you make apple filling.

Peel 11 of the apples, core and cut in ½″ pieces. Put apples in large heavy bottomed skillet with walnuts, raisins, lemon juice, sugar, cinnamon, and coriander. Add 1½ c. water. Cook over medium heat, stirring often, until apples are just tender and liquid is almost all evaporated. Cool. Spoon inside shell and level.

Put oven rack in lower third of oven and preheat oven to 375 degrees. Peel, core and thinly slice remaining apples. Arrange slices in overlapping circles on top of cooked apple filling. Brush with melted butter. Bake until crust is golden brown, about forty minutes.

Serve warm or at room temperature with sweetened whipped cream.

Joseph's Pie Dough

makes enough for one 10" apple cake or 12" tart

2 c. flour
½ c. sugar
1 t. salt
1 t. baking powder
½ t. baking soda
1 stick butter
1 egg and 1 yolk
½ t. vanilla extract

In large bowl by hand or in food processor fitted with metal blade, mix flour, sugar, salt, baking powder and baking soda. Cut in butter until mixture resembles cornmeal.

Mix egg and yolk with 2 T. cold water and vanilla extract. Add to flour mixture and combine with minimum of mixing, just until dough comes together. Wrap dough in plastic wrap, flatten, and refrigerate for several hours.

Joseph's Fruit Tart
makes one 12" tart

1 recipe Joseph's pie dough (preceding recipe)
1 stick butter
1 c. sugar
2 T. flour
½ t. vanilla extract
2 large eggs
2 quarts washed and hulled strawberries or 2 pints
  unwashed raspberries
¼ c. currant jelly
1 T. Kirsch or rum

Roll dough out into 16" circle. Gently drape in half and then in quarters and carefully place with tip in center of a 12" tart pan with removable sides. Unfold dough and lightly press into pan. Use scissors to trim dough ⅓" above pan. Refrigerate for a half hour or more.

Preheat oven to 350 degrees.

Brown and clarify butter by cooking over medium high heat in a small saucepan with a heavy bottom. Watch attentively, shaking pan from time to time. When butter is light brown, remove pan from heat. Cool slightly. Spoon off and discard any impurities that may have risen to the top. Pour butter slowly into a bowl leaving behind any particles that have collected at the bottom of the pan.

Add sugar, flour, vanilla extract, and eggs to brown butter. Whisk together thoroughly. Pour filling into tart shell. Bake until golden brown and set, about a half hour.

Cool. Top with fresh berries. Melt jelly in saucepan over low heat, thin with Kirsch or rum, and brush berries with warm jelly to make them glisten.

My job at Rothschild was too good to be true, and when I moved to Long Island, I passed it along to Sturgess.

Clam pie entered my repertoire when Patti Scott, my partner in a fledgling catering enterprise, received a phone call from Barbara Costikyan. Ms. Costikyan was writing an article on prepared foods on the East End of Long Island for New York Magazine *and she wanted to know if "Michelson & Scott" made clam pie. Naturally we did! This is what we came up with after we were able to inform ourselves about what on earth a clam pie is.*

Clam Pie
serves eight

2 carrots, peeled and cut in julienne strips
2 onions, thinly sliced
2 stalks celery, cut in julienne strips
2 c. potato, peeled and cut in ½″ cubes
1 lb. mushrooms, wiped clean and sliced
1 t. lemon juice
1 c. dry white wine
4 dozen cherrystone clams, well washed
5 T. butter
⅓ c. flour
½ c. cream
pinch white pepper
2 T. dry sherry
1 recipe basic pie dough, amount for 10″ shell (p. 112)
1 egg yolk
2 T. milk

In a large pot with ample boiling water, blanch carrot, onion, celery and potato for five minutes. Drain and put in shallow casserole capable of holding 12 cups.

Put mushrooms, 1 T. water and lemon juice in the same pot. Cover and cook over medium heat until mushrooms release their liquid. Use slotted spoon to add mushrooms to casserole.

(continued) ☞

To the mushroom liquid left in the pot, add the wine. Add half the clams, cover and cook over medium high heat. Remove cooked clams as they open wide and, when all have been removed, cook remaining raw clams in the same liquid.

When clams are cool enough to handle, remove them from shells. Trim away and discard any hard bits of clam and cut each clam into quarters. Add to casserole.

Strain the clam juice through a fine strainer lined with a coffee filter paper or paper towel to remove all sand. Measure three cups and reserve for the sauce.

Melt butter in a saucepan over low heat. Whisk in flour. Add hot reserved clam broth all at once whisking vigorously, or if clam broth has cooled, add it gradually, whisking well between each addition. Simmer a few minutes. Whisk in cream and white pepper. Turn off heat and add sherry. Mix sauce into contents of casserole and let cool.

Roll dough to ⅛" thickness and to a shape that will cover the casserole with 1" to spare all around. Drape dough over casserole and brush with water along the under side of overhanging dough. Press moistened dough to casserole to form a tight seal. Make egg wash by beating egg yolk and milk together with a fork.

Brush egg wash over surface of pie dough. Use a small knife to poke a hole in the center of the dough to allow steam to escape.

Preheat oven to 400 degrees. Bake clam pie until top is golden brown, about forty-five minutes.

Patti and I had met when we each took our six month old babies to a class in infant swimming. We hit it off and we imagined our babies did too. Eventually we started a catering business that we ran for a few years. Although we've lost touch, as an East End newcomer I valued Patti's friendship and enjoyed getting to know a family (the Osbornes) that had been around to receive one of the original land grants in East Hampton. One of the highlights from the time of our friendship was an invitation to the very exclusive Maidstone Club. Even in the early 1980's it was easy to imagine we were the first Jews ever to set foot inside (as guests anyway,) and Jim was certainly the first man ever to attend an event there dressed neither in Madras nor whale print pants!

Anyhow, that clam pie led to lots of business. And then it led to chicken pot pie and, much later, to my own version of shepherd's pie.

Chicken Pot Pie
serves eight

Use same ingredients and procedure as clam pie except substitute six cups cooked boneless chicken cut in ½″ pieces and three cups well salted chicken broth for their clam counterparts.

Shepherd's Pie
serves four or more

3 T. vegetable oil
2½ lb. well trimmed beef stew meat, cut into 1″ cubes
salt
good grinding black pepper
2 c. thinly sliced onions
1 t. minced garlic
1 T. flour
1–2 bottles of good quality beer as needed
1 bouquet garni
1 c. baby carrots
16 small pearl onions, peeled
1 c. frozen peas
2 lb. freshly harvested sweet potatoes
2 T. butter
1 T. minced parsley
1 T. snipped chives, optional
¼ t. white pepper
¼ t. freshly grated nutmeg

Put oil in large heavy bottomed skillet and place over medium high heat until oil is quite hot but not smoking. Put in stew cubes with room between pieces so they will brown and not steam. Add more cubes as space becomes available. Cook turning from time to time until pieces are nicely browned on all sides. Adjust heat as needed to keep things moving along without scorching. Remove meat to a small ovenproof dish with lid and generously season meat with salt and pepper.

Pour off and discard most of the grease in skillet, leaving behind a generous tablespoon. Return pan to stove and over medium low heat stir in onions and garlic, scraping up browned bits at bottom of pan. Sprinkle in flour and mix well. Add a cup of beer to pan and mix well. Pour liquid over beef and add more beer to just cover meat. Tuck in bouquet garni.

(continued) ☞

Cover surface of meat with a round of baker's parchment or aluminum foil, cover pan with lid and bake for one and a half hours in preheated 375 degree oven. Meat should be tender when pierced with a cake tester. Stir once or twice as meat cooks. When meat is done remove bouquet garni and adjust seasoning.

Meanwhile steam carrots until tender. Refresh under cold water and drain. Cook pearl onions over medium heat until tender. Drain well. Mix carrots, pearl onions and peas into stew.

Peel the sweet potatoes, rinse and cut into large chunks. Put in a large saucepan, salt generously, and cover with cold water. Bring to boil, then simmer until tender about half an hour. Drain well, return to pan and dry out over low heat for about thirty seconds. Off heat mash with a potato masher and add butter, parsley, chives, salt, white pepper and nutmeg. Adjust seasoning.

Pour stew into large shallow ovenproof dish.

Cover with mashed sweet potatoes. Put pan in oven and bake for a half hour or so, until topping is lightly browned.

Patti and I used to make this delicious, easy cake frequently. Like many great dessert recipes it originated in Maida Heatter's Book of Great Desserts, *although it's probably less sweet than the original.*

Orange Chocolate Torte
serves eight

dry bread crumbs as needed
3 oz. semi-sweet chocolate, chopped into ½" pieces
1 oz. unsweetened chocolate, chopped into ½" pieces
1 c. blanched almonds
⅔ c. sugar
1 stick soft butter
3 eggs
½ t. almond extract
2 t. grated orange zest

Pass a small amount of bread crumbs through a fine strainer until you have ¼ c. Set those aside and sift 1 T. more to sprinkle in pan.

Preheat oven to 325 degrees. Oil an 8" cake pan, line with wax paper or baker's parchment and oil paper. Pour in 1 T. sifted bread crumbs and distribute around bottom and sides of pan. Dump out excess.

In large bowl set over simmering water or in microwave, melt chocolate. Stir until smooth.

In food processor fitted with metal blade, grind almonds with 2 T. of the sugar until very fine.

Cream butter and remaining sugar until fluffy. Add eggs one at a time, beating well after each addition. Add chocolate, ¼ c. bread crumbs, almonds, almond extract and orange zest. Mix just until combined.

Pour batter into pan. Tap pan on counter to remove air pockets and use a metal spreading spatula to level. Bake for forty

(continued) ☞

minutes. Cake will still be quite wet. Set pan on rack until cool. Invert on rack and remove paper. Cool for several hours to permit cake to dry out a bit. Make chocolate glaze. Put a plate under cake on rack. Pour glaze over cake and spread over top and sides with metal spreading spatula. Let cake stand until glaze solidifies before serving.

Chocolate Glaze
2 oz. semi-sweet chocolate, chopped into ½" pieces
2 oz. unsweetened chocolate, chopped into ½" pieces
4 T. butter

In large bowl set over simmering water or in microwave, melt chocolate and butter. Stir until smooth. Let cool until just slightly thickened, stirring occasionally.

For six months before Jim & I opened Local Talent, I worked for Aldo Maiorano, owner of Aldo's, at that time a catering and prepared foods shop in Greenport. From Aldo, I learned much about bread baking and pastry, but I also learned quite a few things about what not to do.

Aldo was notorious for asking staff to make something without saying how, then leaving the shop for a few hours. Upon his return, he'd have a great deal to say about what had been done wrong which always seemed like an expensive way to write a recipe.

Nonetheless, Aldo is a tremendous talent, and his rendition (once you finally figured out what it was) was invariably the definitive one. When I credit him with something like this recipe for caponata, I'm not a bit sure he'd even agree it resembles his.

Caponata

serves six

1 large eggplant
1 t. salt
1 c. celery, cut in ¾″ chunks
olive oil as needed
1 c. onions, cut in 1″ chunks
2 t. minced garlic
2 medium tomatoes, peeled, seeded and cut in ¾″ chunks
3 T. pitted green olives, coarsely chopped
2 T. red wine vinegar
1 t. capers, preferably the salt packed type rinsed well
good grinding black pepper
1 T. extra virgin olive oil
1 t. balsamic vinegar

Rinse eggplant, cut and discard top and "zebra" peel, leaving alternating stripes of peel. Cut in 1¼″ chunks. Toss with salt and leave to drain in colander an hour or so while you prepare other ingredients.

Blanch celery in boiling water until crisp-tender. Drain, refresh under cold running water and drain well.

(continued) ☞

In large saute pan over medium high heat, cook onions in a tablespoon of ordinary olive oil until golden brown, stirring often. Add garlic and cook a minute or so longer. Set aside.

Put a ¼″ layer of olive oil in same pan and heat until smoking hot. Towel dry eggplant, put half in oil and cook, flipping cubes once or twice until golden brown. Remove with slotted spoon to clean colander set over a bowl. Replenish oil in pan if necessary. Cook rest of eggplant and drain in colander.

Discard oil in pan, return onion and garlic, and over high heat add tomatoes. Cook a few minutes, stirring once or twice until tomatoes give up their liquid and it boils away. Add olives, red wine vinegar, capers and pepper. Cook a minute or two stirring often. Fold in eggplant and celery. Cool. Mix in extra virgin olive oil and balsamic vinegar and salt if needed. Let stand an hour. Serve at room temperature.

This recipe uses lentils de Puy, a special variety of lentil imported from France that holds its shape during cooking. The lentils must be cooked very gently and not too long, so it is important to be attentive. Aldo used to test for doneness by dropping a piece from a height into a metal bowl and listening for a particular plinking sound. But that's because Aldo cooked more by sight, sound and smell than by taste which is somewhat unusual. What works for me is seeing that the lentil yields to the tooth and has lost its raw taste. This salad is great with salami, ham or pâté.

Lentil Salad

serves six

½ lb. or 1⅓ c. lentils de Puy
½ c. safflower oil
3 T. red wine vinegar
1 T. balsamic vinegar
¼ c. sliced scallions
2 T. minced parsley
½ t. salt
good grinding black pepper

Put lentils in large saucepan with cold water to cover amply and bring to a boil over medium heat. Simmer gently until just cooked. Let stand a minute and drain. Cool.

In medium size bowl, mix oil, red wine vinegar, balsamic vinegar, scallions, parsley and salt. Fold in lentils.

Let stand at least fifteen minutes.

Marinated Shrimp

serves twelve

3½ lb. large shrimp (16/20 count)
1 recipe court bouillon (p. 154)
¼ c. lime juice
¼ c. lemon juice
½ c. safflower oil
¾ t. minced ginger
½ t. minced garlic
½ t. salt
¼ t. white pepper
¼ c. minced parsley
2 T. minced coriander leaves

Shell shrimp leaving last shell segment at tail still attached. Devein.

Bring court bouillon to boil. Put in shrimp. Cook until they just begin to curl, stirring once or twice. Drain and let cool.

Combine remaining ingredients except parsley and coriander. Pour over shrimp, mix well and let stand in refrigerator for two hours. Mix in parsley and coriander and serve.

My first job ever was as a salesgirl in Bloomingdale's bread department. Little did I know I'd be spending the better part of my working life around bread. When a customer asked for a sliced rye or pumpernickel I always managed to leave one of the end pieces behind in the slicer. When the customer left, I'd discover it and put it in my pocket for future snacking. I felt like doing exactly the same when I encountered this fabulous roast beef. I just could not resist the end pieces and I probably never did.

Aldo uses filet, but I use boneless rib roast.

Roast Beef with Black Peppercorns and Sea Salt
serves 20 or more as part of a buffet

7 lb. boneless rib roast, tied with twine
½ c. crushed black peppercorns
1 T. coarse sea salt
2 t. thyme leaves
few sprigs fresh rosemary

Have roast at room temperature. Preheat oven to 475 degrees.

Rub filet with peppercorns, sea salt, and thyme leaves. Pierce with rosemary leaves every inch or so of surface.

Put beef in a roasting pan and roast at high heat for twenty-five minutes. Lower heat to 325 degrees and finish roasting until rare or medium rare, about an hour and a half longer. The best way to check is by using an instant reading meat thermometer, the type with a small probe. Cook to 120 degrees as temperature will continue to rise.

Let stand for ten minutes before slicing as thin as possible.

This roast beef is delicious at room temperature.

Stuffed Red Peppers

serves six

6 medium red peppers
¾ c. French bread, cut in ¼″ cubes
¼ c. finely chopped parsley
2 T. olive oil
1 T. minced garlic
¼ t. salt
good grinding black pepper

Wash peppers. Use a paring knife to cut out tops, cutting ¼″ outside of green part to form a lid. Remove seeds from lids and insides of peppers and discard. In a small bowl, mix all remaining ingredients. Divide crumb mixture equally among peppers. Replace lids tightly. Place peppers on their sides on a foil lined baking sheet.

Preheat broiler. Put baking sheet about 2″ from broiler and broil until peppers are blackened on top. Turn peppers and continue broiling and turning until all sides are blackened. Peppers should be soft but not limp. Serve peppers at room temperature with their blackened skins on. The diner should remove the skin before eating.

I never made scones until I worked for Aldo. Ultimately I made my own recipe, not better, but different from his. This one's mine.

Lemon Currant Scones
makes two dozen large scones

¾ c. currants
3 T. dark rum
½ t. vanilla extract
grated zest of 2 lemons
5 c. flour
½ c. sugar
2 T. and 1 t. baking powder
1 t. salt
½ t. allspice
5 sticks cold butter, cut in ¼″ cubes
5 eggs
¾ c. milk

Combine currants, rum, vanilla extract and zest. Let stand an hour or longer.

Into bowl of electric mixer, sift together the flour, sugar, baking powder, salt and allspice. Using paddle attachment, cut in butter until mixture resembles cornmeal. Beat eggs and milk together lightly. Add with currants to mixer bowl and mix until just combined.

Use ice cream scoop to dip out large balls of batter. Place with at least an inch between scones on greased baking trays. Let stand for a half hour.

Preheat oven to 375 degrees. Bake scones until golden brown, about half an hour, reversing pans midway through cooking.

NOTE: After scooping, you can freeze unbaked scones for use within the next few weeks. Defrost before baking as above.

I learned how to make buttercream from Aldo who made an unbelievably delicious cake. Actually a cake so delicious that in spite of Aldo's reputation for lateness people kept ordering cakes for special occasions. I'll never forget the wedding I attended as a guest when the cake never arrived at all! Aldo's workers used to say his motto was "late but great."

This isn't Aldo's recipe, but the precept is: The butter has to be truly soft before you add it.

Vanilla Buttercream
enough for a 10" cake

8 egg yolks
1 t. vanilla extract
⅔ c. sugar
1 lb. sweet butter, cut in small pieces and brought to room
    temperature

Beat egg yolks and vanilla well at medium speed, preferably in a standing mixer or in a large bowl using an electric beater. (Buttercream requires too much mixing to be done comfortably by hand.) Start beating before putting sugar and water on to boil and continue until syrup is ready. It will not be possible to over beat the yolks.

Put sugar and ¼ c. water in a small saucepan. Bring to a simmer, stirring occasionally. Before the mixture simmers, dip a clean pastry brush in cold water and brush down any sugar residue on inner edge of pan. When mixture simmers, stop stirring, and put in a candy thermometer. When syrup reaches 230 degrees, immediately take pan off heat. With mixer running at medium speed, add syrup to egg yolks in a thin stream. Keep beating until mixture cools to room temperature.

Meanwhile, beat softened butter until smooth, either by hand beating with a wooden spoon or by processing in the food processor with the plastic blade.

With mixer running, add butter gradually spoonful by spoonful. After about half the butter has been incorporated, butter can be added more quickly.

Coffee Buttercream
enough for a 10" cake

8 egg yolks
1 T. instant espresso
⅔ c. sugar
1 lb. sweet butter, cut in small pieces and brought to room
    temperature

Add the instant espresso to the egg yolks in place of vanilla and follow directions for vanilla buttercream.

Hazelnut Buttercream
enough for a 10" cake

8 egg yolks
¼ c. hazelnut paste
½ t. almond extract
⅔ c. sugar
1 lb. sweet butter, cut in small pieces and brought to room
    temperature

Add the hazelnut paste and almond extract to the egg yolks in place of vanilla and follow directions for vanilla buttercream.

Every once in a while, in my current life as a journalist, someone gives me a recipe so good, I can't believe I am getting paid (albeit a pittance!) to learn it. Claudia Helinski, proprietor of Salamander General Store in Greenport, NY gave me this recipe for Mole Poblano. It's the sort of recipe I'm usually too lazy to make on my own with its round up of many, many ingredients and painstaking prep work, but as I needed to test the recipe, I exerted myself. The quantity the original recipe made was on the grand scale and I put a number of containers away in the freezer. When the sudden need to feed arose I was always able to buy a rotisserie chicken and pull out some of this delicious sauce for a fabulous meal, so I became very devoted to it.

Claudia's Mole Poblano

makes six cups

6 ancho chiles
4 mulatto chiles
2 pasilla chiles
2 chipotle chiles
4 c. chicken broth
4 allspice berries
3 cloves
1" piece stick cinnamon
1½ t. coriander seed
½ t. anise seed
¼ t. Mexican oregano
2 corn tortillas, broken into pieces
1 medium onion, unpeeled and quartered
3 unpeeled garlic cloves
3 tomatillos
2 fresh plum tomatoes
½ c. vegetable oil
½ c. unsalted peanuts
½ c. blanched almonds
½ c. pumpkin seeds
¾ c. sesame seeds
1 small ripe banana
1 T. raisins
¾ t. salt

(continued) ☞

2 oz. Mexican chocolate or unsweetened chocolate, chopped into ½″ pieces

1 T. white vinegar

Discard stems and remove seeds from all four kinds of chiles, reserving 1 heaping T. of the seeds and discarding the rest or saving for another use.

Heat a cast iron pan over medium heat and toast chiles in it until blistered but not burned.

Put chicken broth in a small saucepan, bring to boil, then turn off heat and add chiles. Let stand for an hour. Wipe out pan and toast allspice, cloves, cinnamon, coriander, and anise over medium heat until smoking, stirring occasionally. Turn off heat, add oregano, stir once or twice, then dump spices into bowl.

Again wipe out pan and over medium heat toast chile seeds and tortilla, stirring often, until tortilla is brown. Chile seeds will be black. Add to other spices and grind to a powder in blender.

Wipe out pan and line it with foil. Set onion, garlic, tomatillos and tomatoes on foil. Brown these vegetables over medium high heat. Watching attentively, turn as they brown and remove them individually when brown all over. Peel onion, garlic and tomato and discard peels.

Remove foil from pan. Heat 1 T. of vegetable oil. Add peanuts and cook over medium heat until golden brown, stirring often. Remove. Repeat for almonds, then pumpkin seeds, then sesame seeds. Use a bit more oil to brown banana and plump raisins over medium heat.

Combine ground spices, charred vegetables, nuts and seeds and fruit in bowl. Blend in small batches to a puree.

Heat remaining few tablespoons of vegetable oil in same skillet. Add puree and salt to pan and cook over medium heat, stirring often for twenty minutes. Stir in chocolate and cook ten minutes longer, continuing to stir. Turn off heat. Stir in vinegar and adjust seasoning.

This recipe became a personal favorite of my daughter, Claude's as soon as she tried it, and it has proven to be a favorite of all carnivores. Sue Kim was one of my favorite "discoveries" actually introduced to me by a mutual friend at the newspaper. She is a brilliant but self-effacing cook and a strong personality which makes for a great lunch and a great interview.

Sue told me to put the meat and marinade in freezer baggies to marinate over the course of time spent becoming frozen and thawing out. So not only is her bulgogi delicious but it can always be on hand for one of those— voila!—instant company dinners.

Sue Kim's Bulgogi
serves four to six

26 oz. flank steak, more or less, sliced thin
⅔ c. soy sauce
2" chunk carrot, peeled and minced
1 minced scallion
2 minced garlic cloves
½" chunk fresh ginger, peeled and minced
3 T. honey
2 T. sesame oil
1 T. sesame seeds
1 T. lemon juice
2 t. light brown sugar
1 t. cayenne pepper
½ t. salt
¼ t. freshly ground black pepper
1 large head of leaf lettuce, well washed and dried
20 mint leaves

Put beef in a large bowl and add all the ingredients except lettuce and sesame leaves. With clean hands mix and rub marinade into the meat. Refrigerate for forty-eight hours or freeze in a freezer bag until needed and defrost in the refrigerator. Bring to room temperature. Heat outdoor gas or charcoal grill until medium hot. Cover with a perforated broiler pan or special pan designed for grilling small objects. Quickly cook pieces of meat until brown on both sides. Serve with lettuce and mint.

To eat, wrap a piece in a lettuce leaf with a bit of mint leaf tucked inside.

Paternal grandparents Max & Erna Michelson

Erna, her mother, and three of her sisters

Erna's family home in Krakow, Poland

Horace Michelson

Munie & Lee Libman with Michael & George

"Dusty" Michelson with Janet

Gertrude Eckel with John

Janet, Gertrude, Munie, Erna, Horace, Max, Lee, Dusty, Henry & G.G.

G.G.'s grandfather Abraham Rosen

Tom & Celia Rosen

G.G. Michelson

Sadie Lipsett & Betty Lipsett

The Julie & Morrie Lipsett Families & Friends

Susan Lipsett with daughters Robin & Debbie

Mildred Terr

Mildred with daughters Nancy & Dana

Lewis Terr (standing), Jeffrey Terr & Dana Terr Konno

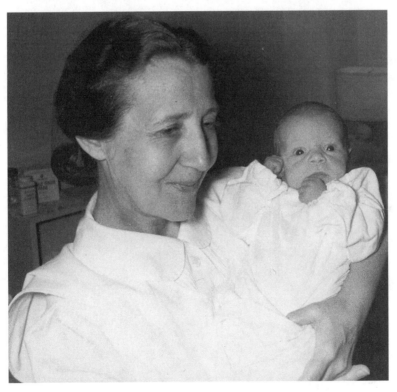

Miss Brumm & Martha Michelson

Lossie Reidout & friend

Martha & Barbara Michelson

Martha & friend

Horace & Phoebe Heffron

G.G.

Erna & Dave Meller

Jim Heffron

Erna, Sarah, Phoebe & Stella Heffron

The Heffron Family

Jim & Barbara

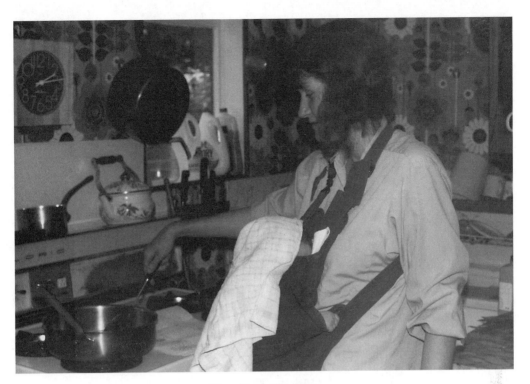

Phoebe & Barbara

Jim & Phoebe

Phoebe & Sarah

Claude Heffron

Sarah

Jim, Claude, Sarah, Phoebe & Stella in Cafe Amore

Joy Lokey & Barbara at The Cordon Bleu

Monsieur Tric

Monsieur Simon

Barry Wildman

Joy

Barbara at Local Talent

Sarah & Phoebe in France

Barbara, Claude, Phoebe & Jim in Ireland

Barbara Butterworth and friend in Nepal

Joe Rosen

Dale Rosengarten & Dana Sardet

Marcia & Jerry Brown

Jane Vris

Jim, Zanya Gissler & Sturgess Spanos

Maggie Megaw & Steve Monas

Paula Dagen & friend

The Family We Made

Jim, Stella & Erna

*J*im was so food pampered that it was probably inevitable that he marry a chef. My mother-in-law, Stella Heffron, is a wonderful cook and miraculous and willing baker. According to Stella, Jim had great taste from the beginning and never deigned to eat baby food. (Phoebe took after him; the first meal she ate with satisfaction was eggplant parmagiana chopped baby fine.) When Jim got his first tooth he was ready to attack beef stroganoff, a dish that topped his hit list for years.

Beef Stroganoff
serves four

1½ lb. beef filet
6 T. butter
¼ c. minced shallots
10 oz . mushrooms
½ t. paprika
½ t. salt
good grinding black pepper
¼ c. demi glace (p. 21)
¼ c. sour cream
1 t. lemon juice

Trim all fat from filet. Cut meat into strips about 2½″ × ½″ × ½″. Refrigerate meat until ready to cook.

In large skillet over medium heat, saute shallot in 2 T. butter until soft, stirring frequently. Add mushrooms. Cook until juices have evaporated and mushrooms are golden brown. Season with paprika, salt and pepper. Remove from pan and reserve.

Add remaining 4 T. butter to pan. Raise heat to high. When butter sizzles, add beef strips, enough to fill but not crowd pan. Brown nicely on both sides. Meat should remain pink inside. Remove cooked meat to plate with mushrooms. Add uncooked strips as you remove cooked pieces.

(continued) ☞

When all the meat is done, lower heat and add demi glace to the pan. Cook stirring and scraping to mix in browned bits in pan. Add sour cream and lemon juice. Heat until piping hot but not boiling. Add lemon juice. Adjust seasoning. Fold in meat and mushrooms and heat a minute longer without boiling.

Later Jim put roast beef on his favorites list provided it was served with York-shire pudding made with the drippings.

Yorkshire Pudding (adapted from *The New York Times Cookbook*)
serves eight

½ c. beef drippings (collected from the roasting beef)
2 c. flour
¾ t. salt
½ t. minced fresh rosemary leaves
1¾ c. milk
4 eggs

Preheat oven to 450 degrees.

Put all but 2 T. of beef drippings in a shallow oven to table baking dish with about ten cup capacity. Grease sides of pan well with drippings.

Sift together flour and salt. Add rosemary. Beat together milk and eggs and remaining 2 T. of drippings. Pour liquid mixture into flour mixture. Beat until smooth. Pour into prepared pan. Bake twenty minutes. Lower heat to 325 and bake fifteen minutes longer until puffed and golden brown. Serve along side roast beef.

After spending most of his growing up years in Bethesda, Maryland, this is what Jim now requires for his birthday dinner.

Crab Cakes
serves eight as a first course or four as a main course

3 T. butter
½ c. minced onion
¼ c. minced celery
¼ c. minced green pepper
¼ c. cream
¼ c. minced parsley
1 T. lemon juice
½ t. mustard, preferably Coleman's
½ t. Worchestershire sauce
1 t. salt
¼ t. white pepper
pinch cayenne pepper
1 lb. top quality crab meat
2 slices white bread crusts removed
4 eggs
vegetable oil
flour
unseasoned dry bread crumbs, preferably homemade
lemon wedges

In a small skillet over medium heat, cook butter, onion, celery and green pepper until tender, stirring occasionally. Add cream. Cook until cream is reduced by half. Off heat, add parsley, lemon juice, mustard, Worchestershire sauce, salt, white pepper and cayenne pepper. Let cool.

Pick over crab meat to remove any bits of shell or cartilage.

Chop bread in processor to make soft bread crumbs.

In large bowl beat 3 eggs. Mix in vegetable mixture and soft crumbs. Gently fold in crab meat until well mixed. Divide

(*continued*) ☞

into 16 balls and flatten to form 1″ thick disks. Let stand covered in the refrigerator for about an hour.

In a large heavy bottomed skillet, pour oil to a depth of ¼″. While oil heats, beat remaining egg with 1 T. water.

Lightly dredge crab cakes in flour, then dip in egg, and finally coat well with dry bread crumbs.

When oil is hot enough to immediately sizzle a drop of water, slip in crab cakes. Cook until golden brown on each side. Drain on paper towels. Serve with lemon wedges.

Stella's oatmeal cookies were the daily special when Jim and Bobby, his brother, were growing up. According to family legend, Jim could eat a double batch by himself after school no problem

Oatmeal Chocolate Chip Cookies
makes about six dozen

2 sticks room temperature butter
1 c. lightly packed light brown sugar
1 c. sugar
2 eggs
1 t. vanilla
2 c. flour
1 t. baking soda
pinch salt
2 c. old fashioned oatmeal
12 oz. chocolate chips

Preheat oven to 350 degrees. Grease several baking sheets.

Cream butter and sugars well. Add eggs and vanilla. Beat well.

Sift together flour, baking soda and salt. Add to batter with oatmeal. Stir to just combine. Add chocolate chips and mix to distribute.

Drop heaping tablespoonsful onto baking sheets leaving plenty of space around each cookie. Bake for twelve minutes. Cookies will look slightly underdone, but will crisp up as they cool. Remove warm cookies to cooling rack. Regrease pan and repeat with remaining batter.

I met Jim when I was sharing an apartment on East Tenth Street in NYC with Sturgess, my friend from cooking school. I was then in the phase Sturgess refers to as my three year man hunt. Sturgess had been promising to serve up to me this tantalizing Swiss jazz pianist friend due to visit at any time, but before he arrived, Jim passed through. Jim had been Sturg's friend at Vassar College and was showing a Dutch friend the states. He stayed in our apartment, and we met—actually remet since apparently we had met once before when I was NOT man hunting and the meeting left no impression. After that the Swiss man was academic.

Jim was supposed to go clerk for a federal judge in Texas, but decided to stay in NYC. So for a long while he was job hunting. While I worked, he would bake bread for my homecoming. If that isn't endearing, and he was good at it too!

If I could only take one food to a desert island, it would be cheese bread. But only if I'd have a toaster there.

James Heffron's James Beard's Cheese Bread (adapted from *Beard on Bread*)

two loaves

1 package dry yeast
1 T. sugar
1 stick melted butter
6 c. flour
1 T. salt
1 t. Tabasco sauce
¾ c. grated Gruyere cheese
¼ c. grated Parmesan cheese

Put yeast and sugar in ½ c. warm water and stir to dissolve. Let stand five minutes. Add butter, flour, salt and Tabasco sauce. Mix by hand or in mixer with dough hook adding up to 1½ c. more warm water as needed to make a soft but not sticky dough. Knead at low speed or by hand for ten minutes.

Put in oiled bowl, cover with dishcloth and let rise until doubled, about two hours.

Punch down dough, add cheeses and knead for several minutes to thoroughly distribute.

(continued) ☞

Divide dough into two halves, shape each into a round, cover with cloth and let rest five minutes.

Oil two loaf pans. Form dough into loaves. Put dough in pans, cover with cloth and let rise until above the pan.

Toward end of rising, preheat oven to 375 degrees.

Bake breads for about half an hour, remove from pans, return to oven and bake about ten minutes longer. Loaves should sound hollow when rapped on the bottom.

This recipe also derives from Beard on Bread, *Jim's bread baking bible.*

Walnut Bread
makes three loaves

2 packages dry yeast
1½ T. sugar
5 ½ c. flour
1 T. salt
½ c. olive oil
1½ c. warm milk
¾ c. minced onion
½ c. coarsely chopped walnuts

Put yeast and sugar in ½ c. warm water. Stir to dissolve. Let stand five minutes. Add flour, salt, olive oil and milk. Mix by hand or in mixer with dough hook, adding more warm water as needed to make a soft but not sticky dough. Knead at low speed or by hand for ten minutes.

Put in oiled bowl, cover with dishcloth and let rise until doubled, about two hours.

Punch down dough, add onion and walnuts and knead for several minutes to thoroughly distribute.

Divide dough into three pieces, shape each piece into a round, set on baking trays and cover with cloths. Let rise until doubled in size.

Towards end of rising, preheat oven to 375 degrees.

Bake for forty-five minutes. Loaves should sound hollow when rapped on the bottom.

When Stella was eleven in 1938, she and her parents emigrated to the U.S. from rural Austria where her father had run a factory producing fine plum brandy or "slivovitz." Since she spoke no English, she was put into kindergarten. That was quite an indignity, but not quite as bad as learning that, in Peoria, no one sold sour cream! Stella's mother, Erna, was delighted to leave domesticity back in the old country and labor at the five and dime store she was soon running in Brooklyn with her husband, David Meller.

When I came on the scene, everyone called Erna "Grandma Erna", presumably to distinguish her from some once co-existing other grandmother. It always amused me because my grandmother was Erna too, and therefore the name only muddied the waters in my household. Sarah solved the dilemma by calling her Ernie. I always hoped my dignified grandmother-in-law realized that Sarah was thinking of Bert and Ernie, and that the name was a term of great endearment.

While "Ernie" didn't cook, she was much remembered for her housecleaning. Jim recollected that on the occasions when his parents travelled and his grandmother came to stay, he would often be awakened by the sound of her vacuuming—right around the bed as he slept! Her tidiness was ridiculed in Jim's family, yet I loved it that during sporadic visits to our home, she got her very fit eighty year old self up on a step stool and cleaned the top of the refrigerator, a spot that surely hasn't been revisited since her death. Stella told me Ernie chromed her silver candelabra so she wouldn't have to clean it, and has asked me to remind everyone about its underlying value so we can fight over it not pitch it if Stella predeceases us. Done!

Grandma Erna's cleanliness was next only to her frugality. Jim claims if you left a bit of hamburger at dinner, Grandma Erna would squirrel it away in the freezer for future soup making. Recipe intentionally omitted.

But let's not remember her by soup, but by Austrian almond cookies not of her own making, but from a recipe of Stella's.

Vanilla Kipfurl

makes four dozen

2¼ c. blanched almonds
¼ c. sugar
2 sticks soft butter
1½ t. vanilla
½ t. almond extract
2 c. flour
½ c. vanilla sugar (following recipe)

(continued) ☞

Preheat oven to 350 degrees.

In food processor with metal blade, grind almonds with sugar to a fine powder. Combine all ingredients except vanilla sugar. Scoop tablespoon size pieces and roll into balls. Form balls into small crescents. Bake until just about to brown, about 15 minutes. Roll in vanilla sugar while warm.

Vanilla Sugar
makes two cups

2 c. sugar
1 vanilla bean

Put sugar in jar. Split vanilla bean lengthwise and bury in sugar. Let stand at least a week. Will keep indefinitely.

While on the subject of the home country, desserts we all feel nostalgic for because Stella has made them for us often are all the following. Whenever Stella bakes she waxes analytical about how this batch differs from or most likely falls short of a previous batch. But we never listen because we are too busy enjoying.

This is my own recipe for Linzer Torte, developed from Stella's and Maida Heatter's. It tastes better the day after it's baked.

Linzer Torte
serves eight

2 c. almonds
⅔ c. sugar
1¼ c. flour
¼ t. salt
pinch cloves
pinch cinnamon
10 T. cold butter, cut in ¼″ cubes
2 egg yolks, lightly beaten and 1 egg white
1 c. best quality or homemade raspberry jam
1 t. lemon juice
3 T. sliced blanched almonds

In food processor fitted with metal blade, process almonds and sugar to a powder. Add flour, salt, cloves and cinnamon to processor and pulse to mix. Add butter and pulse until very well mixed. Add egg yolks and pulse to form a stiff dough.

Take ⅔ of dough and press into 10″ spring form pan to cover bottom and halfway up sides. Form remainder of dough into thin ropes, lay on cookie sheet, and refrigerate for a half hour or more. (Or very lazy bakers like me can skip this step and merely scatter the remaining dough as "crumbles" over the jam. In this case, no need to wait nor to bother brushing with egg white.)

(continued) ☞

Set rack in lower third of oven and preheat oven to 325 degrees.

Mix jam with lemon juice and spread jam over dough in pan. "Basket weave" ropes of dough over top to make a lattice top.

Beat egg white with 1 t. water. Brush over lattice. Sprinkle sliced almonds on top. Bake until very lightly browned, about one hour.

Rugelach

makes about three dozen pieces

2 c. flour
⅔ c. sugar
½ t. salt
12 T. cold butter, cut in ¼″ cubes and 1 stick melted butter
1 egg yolk
1 T. grated orange rind
¼ c. orange juice
2 t. cinnamon
2 c. raisins
2 c. coarsely chopped pecans

In food processor with metal blade, mix flour, 2 T. sugar and salt. Cut in butter cubes until mixture has cornmeal consistency. In a separate bowl combine egg yolk, orange rind and juice. Add to dough, mixing with the minimum number of strokes until dough holds together. Divide into three balls. Wrap in plastic wrap. Let dough rest in refrigerator for thirty minutes or more.

Preheat oven to 350 degrees.

Roll a ball of dough into a thin rectangle. Mix together remaining ½ c. sugar and cinnamon. Brush dough with a third of the melted butter. Sprinkle with a third of sugar mixture, raisins and pecans. stopping 1″ from edges of dough. Roll dough from the long side into a long cylinder, brushing last inch of dough with water and pressing to seal. Set seam side down on oiled baking sheet. Cut ¾ of the way through roll. Repeat with rest of ingredients.

Bake until golden brown, about thirty minutes. Cool. Cut pieces completely.

Cooking For No Reason

*O*ut of literally hundreds of great dishes and baked goods we've enjoyed at Stella and my father-in-law Howie's house, these are my family's favorites. The all time favorite is marble cake because as Ceci says. "When we visit, our grandmother makes us a cake for no reason."

Stella's Marble Cake
serves twelve

2¾ c. flour
2 t. baking powder
½ t. salt
2 sticks butter, at room temperature
2 c. sugar
3 eggs
1½ t. vanilla extract
1 c. milk
¾ c. chocolate sauce (p. 126), at room temperature
¼ t. baking soda
¼ t. almond extract

Grease and lightly flour a 10″ bundt or tube pan. Set rack in the center of the oven and preheat to 350 degrees.

Sift together flour, baking powder and salt.

Use an electric mixer to cream butter well. Add sugar and cream for several minutes until fluffy. Add eggs one at a time, scraping bowl and beating well after each addition, Add vanilla. Beat a minute or two longer. Alternately add milk and flour mixture in several additions. Stir only until combined.

Spread ⅓ of batter in pan. Set ⅓ aside in a small bowl. To the ⅓ remaining in large mixing bowl, add chocolate sauce, baking soda and almond extract. Mix to combine thoroughly.

(continued) ☞

Add chocolate batter to pan. Level it. Top with remaining plain batter. Level by tapping pan on counter and by spreading with a metal spatula. Use a table knife to "marbleize" by swirling through batter several times in each area. Bake for forty-five minutes. Cover top with foil and bake another fifteen minutes or so until done. (Cake tester will come out clean and cake will be springy to the touch.) Set pan on wire rack for five minutes before unmolding cake onto wire rack.

All breakfasts at Stella and Howie's house require the best available bagels and fresh vegetable cream cheese.

Vegetable Cream Cheese
makes four cups

1 lb. cream cheese at room temperature
1 c. finely chopped carrots
1 c. finely chopped scallion
½ c. finely chopped radish
½ c. finely chopped green pepper
¼ c. finely chopped celery
¼ t. salt
pinch white pepper

Beat cream cheese until light. Add remaining ingredients and beat until well mixed.

Let stand a half hour before serving.

There may be homemade granola in the jar.

Granola

makes approximately twenty-four cups

16 c. oats
3 c. toasted wheat germ
3 c. dried unsweetened coconut
3 c. sunflower seeds
1½ c. sesame seeds
1½ c. honey
2 c. vegetable oil
3 c. coarsely chopped nuts

Preheat oven to 275 degrees. In very large bowl, mix all ingredients. Spread in two baking pans. Bake, stirring often, until light brown. The granola takes a long time, but it comes out best when baked very slowly.

Depending on how long we stay, we may have any of these things, too. Don't think it would require a long visit, as we eat more or less continuously when we visit.

Vegetable Frittata
serves twelve

1½ c. sliced mushrooms
1½ c. grated zucchini
¾ c. chopped green pepper
¾ c. coarsely chopped onion
1 t. minced garlic
1 T. oil
6 eggs, beaten
¼ c. cream
1 lb. cream cheese, cut in small cubes
1½ c. grated cheddar cheese
2 c. cubed bread, slightly stale
1 t. salt
good grinding black pepper

Preheat oven to 350 degrees. Oil a 10″ spring form pan.

In large skillet over medium heat, saute mushroom, zucchini, pepper, onion and garlic in oil until crisp-tender, stirring often. Cool.

Beat eggs with cream. Add cream cheese, cheddar, bread, salt and pepper and mix well. Add sauteed vegetables and mix well. Pour mixture into pan.

Bake until set in center, about one hour.

Cool ten minutes before unmolding and cutting into wedges.

These are perfect with a plain roast chicken.

Stella's Garlic Mashed Potatoes
serves six

3 lb. Yukon Gold potatoes
salt as needed
2 T. butter
30 large cloves of garlic separated but not peeled (about two
  heads)
2 T. flour
1¼ c. milk
large pinch white pepper
good grinding nutmeg

Peel potatoes and cut into large chunks. Put in a large saucepan and cover with cold water. Add a generous amount of salt. Cook over medium low heat until tender when pierced with a cake tester. Drain, return to pot and cook over low heat a minute or so to evaporate excess moisture. Mash with a potato masher or put through a food mill, depending on whether you favor lumpy or smooth mashed potatoes.

While potatoes cook, put butter and garlic in small covered saucepan over low heat. Cook for fifteen minutes, stirring occasionally until garlic is tender. Whisk in flour and then add milk in small additions, whisking each addition until smooth. Simmer sauce for ten minutes. Add pepper and nutmeg. Put sauce through food mill. Whisk sauce into mashed potatoes, whipping as you add. Adjust seasoning.

Potatoes will improve if made ahead of time and reheated in double boiler or in microwave.

Curry Chicken Salad
serves eight

3 lb. cooked chicken breast, cut into ¼" pieces
¾ t. salt
¼ t. white pepper
3 T. butter
1 c. minced onion
¼ c. curry powder
¼ t. cayenne pepper (optional)
1¼ c. Hellman's mayonnaise
½ c. Major Grey's chutney, chopped
1 c. finely chopped, blanched celery
⅔ c. seedless grapes, cut in halves
¼ c. unsalted, dry roasted peanuts or other nuts

Season chicken with salt and pepper. Cook onion in butter in small saute pan over medium low heat until onions are soft. Add curry powder and cayenne if using and cook stirring for thirty seconds, just long enough to release fragrance of spices. Set aside to cool. Mix with mayonnaise and chutney. Fold in chicken and celery. Let stand at least an hour in the refrigerator. At serving time, adjust seasoning and fold in grapes. Sprinkle nuts on top.

Stella's recipe by way of the Time Life *cookbook series.*

Chicken Liver Mousse
makes one loaf pan, enough to serve twenty

1 lb. chicken livers
¾ c. heavy cream
⅓ c. rendered chicken fat
1 small onion, peeled
¼ c. flour
1 egg and 1 egg yolk
3 T. brandy
2 t. salt
½ t. powdered ginger
1 t. white pepper
½ t. ground allspice
good grating nutmeg

Grease a loaf pan. Preheat oven to 325 degrees.

Use a sharp paring knife to remove any discolored bits and connective tissue from chicken livers. Discard trimmings. Combine all ingredients in blender. Strain mixture through a fine sieve to remove any lumps. Pour mixture into loaf pan.

Bring a quart of water to boil. Set pan in a baking dish and pour in boiling water to a depth of an inch. Put baking dish in the oven and bake approximately one and a half hours until mousse is set (contents won't move when pan is shaken lightly.) Take loaf pan out of water bath and cool on a cake rack. Gently unmold mousse onto a plate and wrap well with plastic wrap. Serve with crouton rounds.

Lamb Tagine
serves six

3½ lb. lean lamb stew meat
4 T. melted butter
2 T. oil
3 T. grated onion and 1 c. thinly sliced onion
pinch saffron
1 heaping t. ground cinnamon
1 t. ground ginger
½ t. ground coriander
¾ t. salt
good grinding black pepper
12 oz. pitted prunes
1 T. honey
4 tart apples
1 T. sesame seeds

Trim almost all fat from lamb and cut into 1″ cubes.

Combine 3 T. butter, oil, grated onion, saffron, cinnamon, ginger, salt and pepper. Mix well with meat. Put in Dutch oven, add water to almost cover, cover pot and simmer one hour, stirring from time to time.

While stew cooks, soak prunes in cold water for thirty minutes. Drain and add to lamb along with sliced onion. Stir in, cover and simmer thirty minutes longer.

Stir in honey and cook uncovered until sauce reduces to about one cup.

Make garnish by peeling, coring and slicing apples into wedges. Saute in skillet with remaining 1 T. butter until tender.

Toast sesame seeds in oven until golden brown.

Put lamb in serving dish. Surround with apples and sprinkle with sesame seeds.

I hope to be forgiven for adding cooked corn to Stella's recipe.

Cold Zucchini Soup
serves four to six

5 medium zucchini
1 large onion, thinly sliced
2 T. butter
1 heaping t. curry powder
3 c. chicken broth
2 ears of corn
1 c. cream
½ t. salt
large pinch white pepper
3 T. snipped chives

Cut one of the zucchini into fine julienne strips. Bring a small pot of water to boil and cook strips one minute. Drain and reserve.

Coarsely chop rest of zucchini. Put in large pot with onion, butter and curry. Cook over low heat a few minutes, stirring often to release fragrance of curry. Add broth, salt and pepper. Simmer until zucchini is tender, about thirty minutes.

While soup cooks, shuck corn and steam a few minutes until just cooked. Cool, cut kernels from cob and reserve.

Cool soup slightly and blend in batches in blender until smooth. Add cream and corn. Chill.

Adjust seasoning. Garnish with chives.

Stella refuses to eat noodles of any kind on the grounds of some form of phobia. In spite of this, she makes the universe's best lasagna. Her lasagna is tons of work, and it spoils you for all other lasagnas, so I'm not sure we should thank her for it. The basis for this recipe is one by Ed Giobbi in The New York Times *a few decades ago.*

Stella's Lasagna
serves eight

1 lb. lasagna
salt
1 lb. ricotta
3 eggs
1 c. Parmesan cheese
2 T. minced parsley
1 recipe Bolognese sauce (following recipe)
1 lb. mozzarella, cut in ¼" cubes

Cook lasagna in a large pot of well salted water. Stir gently several times so lasagna doesn't stick together. Remove when a bit harder than al dente. Drain, rinse under cold water. Drain and spread on dish towels to dry completely.

Mix together ricotta, eggs, cheese and parsley.

Spread a thin layer of sauce in a deep rectangular baking dish approximately 9" × 13" × 3" in dimension. Lay a layer of lasagna on top, overlapping noodles slightly. Cut noodles to fit if necessary. Spread a layer of sauce. Use a spoon to add ricotta in dabs that are practically touching. Use one third of the ricotta mixture. Scatter one third of the mozzarella on top. Repeat with another layer of noodle, sauce and cheeses. Finish with a third layer.

If any meat sauce remains, freeze it for another meal.

Cover pan with aluminum foil.

Lasagna can be refrigerated for a day or so or frozen for a month or so.

(continued) ☞

To bake, preheat oven to 375 degrees. Put in just made, refrigerated or frozen lasagna and bake until piping hot. Time varies greatly, and may take up to over an hour for frozen lasagna. When lasagna is heated, remove foil and raise heat to 425 degrees. Bake fifteen minutes longer until top is nicely browned. Remove from oven and let stand for ten minutes before cutting into squares.

Bolognese Sauce
makes ten cups

1 lb. sweet sausage
1 lb. lean ground beef
8 oz. finely chopped mushrooms
1 t. minced garlic
½ t. salt
good grinding black pepper
1 recipe marinara sauce (p. 39)
3 T. butter
3 T. flour
1 c. milk
1¼ c. cream
¼ t. freshly grated nutmeg

In a large skillet with high sides cook sausages over medium low heat until golden brown all around. Drain on paper towels. Cool sausages, remove and discard casings. Chop sausage meat into small pieces. Pour off grease in skillet and discard. Add ground beef and cook over medium heat stirring frequently until meat is lightly browned. Add mushrooms, garlic, salt and pepper. Cook stirring from time to time until mushroom liquid evaporates. Add marinara sauce and sausage meat. Simmer over low heat for forty-five minutes. Turn off stove.

While sauce cooks, melt butter over low heat in a medium saucepan. Whisk in flour. Add milk in several additions whisking well after each. Whisk in cream. Season with nutmeg, salt and pepper. Simmer five minutes. Add to meat sauce. Combine well.

Chocolate Chip Coffee Cake
serves twelve or more

2 packages dry yeast
½ c. milk
¾ c. sugar
½ t. salt
4 egg yolks
2 sticks soft butter
5 c. flour, more or less as needed
½ c. warm water
4 oz. semi-sweet chocolate, chopped fine or 1 c. chocolate
   mini chips
½ t. cinnamon
½ c. coarsely chopped walnuts
1 recipe crumb topping (following recipe)

In bowl of standing mixer, put yeast and ½ c. warm water. Let stand five minutes.

Add ¼ c. milk, sugar, salt, yolks, butter and 4 c. flour. Use paddle attachment to beat until smooth.

Remove paddle and attach dough hook. Add remaining flour as needed to make soft but not sticky dough. Knead five minutes. Put dough in oiled bowl, cover with a cloth and let dough rise until double, several hours.

Heat remaining ¼ c. milk in small saucepan until it almost boils. Turn off heat and stir in chocolate and cinnamon. Stir until smooth. Let cool.

Punch down risen dough. Put on floured counter and roll to 10″ × 15″ rectangle. It may be easiest to roll a bit, then let dough rest a minute or two before rolling again. Spread with melted chocolate. Sprinkle with chopped walnuts. Roll from long side. Place seam side down in tube pan, pressing ends together. Make crumb topping and sprinkle over dough.

(continued) ☞

Cover with dishcloth and let rise until light looking and quite high, about one hour.

About fifteen minutes before dough has fully risen, preheat oven to 350 degrees.

Bake risen cake until golden brown, about forty-five minutes. Cool in pan for ten minutes. Unmold and cool.

Crumb Topping
makes two cups

½ c. flour
½ c. small chocolate chips
½ c. coarsely chopped walnuts
¼ c. soft butter
¼ c. sugar
1½ t. cinnamon

Combine all ingredients.

Almond Biscotti

makes about five dozen

2¼ c. almonds
1¾ c. flour
1 c. sugar
½ t. baking powder
¼ t. salt
2 eggs plus 1 yolk, beaten together
1 t. vanilla
½ t. almond extract

Preheat oven to 400 degrees. Put almonds on baking sheet and bake until light brown inside, about fifteen minutes. Cool and coarsely chop.

Turn oven to 350 degrees.

In food processor with metal blade, mix flour, sugar, baking powder and salt. Add eggs, vanilla and almond extracts, and almonds and pulse until mixture forms dough. Divide into three parts.

With wet hands squeeze/shape dough into logs, about 1¼″ in diameter. Place on cookie sheets with room between logs and bake until very lightly browned and set, but not cooked through, about twenty minutes.

Take from oven and slice on the bias into ½″ slices. Lay slices flat on baking sheets and bake until dried out and light brown, about fifteen minutes longer. Flip slices once, halfway through second baking.

Almond Biscotti with Chocolate Chips
makes about five dozen

2¼ c. almonds
1¾ c. flour
1 c. sugar
½ t. baking powder
¼ t. salt
1 t. vanilla
½ t. almond extract
2 eggs plus 1 yolk, beaten together
1¼ c. small chocolate chips

Make like almond biscotti. Add chocolate chips with almonds.

Hazelnut Anise Biscotti
makes about five dozen

2¼ c. hazelnuts
1¾ c. flour
1 c. sugar
½ t. baking powder
¼ t. salt
1 t. vanilla
½ t. almond extract
2 eggs plus 1 yolk, beaten together
2 T. coarsely crushed anise seeds

Bake hazelnuts at 400 degrees until skins begin to loosen. Rub hot nuts by the handful inside a dish towel to remove skins. Coarsely chop.

Follow recipe for almond biscotti, substituting hazelnuts for almonds. Mix hazelnuts and anise seed into dough.

My Three Best Creations

The Inner Dinner Circle

*J*im's cooking talents atrophied when he met me, since in the interest of effi-
ciency, usually I produce the meals. Still there are one or two family specialties which he makes so painstakingly, they are only acceptable when
they come from his hands.

Spaghetti Carbonara
serves four

1 c. finely chopped onion
2 T. olive oil
1½ c. fresh young peas or ½ box frozen peas
1 lb. low salt bacon
salt
1 lb. spaghetti
2 eggs
¼ c. milk
1 c. Parmesan cheese
good grinding black pepper
good grating fresh nutmeg

In large pot over medium heat, saute onion in olive oil until
soft, stirring often. Remove and set aside.

In steamer or small pot, cook peas for five minutes. Add to
onion.

Fry bacon in the unwashed large pot over low heat. When
crisp remove and drain on paper towels. Pour off all but about
1 T. bacon fat from pan and discard.

Fill stock pot with water, salt amply, and bring to boil.

Cook the spaghetti in boiling water until cooked al dente.
Drain.

(continued) ☞

Beat the eggs with milk, ⅔ c. cheese, pepper and nutmeg.

Return cooked spaghetti to pot over low heat. Add the egg mixture, stirring vigorously until spaghetti is coated. Mix the bacon, onion and frozen peas into the spaghetti.

Serve piping hot. Serve remaining cheese on the side.

Chicken Nuggets
serves four

1½ lb. boneless chicken breast
2 eggs
¼ c. milk
flour
dry bread crumbs
vegetable oil
salt
1 lemon, cut into wedges

Trim fat and gristle from chicken. Cut into "finger" shapes.

Beat eggs and milk in flat bowl.

Spread flour and bread crumbs on two separate plates.

Pour oil into fryer or deep sided skillet to a depth of about two inches.

Dredge each piece of chicken in flour, then dunk in the egg mixture. Roll in bread crumbs until well coated.

Heat oil until it is hot enough to immediately sizzle a drop of water. Fry a few pieces of chicken at a time until light brown. Drain well in fryer basket or paper towels. Salt to taste.

Serve with lemon wedges.

*One of Phoebe's first tastes was for bitter food like escarole. She would bliss-
fully sit in her high chair ingesting large quantities of this soup. No longer as
sophisticated as she was at one, she now prefers the soup made with
spinach. Now also a vegetarian, she seems to have a grandfather clause for
the chicken broth in this one recipe.*

Escarole or Spinach and Rice Soup
serves six

3 T. olive oil
1 c. finely chopped onion
6 c. spinach or escarole leaves, well washed, drained, and
   cut in thin shreds
9 c. chicken broth
salt
pinch white pepper
⅓ c. Arborio rice
freshly grated Parmesan cheese

Put oil and onion in a soup pot. Cook over medium heat until
onion turns golden brown, stirring from time to time. Add
spinach or escarole and toss in oil for a minute. Add broth,
salt and pepper. Bring to boil. If using escarole, simmer for
twenty minutes before adding rice. If using spinach, add rice
right away. After adding rice, simmer for fifteen minutes.
Ladle into warm soup bowls.

Serve with grated cheese on the side.

Another favorite of Phoebe's and of practically everyone else is fried zucchini. The blossoms are a special summer country treat, fun to gather when the bees are buzzing all about them. If by remarkable chance there are leftovers, they're a great add-in for a last minute spaghetti dish with garlic and Parmesan cheese.

Fried Zucchini and Zucchini Blossoms
serves four as a side dish or more as an hors d'oeuvres

4 medium zucchini, well scrubbed
milk
flour
1 dozen squash blossoms
vegetable oil

Cut off and discard ends of zucchini. Cut into 3" lengths, then into thin strips, discarding any pieces that have no green skin attached. Put in bowl with milk to cover. Let stand for twenty minutes or so. Drain zucchini, saving milk, and dredge strips in flour. Lay strips with a bit of space between them on foil or wax paper. It's fine to stack with foil or wax paper separating the layers. Gently dip squash blossoms in reserved milk and then dredge in flour. Lay on foil or wax paper with space around each piece.

Into a deep fryer with wire basket, pour oil to a depth of 4" and heat until oil is hot enough to immediately sizzle a drop of water.

Gently drop about twenty pieces of zucchini into hot oil. Cook until golden brown. Drain by raising basket over oil, then dump zucchini onto paper towels to drain further. Sprinkle with salt. Serve right away.

Follow with a round of blossoms cooked exactly the same way.

Serve with lemon wedges or a little bowl of marinara sauce.

A popular variant.

Fried Onions
serves four

2 medium onions, sliced into thin rings
milk
flour
vegetable oil

Make like fried zucchini (preceding recipe). You don't have to be as careful to keep pieces from touching.

People who expect more of me are shocked that I think a baked potato can be dinner. When I'm motivated, I make these baked potatoes plus.

Restuffed Potatoes
serves ten

12 large Idaho or other russet potatoes
1½ sticks butter
1 c. sour cream
2 t. salt
½ t. nutmeg
¼ t. white pepper
1 c. grated Gruyere cheese

Preheat oven to 450 degrees.

Scrub potatoes. Pierce with a fork, set on baking sheet and bake until tender about one hour. Cool slightly. Cut a small piece from tops. Scrape flesh from tops and scoop out flesh from bottoms being careful not to cut through skins. Even with the best of care, you usually destroy one or two shells, so sacrifice these potatoes and use all the contents for stuffing and the whole shells for skin.

Put flesh in bowl with butter. Mash well with potato masher. Add sour cream, salt, nutmeg and pepper. Mix well. Fill potato shells. Sprinkle with cheese.

Cut skins into ½" strips and toss with oil. Lay on foil lined baking sheet.

Put skins and potatoes in oven and bake for about twenty minutes.

Serve each stuffed potato with several pieces of crispy skin.

When I serve Stella's Lasagna, I let my vegetarians inhabit a parallel universe.

Vegetable Lasagna
serves eight

2 c. eggplant peeled, cut in ½″ cubes
salt
4 T. olive oil
1 c. mushrooms, cut in wedges
1 lb. spinach, well washed and drained
1 c. broccoli florets
1 c. zucchini cut in ⅓″ cubes
1 lb. lasagna
1 lb. ricotta
3 eggs
1 c. Parmesan cheese
2 T. minced parsley
1 recipe marinara sauce (p. 39)
1 lb. mozzarella, cut in ¼″ cubes

Sprinkle eggplant generously with salt and leave to stand in colander in sink or over bowl for several hours to discharge liquid. Rinse and dry by spreading on dish or paper towels for a half hour.

In medium skillet heat 3 T. oil until smoking hot. Put in eggplant and cook until golden brown. Drain in colander and put in large bowl. Add remaining T. oil to skillet and heat until it smokes. Add mushrooms and cook until golden brown. Add to cooked eggplant.

Cook spinach in a large pot with lid over medium heat, moving spinach with tongs once or twice. When leaves are limp, dump in colander, refresh with cold water. Drain, wring dry and chop coarsely. Put with eggplant and mushrooms in bowl.

(continued) ☞

Steam broccoli and zucchini separately until just tender. Refresh each with cold water and drain well. Put cooked vegetables in bowl. Mix together well.

Cook lasagna in a large pot of well salted water. Stir gently several times so lasagna doesn't stick together. Remove when a bit harder than al dente. Drain and rinse under cold water. Drain and spread on dish towels to dry completely.

Mix together ricotta, eggs, Parmesan cheese and parsley.

Spread a ¼″ layer of sauce in a deep rectangular baking dish approximately 9″ × 13″ × 3″ in dimension. Lay a layer of lasagna on top, overlapping noodles slightly. Cut noodles to fit if necessary. Spread a layer of sauce. Sprinkle half the vegetables on top. Use a spoon to add ricotta in dabs that are practically touching. Use one third of the ricotta mixture. Scatter one third of the mozzarella on top. Repeat with another layer of noodles, sauce, the other half of the vegetables and second third of the cheeses. Finish with a third layer without vegetables. Cover with aluminum foil.

Preheat oven to 375 degrees. Put in lasagna and bake until piping hot, about forty minutes. Raise heat to 425 degrees. Uncover and bake for fifteen minutes longer until top is nicely browned.

Remove from oven and let stand for ten minutes before cutting into squares.

Phoebe will make these anytime you ask. Although I'm not a fan of one use kitchen items, popovers are enough of a specialty of the house to rate special popover pans. The mini pans are best.

Popovers
makes twelve mini popovers or six regular size popovers

1 c. milk
1 c. flour
2 eggs
1 T. vegetable oil
½ t. salt

Preheat oven to 425 degrees.

Grease popover pans.

Beat ingredients until smooth. Fill cups a bit less than halfway. Bake for fifteen minutes. Turn oven down to 350 degrees. Bake ten minutes longer for mini popovers, twenty minutes longer for regular size.

When Sarah was nine she got up at four in the morning for her first horse show ever and was constantly occupied until five in the afternoon. She was much too busy (and probably nervous) to eat. At the end of the day she announced she was starving for "a raw onion."

This gratin is something more socially acceptable that she's glad to eat morning noon or night, and she can eat the whole thing by herself! Hence the name.

Gratin Sarah Rae
serves four to six

1 unpeeled garlic clove
1 T. soft butter
3 lb. potatoes, peeled and sliced into thin rounds
1¼ c. cream
½ t. salt
¼ t. white pepper
¼ t. nutmeg

Preheat oven to 425 degrees. Rub a large shallow baking dish with garlic and discard.

Butter well.

Put potatoes in dish with cream, salt, pepper and nutmeg. Mix well. Bake for twenty minutes. Stir. Return to oven to bake until very well browned, about an hour more.

If you think you can give Sarah a baked potato and call it dinner, you are sadly mistaken. Sarah always requires gastronomy. At least she is willing to whip up a snack like this herself and more or less clean up.

Pad Thai with Vegetables and Bean Curd
serves four

approximately 6 oz. Pad Thai noodles or rice noodles
1 heaping cup fresh mung bean sprouts
3 T. soy sauce
1 T. red wine vinegar
1 t. sugar
1 t. sesame oil
2 T. vegetable oil
1 small onion cut in 1″ pieces
1 c. broccoli florets
½ c. green pepper cut in ¼″ × 1″ strips
½ c. red pepper cut in ¼″ × 1″ strips
1 t. minced garlic
2 eggs, lightly beaten
¾ c. firm bean curd, cut in ½″ cubes
1 t. minced jalapeno pepper
3 T. chopped coriander leaves
¼ c. finely chopped roasted unsalted peanuts
1 lime, cut in wedges

Bring a large pot of water to boil. Boil noodles one to four minutes, according to package instructions which depend on width, until cooked al dente. Stir frequently as noodles cook. Drain. Run cold water over noodles to chill. Drain well.

Remove stringy tails and seed ends from sprouts and discard.

In small bowl mix soy sauce, vinegar, sugar and sesame oil.

In wok or large skillet over high heat, heat oil until hot. Add onion, broccoli, green and red peppers and garlic. Stir fry for two minutes. Make a well in center of pan. Add eggs. Let heat

(continued) ☞

for a minute without stirring to set, then toss until fully cooked. Add noodles and bean curd. Cook for a few minutes, stirring frequently. Add sauce mixture. Heat thirty seconds longer, stirring constantly.

Put noodles on warm serving platter. Sprinkle bean sprouts, jalapeno, coriander and peanuts on top. Garnish with lime wedges.

Another of Sarah's production numbers, usually cooked as a social event with Sabina Martin, Sarah's kitchen co-conspirator.

Vegetable Spring Rolls
makes twenty large or thirty small spring rolls

1 package cellophane noodles
1 T. vegetable oil
2 c. carrot, cut in fine julienne
2 c. onion, cut in fine julienne
2 c. bok choy, cut in thin strips
2 c. green and/or red pepper, cut in fine julienne
2 c. zucchini, cut in fine julienne
2 c. mushroom, cut in fine julienne
1 c. sliced scallion
1 t. grated ginger
1 T. soy sauce or light soy sauce
1 package spring roll skins

Soak cellophane noodles in cold water for a half hour.

Meanwhile heat wok or skillet until smoking hot. Add 1 t. oil and carrots and onion. Stir fry for several minutes until carrots begin to soften. Remove to a large bowl. Heat wok again. Add 1 t. oil, bok choy and pepper and stir fry until peppers begin to soften. Add to onions and carrots in bowl. Repeat procedure with remaining 1 t. oil and zucchini and mushroom. Zucchini and mushroom will release liquid. As the liquid evaporates, add scallion and ginger. Stir for one minute. Turn off heat. Stir in soy sauce and add to vegetable mixture in bowl.

Drain cellophane noodles well. Chop them into 2″ lengths and mix them into vegetable mixture. Cover and set aside in refrigerator until assembly time.

While shaping rolls, heat oil in wok or deep fryer until it is hot enough to immediately sizzle a drop of water. Lower heat to maintain temperature while you shape spring rolls.

(continued) ☞

Lay a spring roll skin on counter at angle so one corner is at top. Just below center, place two heaping tablespoons of filling, a bit less if using small skins. Spread filling to form a 1" wide cylinder that stops ¾" from edges. Fold edges over filling, then roll bottom of wrapper over filling to cover well. Continue rolling to top. Seal top by dabbing with water at inner edge.

Gently place rolls three at a time in hot oil in wok. After about one minute, press gently with slotted spoon or spatula to hold tops under oil. Be careful not to rip skins.

Turn rolls and continue cooking until golden brown all over. Total time should be about three minutes. Drain well on paper towels. Serve hot with dipping sauce.

Dipping Sauce for Spring Rolls
½ c. excellent quality peach jam
1 T. Chinese mustard
1 t. grated ginger
1 t. soy sauce

Combine jam, mustard, ginger and soy sauce. Let stand for thirty minutes.

Rural living has made us self-sufficient in satisfying our cravings for Chinese food. Nonetheless when we head to NYC or Washington DC, a top Chinese restaurant will usually be the food destination.

These scallion pancakes hold their own with the best of them.

Scallion Pancakes
makes six

1½ c. flour, plus extra for rolling
½ t. salt
1 t. melted vegetable shortening
4 T. finely chopped scallion
vegetable oil as needed

In food processor fitted with steel blade, mix flour and salt. Add ⅔ c. boiling water and pulse until dough forms a moist ball. Add a few more drops of water if necessary. Process for one minute. Or make by hand by beating ingredients with a wooden spoon and kneading for eight minutes. Cover dough with plastic wrap and refrigerate for an hour or more. Divide dough into six equal pieces and roll into balls. Flatten a piece of dough and roll into a six inch circle, using extra flour as needed to prevent sticking. Brush dough with shortening and sprinkle with 2 t. of the scallions. Roll up from one edge to form a cylinder.

Flatten slightly by hand to form a rectangle 7″ × 1½″. Roll up from narrow end. Moisten top of last bit of dough with water to prevent unrolling. Turn on side so that dough shows a snail shape. Let rest in the refrigerator an hour or more.

At serving time, roll dough into a 6″ circle. Heat ¼ c. oil in medium skillet for several minutes until hot but not smoking. Slip dough into pan and cook until golden brown but not crispy, about a minute. Flip and cook other side the same way. Drain on paper towels. Repeat for other pieces of dough, replenishing oil as necessary. Cut pancakes in eight wedges. Serve with dipping sauce.

Dipping Sauce for Scallion Pancakes
1″ cube of ginger
3 T. soy sauce
1 t. sesame oil
2 t. rice wine vinegar
1 t. sugar

Peel ginger. Cut in thin slices. Crush slices with side of knife and put in a small bowl. Pour remaining ingredients over ginger. Let stand for thirty minutes, then remove ginger.

Chocolate pudding is one of those desserts that's really satisfying to make, because the way the cream goes from thin to thick in a second is magical. Luckily Sarah is always happy to eat a chocolate cream pie!

Chocolate Cream Pie
one 9″ pie

1 recipe basic pie dough, amount for 9″ shell (p. 112)
2 c. milk
6 egg yolks
¾ c. sugar
¼ c. cornstarch
2 T. butter, at room temperature
1 t. vanilla extract
2½ c. cream
3 oz. semi sweet chocolate, chopped
1 oz. unsweetened chocolate, chopped

Roll dough into 11″ round. Fill 9″ pie pan. Flute edges. Prick dough all over with fork. Put shell in freezer for one hour.

Preheat oven to 400 degrees. Take pie shell from freezer. Cover with aluminum foil and weigh down with beans or rice. (Beans or rice can be reused many times.) Bake about fifteen minutes until dough begins to get dry. Remove foil and weights. Bake about fifteen minutes longer, piercing any bubbles that form, until shell is golden brown.

In large heavy bottomed sauce pan over low heat, bring milk to the verge of boiling. While it heats, beat yolks and sugar until light yellow. Beat the cornstarch in well. Add half the boiling milk, beat in well, then return egg mixture to saucepan. Whisk constantly over low heat until mixture bubbles and thickens. Cook for a minute or so, whisking hard. Off heat, whisk in butter and vanilla.

(continued) ☞

In bowl set over simmering water, heat chocolate and ½ c. cream until chocolate melts. Whisk until smooth, then add to pastry cream. Whisk in thoroughly. Cool slightly.

Spoon chocolate cream into pie shell. Level with a metal spreading spatula. Cover surface of filling with plastic wrap. Refrigerate until cold, at least three hours.

Whip remaining 2 c. cream until stiff. Use a pastry bag to pipe whipped cream over chocolate filling. Serve right away.

This is just embellished chocolate mousse, but the texture contrast of soft mousse and crispy topping makes it extra special.

Chocolate Marquise
serves eight

1 recipe Olga's chocolate mousse cake (p. 12), filling only
1½ oz. semi sweet chocolate
1 oz. unsweetened chocolate
2 t. unsweetened cocoa

Line a large loaf pan with plastic wrap, making wrap as smooth as possible. Fill pan with mousse. Refrigerate for at least six hours. Unmold onto platter.

Melt semi-sweet and unsweetened chocolates in bowl set on top of simmering water or in microwave. Stir until smooth. Use a rubber spatula to spread over top of loaf. Return to refrigerator for thirty minutes or more to harden chocolate.

Sift cocoa over loaf right before serving.

To serve, cut in slices. Serve with whipped cream on the side.

Claude spent her formative first in utero month in Italy and she is forever marked. She can eat pasta twice a day. Here are some of her favorite versions, Italian, improvisational or all American.

Macaroni and Cheese
serves six to eight

6 T. butter
6 T. flour
4½ c. milk
1 t. Dijon mustard
1 t. Worcestershire sauce
1 heaping t. salt
pinch cayenne pepper
pinch white pepper
3 c. grated Gruyere cheese
1¼ lb. macaroni

In medium saucepan over medium heat, melt butter. Whisk in flour. Add milk in several additions whisking well after each. Add mustard, Worcestershire sauce, salt and cayenne and white pepper. Cook over low heat for five minutes whisking frequently. Turn off heat. Whisk in cheese.

Cook macaroni in large pot of heavily salted boiling water. Remove when a bit harder than al dente. Drain. Fold macaroni into sauce. Put in a large shallow oven dish or two medium dishes. Cover with foil.

Put rack in top third of oven and preheat oven to 425 degrees. Bake macaroni until piping hot, about twenty-five minutes.

Uncover and bake fifteen minutes longer until golden brown on top.

This was a spring improvisation that Claude insisted we institutionalize.

Penne with Asparagus
serves four

1½ lb. asparagus
1 c. cream
1 lb. shelling peas
2 leek whites, well washed and cut in ½″ strips
3 T. butter
½ c. good quality smoked ham, cut in ¼″ dice
salt
pinch white pepper
freshly grated nutmeg
¼ c. fresh basil leaves
1 lb. penne
2 c. freshly grated Parmesan cheese

Wash the asparagus well. Snap away asparagus bottoms where they naturally break and discard bottoms. Steam asparagus until tender. Refresh under cold running water. Drain.

Cut off tips and set aside. Puree stalks in blender with cream and strain to remove lumps.

Shell peas and steam until tender, a few minutes or less. Refresh under cold running water. Drain.

In medium skillet over low heat, cook leek whites in butter until limp, stirring often. Add puree, ham, salt, pepper and nutmeg and cook, stirring often, until sauce reduces by half. Turn off heat. Cut basil into fine shreds and add with asparagus tips and peas to sauce.

While sauce cooks, bring a large pot of well salted water to boil. Cook penne al dente. Drain. Mix penne, 1 c. of the cheese, and sauce. Serve remaining cheese at the table.

We met this dish at a party at Will, Sue and Lyndsey Bailey's house. Ceci was sick and couldn't come, and the Baileys sent us home with a big portion for her. The association with cossetting on top of the great taste, puts this pasta at the top of Ceci's list of favorites.

Will's Penne alla Vodka

serves eight

3 T. minced shallot
1 t. minced garlic
2 T. olive oil
¼ c. vodka
1½ c. marinara sauce (p. 39)
¼ c. cream
1 T. shredded fresh basil
salt
1 lb. penne
freshly grated Parmesan cheese

Put shallot, garlic and olive oil in medium skillet. Cook over medium low heat for five minutes, stirring often. Add vodka, ignite by tilting into flame of gas stove, or use a match if your stove is electric. Cook a minute or so, shaking pan continuously. Add marinara sauce, cream and basil. Cook over medium heat for about ten minutes, until sauce is slightly reduced. Adjust seasoning.

While sauce cooks, bring a large pot of water to boil. Salt generously. Add penne to boiling water and stir gently several times so penne doesn't stick together. Strain when al dente.

Return penne to cooking pot, pour sauce on top and mix gently. Adjust seasoning. Serve cheese on the side.

Tubular shape pastas are the family favorite going back to the days when the girls would request "finger noodles." This recipe started with Marcella Hazan, one of my kitchen goddesses.

Rigatoni with Sweet Peppers

serves six

4 large red peppers
2 large yellow peppers
3 T. olive oil
1 t. minced garlic
3 T. butter
¼ c. shredded basil leaves
2 T. minced parsley
salt
good grinding black pepper
1 lb. penne
1 c. Parmesan cheese

Peel thin layer of outer skin from peppers as best you can. Remove and discard cores and seeds. Cut peppers into thin strips about ¼″ × 1½″. Put peppers with olive oil in large skillet and cook over medium high heat, stirring often, until peppers are limp but not browned. Add garlic and cook a minute or so longer. Turn off heat and add butter, basil, parsley, salt and pepper.

In large pot of well salted water, cook penne al dente, stirring often during first few minutes. Drain well.

Return rigatoni to pot and combine with sweet peppers and ½ c. of the cheese. Mix well.

Pass additional cheese at the table.

With her pasta, Claude tolerates one or two side dishes if they are amazing.

Creamed Spinach
serves eight to ten

3 lb. fresh spinach, well washed and drained
⅔ c. minced shallots
4 T. butter
4 T. flour
2 c. whole milk
1½ c. cream
1¼ t. salt
¼ t. white pepper
¼ t. freshly grated nutmeg

Cook spinach in several batches in a large pot with lid over medium heat, moving spinach with tongs once or twice. When leaves are limp, dump in colander, refresh with cold water. Drain, wring dry and chop coarsely.

Put shallots and butter in large heavy saucepan. Over low heat, cook several minutes. Whisk in flour. Cook a few minutes longer, whisking often. Add milk in small additions, whisking well after each. When all the milk is incorporated, add cream, salt, pepper and nutmeg. Simmer for five minutes, stirring often. Add spinach to pan and mix well. Adjust seasoning. Cook a few minutes longer over very low heat, stirring often.

Zucchini with Onions
serves six

3 T. butter
3 c. thinly sliced onion
5 medium zucchini, well scrubbed, sliced thin
salt

In a heavy skillet over medium high heat, heat butter until it sizzles. Add onions and cook a few minutes, stirring often. Add zucchini, sprinkle with salt, and stir well. Cook until most pieces of zucchini are nicely browned, using a spatula to move the pieces around. Zucchini should be just tender.

Ceci usually prevails upon Jim to make this with her several times every summer.

Ceci and Jim's Lemonade
serves four

1 c. freshly squeezed lemon juice
1 c. sugar or more to taste
½ c. raspberries, optional

Mix lemon juice, sugar and 5 c. cold water. Add more sugar, if desired.

For pink lemonade, crush raspberries and strain liquid into lemonade.

Although Claude has the youngest child's brilliant talent for delegation, if coerced to cook, she might make this.

Swiss Fondue
serves eight

2 crushed garlic cloves
1 c. white wine or chicken broth
1 lb. grated Gruyere cheese
1 T. cornstarch
2 T. Kirsch
pinch white pepper
grated nutmeg
slightly stale French bread, cut in ½" cubes

Rub pan with crushed garlic and discard. Put in wine or broth. Bring to simmer over low heat. Add cheese whisking until smooth. Mix cornstarch and Kirsch well. Add to cheese mixture. Heat mixture, stirring all the while until thick and creamy. Season with pepper and nutmeg.

Keep hot at table. Eat by spearing French bread cubes with a fork and dunking them.

In other households, quesadillas are a throw-away meal like grilled cheese sandwiches, but in our home, while they're always proposed in that way, they end up being an elaborate undertaking. Homemade tortillas are so much better than store bought that I can't resist making them. Of course no one will even consider jarred salsa of any type after they have homemade, so next there's that big job which Jim and I usually do together. And after going to all this trouble, it would be a shame not to serve yellow rice, homemade of course. But this is one of those big fusses that is completely worthwhile, a simple meal that everyone loves.

Quesadillas
serves six

14 tortillas (following recipe)
1½ lb. grated Monterey jack cheese
1½ c. salsa (p. 279)
2 c. sour cream
3 c. shredded iceberg lettuce
2 medium tomatoes, cut in ¼" cubes
2 avocados, cut in ¼" cubes
1 red onion, cut in ¼" dice
1 can California olives, drained and cut in rounds

Preheat oven to 350 degrees.

Sprinkle a thin layer of cheese over a tortilla and top with a second tortilla. Repeat using all tortillas and cheese. Make two stacks of tortilla sandwiches and wrap stacks in foil.

Bake until cheese melts, about ten minutes.

Cut quesadillas into wedges. Serve with salsa, sour cream and garnishes.

These taste their absolute best hot from the pan.

Tortillas
makes fourteen

3 c. flour
1 t. salt
1 scant t. sugar
½ c. vegetable shortening

In food processor fitted with steel blade, mix flour, salt and sugar. Add shortening and cut in thoroughly. Add 1 c. hot water and process for sixty seconds. Divide into fourteen 1¼" balls and refrigerate for at least an hour.

Roll a few balls on lightly floured board to a 5" diameter. Let rest a minute or so. Roll again into 8" circles.

Heat heavy cast iron skillet over medium heat until quite hot. Put in a tortilla and cook until it bubbles up and is lightly browned. If pan is at proper temperature this will take about thirty seconds. Flip and cook other side until light brown, for about twenty seconds.

Continue rolling rest of dough as you continue to cook.

Yellow Rice
serves six

2 T. vegetable oil
1 c. finely chopped onion
½ c. finely chopped carrot
½ c. finely chopped green pepper
1½ t. minced garlic
2 c. rice
1 T. tomato paste
3¾ c. hot chicken broth
generous pinch saffron
1 t. salt
pinch white pepper

Put oil, onion, carrot, pepper and garlic in a large saucepan with a heavy bottom. Saute over medium heat, stirring occasionally, for five minutes. Add rice to pot and cook for a few minutes, stirring frequently, until rice is well coated with oil. Add tomato paste and mix well. Stir in broth, saffron, salt and white pepper and bring to a boil. Turn heat to low, cover and simmer for twenty minutes without stirring.

Remove lid, adjust seasoning and fluff rice with a fork. Cover and let stand ten minutes.

Guacamole's even better than diced avocado with the quesadillas. The only trick to making it well is using perfectly ripe avocados. Control the ripening process by buying unripe Haas avocados and ripening them at room temperature in a closed paper bag. That may take several days or longer.

Guacamole
serves eight

2 ripe avocados
1 T. minced red onion
1 jalapeno pepper, seeded and minced
1 t. minced garlic
2 t. lime juice or more to taste
¼ t. salt

Halve and skin avocados. Discard pits. Mash flesh with a fork. Fold in red onion, jalapeno, garlic, lime juice and salt. Adjust seasoning. Serve immediately or pack well into small bowl, placing plastic wrap directly on surface of guacamole.

The coup de grace in the southwestern performance are our family chile favorites, vegetarian (naturally) and con carne.

Vegetable Chile
serves six

1 c. kidney beans
¼ c. vegetable oil
2 c. finely chopped onion
2 T. minced garlic
⅔ c. mild red chile powder
1 T. hot chile powder
½ t. paprika
1 T. cumin
¼ t. dried pepper flakes, or less to taste
¼ t. oregano
2 c. canned tomatoes, drained and chopped
2 c. green pepper, cut in ¾″ chunks
2 c. red pepper, cut in ¾″ chunks
¾ c. celery, cut in ¾″ chunks
2 t. salt
2 c. pearl onions, trimmed and peeled
2 c. baby carrots or regular carrots cut in small sticks
2 c. cauliflower florets
2 c. trimmed brussels sprouts
4 c. zucchini or yellow squash, cut in ¾″ chunks
1½ c. green beans, cut in 1″ pieces
1 c. fresh small okra, if available, sliced into ½″ pieces, tops discarded
1 c. grated cheddar or Monterey jack cheese
1 c. chopped red onion
½ c. pitted black olives, sliced in rounds
1 c. sour cream

Soak kidney beans overnight in cold water to cover amply. The next day, drain kidney beans and put them in a medium saucepan. Add cold water to cover amply, bring to a boil and

(continued) ☞

simmer over low heat until kidney beans are tender, about one hour. Drain.

Put oil and onion in a large skillet. Cook over medium heat, stirring occasionally, until onions soften. Add garlic and cook two minutes longer, stirring a few times. Add chile powders, cumin, pepper flakes, and oregano and cook, stirring continuously, just long enough to release the fragrance of the spices. Add tomato, green and red pepper, celery, 6 c. water and salt. Simmer for fifteen minutes.

Drop pearl onions in boiling water for two minutes. Cut off root end and squeeze to remove skin. Put pearl onions, carrots, cauliflower, brussels sprouts, zucchini, green beans, and okra into chile. Cook over low heat until tender, about thirty minutes. Add cooked beans to the chile and continue to cook over low heat for fifteen minutes. Adjust seasoning.

Serve chile piping hot over cooked brown rice. Pass garnishes of cheese, red onion, olives and sour cream in small bowls.

Chile Con Carne
serves ten to twelve

½ lb. kidney beans
vegetable oil as needed
2 c. onion, coarsely chopped
¼ c. minced garlic
⅔ c. mild New Mexican chile powder
1 T. or more to taste, hot New Mexican chile powder
1 T. cumin
1 t. Mexican oregano
2 t. salt
4 lb. beef chuck, cut in ⅓" cubes
1 lb. lean ground beef

Soak beans overnight. Drain. Put in saucepan with ample water and simmer over low heat until tender, about one hour.

Put ¼ c. oil and onion in deep pot. Cook over medium heat, stirring often, until onions are limp. Stir in garlic and cook a few minutes more, stirring often. Add chile powders, cumin and oregano. Lower heat and cook for several minutes stirring constantly. Add salt.

In large skillet over medium high heat, heat a thin layer of oil until it smokes. Brown as many of the beef cubes as will fit without crowding, turning to brown on all sides. Using slotted spoon, remove and add to chile mixture. Add a bit more oil and continue browning rest of cubes in batches. When all the cubes are done, brown ground beef in skillet, scraping up any browned bits sticking to pan. Strain and add ground beef to beef cubes, discarding grease. Add water to just cover meat. Bring to simmer over low heat, cover, and cook for an hour and a half, stirring often.

Drain beans and add to chile. Simmer a half hour longer. Adjust seasoning.

Serve on top of short grain brown rice with sour cream and chopped red onions on the side.

Cafe Amore

*W*hen they were all small, the girls started a tradition of cooking elaborate multi-course meals for Jim's and my special occasions. Meals were
served in the make believe "Cafe Amore" where Claude, the little four foot tall
maitre d', would welcome us by kissing madame's hand, seating us in the
salon and preparing a drink from the elaborate bar she had set up. The table
(candle lit, of course) was elaborately set with all our best, and the service
was four star.

The meals were usually pretty spectacular too, although once in a while
marred by the sort of blunder that comes with being ambitious. Great as the
meals were, the best parts came before, when banished to the upstairs as the
kids cooked and cleaned away, I listened to the harmonious chatter.

Another favorite feature of meals at Cafe Amore was cocktail hour. Claude
never let being ten years old keep her from mixing a wicked drink of her own
researching!

Claude's Tucson Cocktail
serves two

2 shots or ¼ c. tequila
1 T. honey
juice of a half lemon
crushed ice

Mix tequila, honey and lemon juice well. Put crushed ice in
two short glasses. Pour drink over ice.

The girls came up with the great idea of serving corn on the cob as a separate first course. I've never known anyone else to do this, but it really lets fresh corn have the spotlight it deserves. They also came up with the idea of serving it with pesto, unfortunately at first mistaking the mint in the garden for basil. That's how "minto" was invented, but we'll stick with the recipe for pesto.

Blanching the basil keeps the bright green color and doesn't noticeably affect the fresh basil taste.

Pesto
makes two cups, enough for 1½ lb. pasta or much corn

3 c. basil leaves
1½ c. freshly grated Parmesan cheese
¾ c. extra virgin olive oil
¼ c. coarsely chopped garlic
3 T. soft butter
3 T. pine nuts
½ t. salt
good grinding black pepper

Bring a small pot of water to boil. Drop in basil leaves, stir and cook for ten seconds. Drain. Put under cold running water until cold. Gently squeeze dry. Chop into coarse pieces.

Put cheese, oil, garlic, butter, pine nuts, salt and pepper in blender and puree. While blender runs, add leaves a handful at a time through opening in cap. Blend until all are incorporated but stop before pesto is completely smooth. Put a tablespoon of the boiling cooking water from pasta or corn into blender to thin and warm sauce,

This is best used immediately but can be packed for a few days of refrigerator storage. To store, put in a container and tap a few times to remove air pockets. Cover with a thin layer of additional olive oil. Cover with lid.

Another popular item on the Cafe Amore menu was chicken piccata, made very memorably by the girls on one occasion. I usually keep powdered chicken broth base in the pantry for dishes just like this when a small amount of broth is needed for a sauce. The girls followed the recipe not understanding that they would need to mix the powder with water. Instead they added the full measure of powder and created sauce like a brick. "Madame" was called from the salon to conduct the salvage operation.

Chicken Piccata
serves four

four large boneless half breasts of chicken
flour for dredging
3 T. oil
2 T. butter
salt
good grinding black pepper
3 T. minced scallions
1 c. chicken broth
1 T. or more lemon juice

Trim all fat and gristle from chicken. Dredge in flour.

Heat oil and butter in large skillet until sizzling. Slip in breasts and cook over medium heat until golden brown. Flip and brown second side. Remove chicken to plate and season with salt and pepper.

Discard most of the fat in pan, then set pan over low heat. Add scallions and cook a minute or so, stirring and scraping pan. Stir in a heaping teaspoon of the dredging flour. Whisk in chicken broth and 1 T. lemon juice.

Return chicken to pan, cover and cook several minutes on each side. Add salt or lemon juice if needed.

Poires Belle Helene made a grand finale, and it was completely irrelevant that the crepes didn't work out. Poached pears with vanilla ice cream and chocolate sauce tastes every bit as good. After dessert, the girls offered "hot towels", wet and wrung out wash cloths, rolled in cylinders and heated until piping hot in the microwave.

Poached Pears Belle Helene
serves six

2 c. white wine
1½ c. sugar
3 strips of lime zest
6 large ripe pears
⅓ c. brandy or cognac
6 scoops best quality store bought vanilla ice cream or
    homemade
⅔ c. chocolate sauce (p. 126) with brandy substituted for
    Frangelico

In a medium size non reactive pot over low heat, bring the wine, sugar and lime zest to boil, stirring occasionally to dissolve sugar. Simmer for five minutes. Turn off heat and let stand while you prepare pears.

Peel pears, halve and scoop out cores.

Put pears into syrup and cook over low heat until tender, about twenty minutes. Turn off heat and let stand in syrup for an hour. Remove peel and stir in brandy. Macerate for twelve hours at room temperature.

Put a scoop of ice cream in each of six bowls. Put two pear halves on top, and spoon a few tablespoons of syrup over all. Swirl chocolate sauce on top.

Thanksgiving

I used to cater Thanksgiving, but soon discovered it was the most thank-less holiday. No matter how awful someone's family dishes are, that's his standard and any deviation even as improvement is unacceptable. Stella tells this story about her friends, the Busners. Naomi could never satisfy Phil with her wonderful pot roast until the day she burned it. Then Phil said, "That's delicious. It tastes just like my mother's." That's how it is with holiday fare.

So I wouldn't expect anyone else to like these side dishes, but they're the things—besides roast turkey with bread stuffing and gravy—most likely to be on my family's Thanksgiving table. By the way, once I made a scratch stuffing, a beautiful thing involving garden herbs and homemade bread which I referred to as 'mock Pepperidge Farm,' but which the collective compared negatively to the real Pepperidge Farm.

Around here stick with the package. Once you put all these things on the table, you are free, nay expected, to add others like boiled white rice, another vegetable or two and certainly several desserts involving chocolate and whipped cream.

My mother-in-law's cranberry relish is state of the art, but nonetheless the girls require jellied cranberry, the little ridges proclaiming, yes, it did come right from the can!

Stella's Cranberry Gobbledygook
makes one quart

1 lb. fresh cranberries
1 c. orange juice
1½ c. sugar
2 tart apples, peeled, cored and cut in ⅓" cubes
½ c. yellow raisins
1 t. grated orange rind
½ t. grated lemon rind
4 T. sherry

Wash cranberries and pick over to remove any dried up or under ripe berries. Put orange juice and sugar in a medium saucepan over medium low heat. Cook, stirring to dissolve sugar. Add all the other ingredients except the sherry. Bring to a boil, turn heat to low and simmer, stirring from time to time. In a few minutes the cranberries will pop open. Simmer for ten minutes longer. Take off heat and let cool about five minutes. Stir in sherry. Refrigerate up to one week.

The cinnamon bread topping fills in for the expected marshmallows, and probably no topping at all is the best way to go.

Sweet Potato Casserole
serves twelve or more

6 lb. sweet potatoes
2 t. salt
8 T. butter, melted
¼ c. brandy
1½ t. orange rind
¼ t. white pepper
¼ t. nutmeg
3 slices good quality white bread, crusts removed, cut in ¼″
    cubes
2 T. lightly packed brown sugar
1 t. cinnamon

Peel sweet potatoes. Cut in 1″ chunks. Put in large pot with 1 t. salt and cover with cold water.

Over medium heat, bring to a boil. Simmer until tender. Drain, return to pot and dry out over low heat for a minute or two. Pass through the coarse screen of food mill. Add 3 T. butter, brandy, orange rind, remaining 1 t. salt, pepper and nutmeg. Adjust seasoning.

Make topping by combining bread with brown sugar, remaining 5 T. butter and cinnamon.

Spread sweet potato mixture in an 8″ × 12″ baking dish or other shallow ovenproof dish roughly equivalent in size. Sprinkle bread cubes on top.

Bake at 325 degrees until piping hot and golden brown on top, around thirty minutes.

Pearl Onions in Cream Sauce
serves twelve or more

6 T. butter
6 T. flour
4½ c. milk
1 t. Dijon mustard
1 t. Worcestershire sauce
1 heaping t. salt
pinch cayenne pepper
pinch white pepper
3 lb. pearl onions, peeled & cooked

In medium saucepan over medium heat, melt butter. Whisk in flour. Add milk in several additions whisking well after each. Add mustard, Worcestershire sauce, salt and cayenne and white pepper. Cook over low heat for five minutes whisking frequently. Turn off heat. Fold pearl onions into sauce.

Put in large shallow oven dish or two medium dishes. Cover with foil.

Put rack in top third of oven and preheat oven to 425 degrees. Bake until piping hot, about thirty minutes.

Shelling chestnuts is big work, and only I seem to like this dish. But as I like it a lot, I persevere.

Brussels Sprouts with Chestnuts
serves twelve

1 lb. chestnuts
5 c. trimmed brussels sprouts, all the same size
3 T. butter
¼ t. salt
pinch white pepper

With a sharp paring knife, cut a circle in the hard shell around girth of chestnut, keeping the gash on the surface if possible. Simmer chestnuts in a large saucepan of water. Drain. While chestnuts are still hot—as hot as you can stand—remove shells and husks and discard them.

Cut a small cross in bottom of sprouts with a paring knife. Steam until tender. Refresh under cold running water. Drain well.

In large saute pan, heat butter until sizzling hot over medium high heat. Add chestnuts and cook, stirring frequently, for several minutes. Add Brussels sprouts, salt and pepper. Cook, continuing to stir, for several minutes longer until sprouts are heated through. Adjust seasoning.

Pecan Pie
one 10" pie

1 recipe basic pie dough, amount for 10" shell (p. 112)
1¼ c. sugar
¾ c. dark corn syrup
⅔ c. light corn syrup
8 T. butter, cut in small cubes
5 eggs
1¾ t. vanilla
¼ t. salt
2½ c. pecan halves

Preheat oven to 400 degrees.

In medium saucepan combine sugar and corn syrups. Stir over low heat until sugar dissolves. Turn off heat and add butter. When butter melts, beat in eggs, vanilla and salt. Fold in pecans.

Fill shell. Bake until filling is puffed and firm when shaken lightly, about forty-five minutes.

Variations:

Chocolate Pecan Pie
makes one 10" pie

2 oz. unsweetened baking chocolate, chopped into ½" pieces
2 oz. semi sweet chocolate, chopped into ½" pieces

Add chocolates to hot sugar and corn syrup mixture at same time as butter is added. Proceed as for pecan pie.

Coconut Pecan Pie
makes one 10" pie

1 c. unsweetened shredded coconut

Add to pie mixture at same time as you add pecans. Proceed as for pecan pie.

Pumpkin Pie
makes two 9" pies

1 recipe basic pie dough, amount for two 9" pie shells
   (p. 112)
3 c. cooked and pureed pumpkin
1½ c. cream
¾ c. milk
3 eggs
¾ c. sugar
3 T. molasses
¾ t. salt
1½ t. ginger
1½ t. cinnamon
½ t. allspice

Preheat oven to 400 degrees.

Beat together pumpkin, cream, milk, eggs, sugar, molasses and spices until well combined.

Fill unbaked shells. Bake until filling is puffed and firm when shaken lightly, about forty minutes.

Brown Bagging It

*A*fter Jim left the law, and before we began our lives as market growers and produce brokers, we took Phoebe and Sarah on a three month trip to Europe. It was the first and so far only time I've been to Italy, and while we covered a good bit of Northern Italy, we spent the most time in Santa Margarita on the Ligurian coast, a place I could have moved to in an instant.

We had a number of great meals, although we were hampered by the five and three year old tastes of our daughters. Phoebe insisted on asking for fries, which was bearable, although asking for ketchup was humiliating. In the nicest restaurant we dared enter, Phoebe pounded on the ketchup bottle and the entire contents of the full bottle landed on her plate!

Sarah would only dine in restaurants with pink tablecloths and was ever prepared to back up her preference with remarkable feats of rigor mortis that made carting her away profoundly difficult. When we found a spot she deemed acceptable, she always ordered "spaghetti burro," a plate of perfectly cooked al dente pasta with a dab of the finest butter, served with a flourish and priced on a par with the most elaborate dishes on the menu. But who were we then—or ever—to cross Sarah!

We found the restaurant of my fantasies through reading an article of R. Apple's in "The New York Times." Somewhere in the mountains overhanging the Ligurian coast, there was a restaurant I believe called Ca Peo. We called ahead to be sure the place would be open in early March, and after much getting lost, arrived well over an hour late. The only diners at the odd hour of three in the afternoon, we were seated in a cantilevered alcove with a memorable mountain view. The lady of the house was a fantastic chef who served us a timbale of white beans with radicchio sauce that complemented the season perfectly, presented some of our favorite foods in the most refined manner, and was just fantastic all in all. I'll never know how to replicate it, so these words are my only monument. The second course was a platter of small fish that had been more or less caught to order after we phoned. As we were leaving, the babysitter drove up with two children about the ages of our own. They had clearly been sent off so their mother could minister to the needs of her untimely guests.

I spent years hoping to visit Ireland, and when I finally got there on a riding vacation in Connemara with Phoebe and Sarah, their aunt Susan Heffron, and their good friend Kathleen McKenna, my desires were not assuaged. On the contrary, we all entered into a state of collective addiction that has had us returning in various combinations with all kinds of new recruits, usually on an annual basis.

On our second trip, with our riding instructor Sonja Johanson added to the mix presumably to protect us from the wild riding, I fell in love with a *springer spaniel named Grace. When I called Jim to get his approval on locating and bringing home a similar puppy, he emphatically stated "Do not bring home a dog." Fortunately my one year of law school acquainted me with the doctrine "expressio unius es exclusio alterius" or "the expression of one thing is the exclusion of another." That is how with Sonja's approval and no consultation with Jim, we came to bring back "Jimmy Joe" the pony of our dreams, as a little travel souvenir for Ceci. So far (!) Jimmy Joe has been followed by Miss Pickens, Likely, Matilda, Diamond, Dell Boy, Brownie, Dundee, Scarvagh, and Junior, fortunately most of them going to the homes of friends! A year later, when Susie and David Felton's long hoped for baby arrived, they named her "Grace," after the dog, I've always imagined. What a fateful trip!*

Although we never make soda bread at home, we always look forward to tea with this delicious brown bread after a day riding cross-country with the Leahy family in Loughrea, Ireland. At the end of the day I'm always so happy I survived, I take my Irish whisky straight, but most riders enjoy one of Wlliam's hot whiskeys or hot rums, potent mixes of boiling water and sugar stirred into a big blast of liquor.

Irish Soda Bread

one loaf

2¾ c. all purpose flour
¾ c. stone ground whole wheat flour
½ c. bran
1½ t. wheat germ (optional)
1½ t. salt
1 t. baking soda
¾ t. baking powder
1¾ c. buttermilk

Preheat oven to 400 degrees. Lightly oil a cookie sheet.

In a large bowl, mix flour, whole wheat flour, bran, wheat germ, salt, baking soda and baking powder thoroughly. Add buttermilk and mix in well. Turn dough onto lightly floured counter and knead for three minutes. Shape into a 6" round. Place on cookie sheet. Slash top of loaf with sharp knife. Bake for fifty minutes until well browned.

Our good friends Barbara Butterworth and Mike Gill are on again off again Cutchogue residents and lifelong summer residents. For the past five years they've made their home in Katmandu, Nepal.

One summer while hanging out on our deck we accepted the annual invitation to come visit the following Christmas vacation. With spending time in their home in Kathmandu, trekking around Annapurna, and visiting the jungle to the south, we had the most remarkable visit. Although we're not about to forget it, a little taste of Barbara's chutney brings all the memories back.

Dr. Butterworth's Nepalese Chutney
makes enough for a number of small jars

1 large jar tamarind concentrate
5 small cans of tomato sauce
3 c. sugar
12 large onions, finely chopped
½ c. minced garlic
2 T. minced ginger
¼ c. oil
1 T. ground coriander seed
2 t. curry powder
1 t. ground cloves
1 t. ground cinnamon
1 t. freshly grated nutmeg
1 t. salt
pinch red pepper
good grinding black pepper
3 c. minced fresh coriander

In a large sauce pan, put tamarind, an equivalent amount of water, the tomato sauce and sugar. Stir over low heat to dissolve sugar. Over low heat in large deep skillet, saute onions, garlic and ginger in oil until soft, stirring often. Add coriander seed, curry, cloves, cinnamon, nutmeg, salt, red and black pepper. Cook over low heat for several minutes, stirring often, to release fragrance.

Add onion mixture and fresh coriander to tamarind mixture and simmer for fifteen minutes.

Along the way we've become Vermonter wannabees. We first started coming to Vermont so the girls could train with Denny Emerson, a distinguished combined training competitor and teacher in Strafford. Later we brought Ceci's pony, Jimmy Joe, to Brownsville to be trained to pull a carriage by Robin and Wilson Groves, and we've returned for various shows and riding camps in the area.

We came for the horseback riding, but we stayed for the cooking after we fell in with K. Carriere at the Millbrook B & B and became addicted to her hospitality and her breakfast cooking. Mornings we fill up on her special oatmeal, baked omelettes and spicy ham & cheese creation. Then for lunch we go down the street to the Brownsville General Store for their unique and fantastic sandwiches. For dinner there's any number of great restaurants within a half hour drive.

K. was generous enough to share her recipes with me and then, of course, I've mangled them with frequent repetition.

K's Real Oatmeal
serves at least ten

3 c. oat groats
1 c. oat flour

Put groats in a large bowl. Pour in six cups of boiling water. Stir. Set bowl over a pot filled with plenty of boiling water to create a large double boiler. Cook over medium-low heat for forty minutes, stirring from time to time. Add oat flour and four cups more boiling water. Whisk. Continue to cook for an hour, whisking often and adding a bit more water if needed. Serve with a selection of condiments—milk, cream, butter, maple sugar, brown sugar, cinnamon, raisins . . .

Also from K's breakfast arsenal.

Ovenlettes with Onions and Cheddar
serves six

1 large onion, coarsely chopped
4 T. butter
16 fresh eggs, well beaten
½ t. salt
¼ t. Tabasco sauce
1 c. coarsely grated Vermont Cheddar cheese

Preheat oven to 400 degrees.

In small saucepan, saute onion in 3 T. butter until golden brown. Let cool. Beat onion, salt, Tabasco and Cheddar into eggs. Use remaining 1 T. butter to generously grease a shallow oven proof dish, about 9″ × 12″. Pour in egg mixture. Bake until puffed, set and golden brown, about 20 minutes. Serve wedges right away.

A favorite at the Brownsville General store is its classic "Vermonter," slices of Vermont cheddar and smoked turkey on anadama bread slathered with Vermont mustard and topped with lettuce, tomato, sliced onion, dill pickle slices and alfalfa sprouts. To create your own Vermont mustard, add maple syrup to dry or prepared mustard, preferably Coleman's brand. For a "Veggie Sandwich" leave out the turkey and add more types of raw vegetables, green pepper and cucumber slices for example.

The "Gobbler" may not sound as promising, but is great. White bread gets a veneer of mayonnaise, slices of jellied cranberry, a generous layer of real turkey and a topping of warmed bread stuffing.

Anadama Bread (adapted from James Beard's *Beard on Bread*)

makes two loaves

1 package and 1 t. dry yeast
3 T. butter
⅓ c. molasses
1 heaping T. salt
⅔ c. yellow cornmeal
6½ c. flour

Dissolve yeast in ⅓ c. warm water. Put 1⅓ c. warm water, butter, molasses and salt in a medium saucepan and heat until warm, not hot. Add to yeast along with cornmeal and flour and mix well. Using electric mixer with dough hook at low speed or by hand, mix, adding water as needed for a moist but not sticky dough. Beat with the dough hook using medium speed or knead by hand for ten minutes. As the gluten in the dough is developed by kneading, the dough will begin to show long strands when it is gently pulled apart. At this point stop kneading.

Put dough in a bowl, cover with a dishcloth and set aside in a warm spot until doubled in size, two hours or so.

Punch down. Knead back into a ball and cut into two equal pieces. Shape into loaves by forming rectangles which you let

(continued) ☞

rest a few minutes. Roll up rectangles and pull ends underneath. Put into greased loaf pans. Cover with dishcloths and let rise until doubled.

When dough has almost fully risen, put oven racks in the middle of the oven and preheat oven to 425 degrees. Bake risen dough for fifteen minutes, then turn heat down to 325 degrees. Continue baking for twenty-five minutes longer. Turn hot bread out of pan and return to oven for ten minutes more. Cool before slicing.

This dessert concoction is from Bentley's and Firestone's, two excellent restaurants in the Brownsville area.

Vermont Sundae
serves one

2 scoops best quality vanilla ice cream
1–2 T. best quality maple syrup
1 T. granulated maple sugar, if available
a dollop of whipped cream
1 T. chopped walnuts
1 small maple sugar candy if available

Put ice cream in bowl or parfait glass. Drizzle with 1 T. syrup and sugar. If you do not have maple sugar, use 1 T. more syrup. Top with whipped cream. Sprinkle nuts on top and garnish with maple sugar candy.

What Our Friends Bring to the Table

*M*other of my childhood friend, Lisa, and now my very own Southold friend, Irene "Buffy" Ernest, once brought a groaning platter of her stuffed artichoke creation to my house, and her dish has been fondly remembered ever since. Her "recipe" reflects her Italian home style of cooking where everything depends on the vagaries of the ingredient at hand, but rest assured any permutation of the few ingredients will yield success. Irene also recommends using this stuffing formula on large mushrooms, dabbing each with a bit of butter and baking in an oiled dish.

Buffy's Stuffed Artichokes
serves eight as a first course

lots of Italian parsley
8 artichokes as large as possible
dry bread crumbs, preferably homemade
extra virgin olive oil
several cloves minced garlic
salt
good grinding black pepper
1 lemon, quartered

Wash and dry parsley. Coarsely chop leaves, reserving stems.

Working quickly so artichokes don't discolor too much, cut stems off flush with bottoms of artichokes. Peel stems, discard peelings and chop stems in food processor into small bits. Mix with chopped parsley, bread crumbs, oil as needed to moisten, garlic, salt and pepper.

Cut tips off artichokes and pull away a few rows of tough outer leaves. Use a scissors to cut tips of remaining leaves so artichoke looks like a flower. Pull leaves away from center. Scoop out center choke before stuffing and stuff artichoke centers with crumb mixture, packing tightly.

(continued) ☞

Set artichokes flat in a deep pan, add boiling water halfway up, and drop in lemon quarters. Scatter parsley stems over artichokes.

Set heat medium low and simmer covered until artichokes are tender, replenishing water if needed. Test for doneness by pulling off one of the outer leaves. When leaf comes away without resistance, artichoke is done. Cool slightly, remove from liquid and discard parsley stems.

Serve artichokes at room temperature with additional lemon wedges.

Buffy loves this tart (from a NY Times recipe from Albert Kumin, a former White House chef) with its really puckery lemon taste. I made this a number of times years ago and when she refound the recipe, we celebrated with a mini-Proustian experience.

Lemon Tart
serves eight

1 recipe pie dough, amount for 9″ shell (p. 112)
2 T. cornstarch
5 egg yolks
⅓ c. lemon juice
⅓ c. sugar
1 T. butter
1 t. gelatin
½ c. cream
1 c. coarsely crushed amaretti
½ c. apricot jam
2 large lemons, very thinly sliced
½ c. apricot jam
2 t. rum

Roll dough into 10″ round. Fill 9″ pie pan. Flute edges. Prick dough all over with fork. Put shell in freezer for one hour.

Preheat oven to 400 degrees.

Take pie shell from freezer. Cover with aluminum foil and weigh down with beans or rice. (Beans or rice can be reused many times.) Bake about fifteen minutes until dough begins to get dry. Remove foil and weights. Bake three minutes longer, piercing any bubbles that form, then continue baking until completely baked and golden brown all over.

In small bowl, mix cornstarch with ¼ c. water. Beat in egg yolks.

Put lemon juice, sugar and ⅔ c. water in saucepan. Bring to boil, stirring to dissolve sugar. Beat a few spoonsful of boiling

(continued) ☞

hot lemon syrup into yolk mixture, then beat yolk mixture into saucepan with lemon syrup. Cook whisking continuously over low heat for three minutes. Beat in butter. Put aside to cool.

Put gelatin in a heat proof bowl, mix in ¼ c. cold water, and set over a pan of boiling water to dissolve. Pour gelatin into lemon mixture, beat to combine thoroughly and let mixture cool.

Beat cream until soft peaks form. Fold cream and amaretti into lemon mixture and fill pie shell.

Add rum to apricot jam and melt over low heat. Coat lemon slices with jam and arrange in concentric circles over tart. Refrigerate an hour or so until set.

Two cherished items in my cache of bluefish recipes were given to me by Don Agger. Recently deceased, he was my husband's boyhood fishing mentor and practically world famous for his smoked bluefish. Bluefish, by the way, turn into the most fabulous smoked fish. It goes without saying in these recipes that you will catch and clean the fish yourself.

Don's Smoked Bluefish

the amount of bluefish you have caught
kosher non-iodized salt

Rinse well "any number of bluefish filets with or without skin." In a non-reactive bowl or pot, dissolve enough salt in cold water to float a raw egg. (Put back the egg—it's not in this recipe!) Submerge the filets skin sides up. Cover and refrigerate overnight, about ten or so hours.

In the morning, remove and rinse each filet under cold running water, massaging gently to release all the salt in cracks and crevices. Dry filets well on paper towels.

In a wood smoker, smoke filets skin side down until somewhat darker than golden brown, what Don calls "walnut" color. Smoking will take from five to ten hours, depending on size of filets and how fully loaded the smoker is.

Among Don's trove of simple tricks is a "recipe" for broiling bluefish that has been smeared with a thin layer of mayonnaise. Although it's a slightly repellent idea, the reality turns out to be excellent; the fish comes out moist with a terrific crust.

Broiled Bluefish

serves four

4 bluefish filets, about 8 oz. each
⅓ c. Hellman's mayonnaise

If oven heats separately from broiler, preheat oven to 450 degrees and preheat broiler. Otherwise preheat broiler first.

Place filets skin sides down on foil covered baking tray. Cover fish with generous layer of mayonnaise. Broil until mayonnaise is black, a very short time. Finish cooking filets in oven until flesh just flakes when tested with a fork. Remove from pan leaving skin behind.

This is another great, although non-Agger, way to cook bluefish. It's adapted from More Classic Italian Cooking *by Marcella Hazan, and this seemed like the spot to tuck in the recipe, just in case of a really big catch.*

Baked Bluefish Genoese Style
serves four

1½ lb. potatoes, peeled and cut in very thin rounds
½ c. olive oil
¼ c. minced parsley
1 T. minced garlic
salt
good grinding black pepper
4 bluefish filets, about 8 oz. each

Preheat oven to 450 degrees.

Put potatoes, 4 T. olive oil, 2 T. parsley, 1 heaping t. garlic, ½ t. salt and a bit of pepper in a very large shallow baking pan. Mix well and level potatoes.

Bake on the top shelf of the oven until lightly browned, approximately thirty-five minutes Take the dish from the oven. With a spatula, gently stir the potatoes, scraping up any browned bits that cling to the sides of the pan. Place fish on top with skin sides down. Mix remaining oil, garlic and parsley, and rub on top of fish. Season fish with salt and pepper and put dish in the oven for another ten minutes or so. Before serving, tilt pan, spoon off as much oil as possible and discard.

Years ago Sharon and David Agger, Don's oldest son and Jim's longtime friend, visited from Tucson, Arizona where they were then living. They brought a large jar of homemade salsa and the recipe which I believe they extorted from a local restaurant. No one before or since has contributed so directly to the happiness of our household. During tomato season we make this relentlessly, so much so, that the recipe has perhaps mutated a bit in our hands. I do have one complaint: After eating this salsa, no commercial salsa ever brought us pleasure.

Salsa
makes about seven cups

3 medium jalapeno peppers or more to taste
one 28 oz. can crushed tomatoes
2 c. tomatoes, cored and cut with serrated knife into ¼" dice
½ c. sliced scallions
1 T. minced garlic
⅓ c. minced coriander leaves
2 T. minced parsley
¼ c. cider vinegar
1 T. red pepper flakes
¾ t. freshly ground black pepper
large pinch cayenne pepper

Wear rubber gloves while handling the jalapenos. Cut off and discard the tops. Cut the peppers in half lengthwise, scrape out seeds and discard. Chop peppers very fine.

Put the peppers, canned and fresh tomatoes, scallions, garlic, coriander, parsley, vinegar, pepper flakes, black and cayenne pepper into a large non-reactive container. Mix well.

Salsa will keep for about one week in the refrigerator.

Jane Vris was a great high school friend who married my first cousin Bobby Michelson about twenty years ago. She would never claim cooking as one of her many interests and talents, but Jane is one of those rare quick study people. Everything she attempts she does superbly. So while she's only cooked for me twice (or perhaps cooked twice ever) on both occasions I asked for her recipe. I print only this one, since the other is for veal, a food I no longer make, even though I find it delicious, as the thought of calf farming depresses me.

This recipe was adapted from Diet for a Small Planet *or its sequel, and I must admit it has the vintage appeal of bell bottoms and tie dye.*

Curried Rice with Vegetables
serves ten

⅓ c. olive oil
1 c. coarsely chopped onions
3 T. curry powder
2 c. brown rice
1 t. salt
⅔ c. sunflower seeds
½ c. raw peanuts
½ c. green pepper, cut in ½" pieces
1 medium summer squash, cut in ½" pieces
2 c. peeled, seeded and chopped tomatoes

In large saucepan over medium low heat, combine ¼ c. olive oil and onion. Saute stirring often until onion is soft. Add curry powder and rice and cook stirring often for a few minutes. Add 5 c. water, ½ t. salt, sunflower seeds and peanuts. Cover and simmer over low heat until rice is tender, about fifty minutes.

While rice cooks, put remaining 1 T. olive oil in sauce pan with pepper and squash. Cook stirring often for five minutes. Add tomato and remaining ½ t. salt and cook to reduce liquid slightly.

Serve vegetables over cooked rice.

I have to include one of Paula Dagen's dishes, because she's the best hostess anywhere. Not that she ever cooks. But when you speak she gives you 200% of her total attention. She especially makes the girls feel that she has never heard anything more interesting in her life than what they're saying and that she has never laid eyes on a more precious living being. Although few things are better than good food, this is.

Paula is also an ace procurer—the best bread, the best mozzarella, the best tomatoes, all served in lavish amounts. What really sets this dish apart from everyone else's is the way Paula serves basil, in heaps which you're expected to eat like a vegetable. So of course we do.

Paula's Tomatoes and Fresh Mozzarella
serves six

1 loaf of fantastic bread, sliced thickly
4 large ripe tomatoes, cut in rounds
2 lb. fresh mozzarella, sliced slightly thickly
1 big bunch basil
best quality extra virgin olive oil
salt
good grinding black pepper

Put the bread in a basket and the tomatoes and mozzarella on a big, beautiful platter. Surround with basil, drizzle with oil and season with salt and pepper.

Steve Monas, my good friend from my one year of law school, developed the practice of making migas in his musician years in Austin, Texas when he'd finally get up on Sunday mornings after coming in late from Saturday night gigs. Friends would show up with ingredients and eventually the miga feast would evolve: raw jalapenos halves stuffed with cream cheese, nachos made with refried beans, pickled jalapenos and Monterey jack cheese, and migas with all the fixings. Steve and Maggie brought the tradition to the Upper West Side, gathering Columbia law and literature students for hours long feasts.

Refried Beans

makes about seven cups

1 lb. red kidney beans or black beans
4 T. oil
1 c. minced onion
½ c. minced green pepper
1 T. minced garlic
1 t. salt
good grinding black pepper

Soak beans overnight in water to cover amply. Drain, put in large saucepan and cover amply with water. Bring to boil and simmer over low heat until beans are very tender.

Drain, reserving cooking liquid.

In large skillet, saute onion, pepper and garlic in oil over low heat for several minutes stirring often. Add beans, salt and pepper and cook mashing with a potato masher and stirring up browned bits of bean that form on the bottom of the pan. Cook in this way, mashing from time to time until beans are coarsely mashed throughout, about half an hour, adding additional bean liquid as necessary to keep from getting too dry.

Nachos
serves twenty

corn tortillas
vegetable oil as needed
1 recipe refried beans
1 jar pickled jalapeno peppers, cut into thin rings
1 lb. grated Monterey jack cheese

Preheat oven to 400 degrees.

Cut tortillas in wedges. Deep fry or shallow fry in small batches until golden brown. Drain well. Spread each wedge with generous layer of refried beans. Top with a round of jalapeno and sprinkle cheese on top.

Set on foil lined baking tray. Bake until cheese is melted and beginning to brown.

Migas

serves twelve

8 corn tortillas, cut in small wedges
vegetable oil as needed
30 eggs
1½ c. coarsely chopped raw onion
1 serrano pepper, seeds removed and minced, or more to
   taste
¼ c. oil
4 small tomatoes, cored and cut into ⅓″ dice
¾ t. salt

Cook tortillas in vegetable oil as in preceding recipe. Drain on paper towels.

Break eggs into bowl but do not scramble.

In a large skillet over medium heat, saute onion and serrano pepper in oil for a minute or two, stirring often. Add tomatoes, salt and eggs. Cook stirring often to break up eggs and mix. As eggs begin to set, add fried tortilla. Cook until eggs are done. Adjust seasoning.

Serve with bowls of homemade salsa (page 279), guacamole (p. 249), and chopped raw onion.

Alice Gordon, my friend through Maggie Megaw, gave me this recipe for these fantastic cookies. The flavors formed the basis for our mail order cookie "Negril."

Alice's Brownie Cookies
makes five dozen or more

1⅔ c. flour
¼ c. unsweetened cocoa
½ t. salt
2 sticks butter, at room temperature
½ c. sugar
2 t. instant espresso
2 t. vanilla extract
2 c. finely chopped walnuts
confectioner's sugar

Preheat oven to 325 degrees.

Sift together flour, cocoa and salt.

Cream butter and sugar together well.

Dissolve espresso in 1 T. hot water and vanilla. Add to butter mixture and beat. Fold in flour and as it begins to disappear, add walnuts.

Shape into 1″ balls. Bake for fifteen minutes.

While still warm, roll in confectioner's sugar.

Flo Liso worked for me in the many incarnations of my business and when I was chef at Aldo's. She is the warmest, most loving person and some of those qualities seem to get bottled up in the jam she is always making and dispensing. Flo taught me to overcome my fear of canning.

Flo's Strawberry Jam
makes eight half pint jars

2 quarts strawberries, hulled
1 t. butter
1 package Sure Gel
7 c. sugar

Put clean canning jars, screw top rings and large Pyrex measuring cup through dishwasher cycle to sterilize. Meanwhile boil flat lid tops in a saucepan of water for three minutes. Remove and drain on a paper towel.

Wash berries by putting in a basin of water, agitating gently and removing right away. Drain. Crush berries with a potato masher.

Put five cups mashed berries in a large pot with butter and Sure Gel. Sir over medium heat until berry mixture comes to a full rolling boil. Add sugar, bring back to rolling boil while stirring constantly. Lower heat slightly and while stirring constantly, cook for exactly one minute.

Take pan from heat. Remove foam from on top of jam.

Scoop jam from pot into Pyrex cup and pour into jars, leaving ⅛" headroom. Wipe outside of jars with clean cloth. Cover with lids and screw rings on tightly. Turn jars upside down for five minutes, then turn upright and cool.

To make more, repeat without bothering to wash pot, but do not increase batch size.

Marcia Brown is among the very few clients I ever had who became a personal friend, which might seem surprising since Marcia was also one of the most painstaking and demanding clients ever. But none of the many requests were in service of vanity or pretension. Everything just had to be perfect because she was planning a birthday party for Jerry!

As a friend, I've gotten to be on the receiving end of the fuss and care. It's fine on both sides of the fence, but it's particularly good to be friends when Marcia and Jerry are serving up pumpkin soup.

When I started writing my column they agreed to be my first subjects, and this recipe got my journalism career off to a good start.

Pumpkin Soup
serves eight or more

12 lb. Cinderella pumpkin or other great looking cooking
   pumpkin of that size
1 stick butter
1 c. minced onion
2 c. dry bread crumbs, preferably homemade
1 c. grated Emmenthal or Gruyere cheese
1 heaping T. fresh sage or 1 t. dried sage
1 t. salt
pinch white pepper
8–9 c. chicken broth
1 c. cream
2 T. minced parsley

Take one rack out of oven and put other in bottom third. Preheat to 400 degrees.

Cut a lid from the pumpkin up near the stem as for a jack o'lantern. Make one tiny slash through the lid and base where they meet to indicate how to refit the lid later. Use a spoon to scrape out seeds and fiber. Set pumpkin in an ovenproof serving dish.

Put butter and onion in a small saute pan and cook over low heat for about fifteen minutes until onion is tender, stirring from time to time.

(continued) ☞

Put onion, bread crumbs, cheese, sage, salt and pepper into the pumpkin. Pour in chicken broth to within 1¾″ of top and replace the lid.

Bake the filled pumpkin in the oven at least one and a half hours, rotating the dish once or twice so it cooks evenly. When pumpkin flesh is tender when pierced with a fork, heat the cream in a small pan until piping hot. Add to pumpkin, stirring contents well.

Bring the pumpkin to the table immediately. Use a ladle to scoop some pumpkin flesh into each serving of soup. Top with fresh parsley.

This recipe delivers the maximum taste with the minimum bother, the definition of a treasure.

Marcia and Jerry's Frico
serves six

1 c. Parmesan cheese, coarsely grated into the longest
possible shreds

Preheat oven to 375 degrees. Drop cheese onto a large foil covered baking sheet in 1 T. size mounds leaving lots of room between pieces. Bake until cheese spreads and turns golden brown. Use a metal spatula to remove from tray. Serve warm.

Marcia and Jerry have a permanent labor division whereby Jerry is the chef and Marcia is the chef garde manger and pastry chef. Since most households don't keep a pastry chef on staff, you don't usually get a homemade dessert as nice as at the Browns'. This tart is one of Marcia's specialties.

Blueberry Tart (originally from *The New York Times Magazine*)
serves eight

2 c. walnuts
¾ c. flour
2 T. sugar
pinch salt
6 T. cold butter, cut in small cubes and 2 T. melted butter
¾ c. lightly packed brown sugar
1 pint blueberries, washed, drained and picked over

Preheat oven to 425 degrees.

Pulse walnuts in food processor or chop by hand until fairly fine. Set one cup aside.

To the remaining nuts, add flour, sugar and salt and process until the nuts are finely ground. Add cold butter and mix in well. Add 3 T. cold water and pulse to form dough into a ball.

On floured counter, roll dough into circle ½" thick. Put in 9" tart pan with removable bottom.

Press dough into pan allowing sides to rise above pan by ½".

Mix reserved nuts with brown sugar. Sprinkle half of mixture in bottom of pan. Spread blueberries on top. Sprinkle remaining nut mixture over berries. Drizzle with melted butter.

Bake until pastry and topping are lightly browned, about thirty or forty minutes.

We lost track of our friend, Jeff Morgan, when he and his family moved to the San Francisco area. Jeff made a successful career switch from playing the saxophone to writing about wine. Because of our common interests, we had many great dinners together, and we're happy to have two of his recipes to remind us of him when dining.

Tahini Vinaigrette
makes one cup

3 T. tahini
½ c. extra virgin olive oil
2 T. white wine vinegar
½ t. minced garlic
salt
pinch white pepper

Combine tahini, olive oil, vinegar, garlic, salt and pepper in blender jar and blend. Let stand for at least several hours in refrigerator and adjust seasoning.

Mussels with Soba Noodles

serves six

3 lb. mussels
¼ c. white wine or sherry
1 t. minced ginger
¼ t. minced garlic
pinch red pepper flakes
salt
⅔ lb. soba noodles (Japanese buckwheat noodles,
  preferably wide)
2 T. minced coriander

Scrub mussels and pull out beards. Put in large pot with wine or sherry and ginger, garlic and pepper flakes.

Fill another large pot with water, salt it well, and bring to boil.

Cook mussels over medium heat, stirring gently once or twice until they are wide open. Turn off heat.

Put soba noodles in boiling water and cook al dente. Drain.

Divide noodles in large soup plates and top with mussels and broth. Garnish with coriander.

Alphenic "Tiny" Martin is one of my dearest friends. I got to know her really well because she worked at Local Talent for all the days we were in business, and while our hands were busy we chattered away. Jim and I couldn't have managed without Tiny's help and her incredible talents in the kitchen.

Before Tiny came to work, we got to know La Toya, Sabina and Silvia, the three oldest girls among Tiny's six kids, who became Phoebe and Sarah's friends when they rode the school bus together. Now La Toya and Sabina are off at college in NYC, at Long Island University and Fashion Institute of Technology, and Tiny and I are plotting future cooking business ventures.

This is Antiguan comfort food.

Fungi, Saltfish and Spinach
serves eight

1 lb. dried codfish, soaked overnight in cold water
3 c. tomatoes, peeled, seeded and diced
2 c. onion, coarsely chopped
2 t. minced garlic
½ c. olive oil
salt
good grinding black pepper
2 lb. spinach leaves, well washed and drained
2 T. butter, plus extra for buttering bowls
½ lb. fresh okra, sliced in ½" rounds
1 lb. fine cornmeal, Goya brand

Drain codfish, put in saucepan, cover with 1 gallon cold water, cook gently until it flakes apart, about three minutes from time water simmers. Break codfish into little pieces.

Over low heat, cook onion and garlic in olive oil in skillet until tender, stirring from time to time. Add tomato and saute a few minutes. Fold in codfish, simmer for two minutes. Season to taste.

Put spinach in pot with just the water clinging to the leaves. Cover and cook over medium heat until limp, stirring once or twice. Drain well, press out most of liquid and chop coarsely. Return to pot, mix in butter and cover to keep warm while cornmeal cooks.

(continued) ☞

Cook okra in 3 c. water until tender. Drain and reserve water.

Put cornmeal in a small bowl and mix with a small amount of cold water to moisten, stirring with a spoon.

In large saucepan, put half of reserved okra cooking liquid. Bring to simmer over low heat. Add soaked cornmeal, beating with a wooden spoon as you add. Stir until cornmeal starts getting firm. Add rest of the reserved okra liquid while stirring constantly for three minutes.

Fold okra into spinach. Scoop small portion of cornmeal into ball and roll. Serve one cornmeal ball in a bowl with spinach and codfish in separate scoops on the side.

My Repertoire by Repetition

*T*hese recipes are for deeply cherished and much cooked favorites that haven't fallen into any of the other categories.

Herb Dip
makes two cups

¼ c. minced shallot
2 T. white wine vinegar
2 heaping T. minced fresh tarragon or 2 t. dried tarragon
1 lb. cream cheese, at room temperature
4 oz. butter, at room temperature
1 T. minced garlic
3 T. minced parsley
1 T. snipped chives
¼ t. salt
pinch white pepper

Put shallots, vinegar, most of fresh or all of dried tarragon in a small skillet with 2 T. water. Cook over low heat stirring occasionally until all liquid evaporates. Let cool. Beat cream cheese and butter well. Add shallot mixture, garlic, parsley, chives and remaining fresh tarragon if using, salt and pepper. Let stand at least one hour before serving.

Serve with crudites.

Crab Dip
serves six

3 T. butter
½ c. finely chopped onion
½ c. finely chopped celery
⅓ c. finely chopped green pepper
1 t. minced garlic
2 T. ballpark mustard
1 T. minced parsley
1 T. Worcestershire sauce
1 heaping t. salt
1 t. cayenne pepper
1 t. Tabasco sauce
¼ t. white pepper
¼ t. freshly ground black pepper
⅓ c. homemade or Hellman's mayonnaise
1 lb. best quality crab meat

In a small skillet over low heat put butter, onion, celery, green pepper and garlic on to cook until limp, stirring from time to time. Cool. Combine cooked vegetables with mustard, parsley, Worcestershire sauce, salt. cayenne, Tabasco, white pepper, black pepper and mayonnaise and mix well.

Gently pick over crab meat to remove any bits of shell or cartilage without breaking up lumps of meat. Fold crab meat and celery into mayonnaise mixture. Gently heat until warm and serve in a shallow chafing dish or a fondue pot with a basket of thinly sliced French bread on which to spread the warm dip.

Stuffed Mushrooms with Porcini and Wild Rice

serves six

⅓ c. dried cepes, otherwise called porcini mushrooms
2 T. butter
24 large mushrooms, wiped clean
1 T. minced shallot
2 T. brandy
salt
good grinding black pepper
3 T. cream
½ c. cooked wild rice
1 egg
1 T. minced parsley

Soak cepes in 1 c. hot water for thirty minutes. Lift from water, rinse in several changes of water to remove all traces of sand, squeeze dry and chop fine. Filter soaking liquid through coffee filter or paper towel lined strainer. Reserve.

Melt butter in a small saute pan. Remove from heat.

Select eighteen perfect mushrooms. Remove stems and save. Brush caps with melted butter.

Coarsely chop stems and remaining mushrooms. Add shallots to butter remaining in skillet and cook over medium heat a few minutes to soften. Raise heat to high, add chopped mushrooms and cook stirring often until liquid evaporates and mushrooms turn light brown. Turn heat to low, add chopped cepes, filtered soaking liquid, brandy, salt and pepper. Cook to evaporate liquid, stirring from time to time. Add cream and again cook to evaporate, stirring a bit. Fold in wild rice. Cool. Adjust seasoning. Beat in egg and parsley.

Heap mixture into caps. Set caps in baking dish. Add 2 T. water to dish.

Preheat oven to 400 degrees. Bake mushrooms until cooked through and slightly crisped on top, about twenty-five minutes. Cool slightly before serving.

Clams Florentine (adapted from a recipe of Craig Claiborne's)
makes sixty

60 littleneck clams
1 lb. fresh spinach leaves
8 T. butter
½ c. finely chopped celery
3 T. minced shallot
1 T. minced garlic
1 T. white wine
1 T. Pernod
1 c. unseasoned dry bread crumbs, preferably homemade
2 T. minced parsley
1 T. minced fresh tarragon or 1 t. dried tarragon
1 T. snipped chives
1 T. lemon juice
good grinding black pepper
1 egg yolk
½ c. freshly grated Parmesan cheese
lemon wedges

Put half of clams in a large heavy pot. Add ¼ c. water. Over medium heat cook until clams open, stirring from time to time and removing to large bowl as they open. When all are done, repeat with remaining clams. Filter clam juice in pot through coffee filter or paper towel lined strainer. Reserve ¼ c. and save the rest for another use.

Remove clams from shells, reserving 60 half shells and discarding the rest. Remove and discard hard part of clams and chop tender part into tiny pieces. Set aside. Clean pot.

Wash and dry spinach thoroughly. Put spinach in pot and cook covered over medium heat until just limp. Drain and refresh under cold running water. Wring dry and chop fine.

(continued) ☞

Heat butter in skillet over medium heat. Add celery, shallot and garlic. Cook a few minutes to soften celery, stirring from time to time. Add spinach and stir to mix in well. Add clam juice, wine and Pernod. Cook a minute or two to evaporate much of liquid. Off heat add bread crumbs, parsley, tarragon, chives, lemon juice, pepper and egg yolk. Add chopped clams and mix well.

Divide mixture among shells. Set shells on baking sheets. Sprinkle cheese over each clam.

Preheat oven to 400 degrees. Cook clams until piping hot and slightly browned. Serve with lemon wedges and tiny forks.

This comes out even better with home made puff pastry.

Cheese Straws
makes about three dozen pieces

1 c. finely grated Parmesan cheese
¾ t. paprika
¼ t. cayenne
1 package frozen puff pastry dough or ½ recipe homemade
  (p. 356)

Preheat oven to 350 degrees.

Combine cheese, paprika and cayenne, mixing well.

If using homemade dough, cut 1 lb. slab into two pieces. Roll each piece evenly into approximately 7″ × 16″ rectangle and proceed with covering with cheese and folding as described below.

If using frozen dough, thaw according to package instructions. Gently unfold one piece of dough. Place half the cheese mixture in the center of it and fold up sides of dough to enclose filling, letting edges overlap slightly. Dab place where dough overlaps with a bit of water to seal. Press on edge.

Lightly flour underneath and on top of dough and roll into a rectangle 7″ wide and ¼″ thick, picking up dough often while rolling so it doesn't stick to the counter. Cut into strips ⅓″ wide.

Starting at the center, twist each strip several times into a corkscrew shape and set on lightly greased baking pan. Bake until golden brown, about thirty minutes. Cool on wire rack.

Sausage Straws
1 package Park's sausage meat, the loose type in the cylinder
1 package frozen puff pastry dough or ½ recipe homemade
  (p. 356)

Cook sausage until brown in large skillet, using a wooden spoon to break it up as it cooks.

Cool and chop fine in food processor.

Make straws as above, substituting sausage for cheese mixture.

Meatballs
makes sixty

2½ lb. ground beef round
2 slices white bread, without crust
½ c. milk
⅔ c. finely grated Parmesan cheese
½ c. finely chopped onion
2 eggs
vegetable oil as needed
2 T. minced parsley
1 t. minced garlic
1 t. salt
good grinding black pepper
unseasoned dry bread crumbs as needed
one 28 oz. can whole tomatoes, drained and chopped

Put meat in large bowl. Break up with a fork. In a small pan over low heat, mash bread and milk together with fork. Cool while you prepare other ingredients.

Add mashed bread, cheese, onion, eggs, 2 T. vegetable oil, parsley, garlic, salt and pepper to meat, mixing well. Use a small scoop and wet hands to form into 1¼″ balls. Refrigerate balls for at least thirty minutes.

Into a large heavy bottomed skillet, pour enough oil to amply cover bottom. Heat oil until quite hot as you roll meatballs in bread crumbs. Place half the meatballs in skillet and cook, turning occasionally until well browned on all sides. Remove meatballs to a bowl. Pour out and discard fat. Deglaze skillet with ¾ c. water, scraping up browned bits in pan. Pour liquid over browned meatballs. Dry out pan over heat, add oil as before, heat it and brown remaining meatballs. Remove meatballs to bowl and discard fat in skillet. Add tomatoes to pan. Over low heat scrape up browned bits in bottom of pan. Return meatballs and liquid to pan. Sprinkle with salt and pepper. Cover and cook over low heat for thirty-five minutes, stirring occasionally.

To me there's no better dinner than soup and bread or soup and salad. This soup's nutritional profile is impeccable, and it's also delicious. Just as the different beans complement each other's proteins, they really fill in the gaps tastewise too.

Bean Soup
serves six or more

½ c. navy beans
½ c. kidney beans
½ c. black beans
⅓ c. black-eyed peas
3 T. green split peas
2 T. yellow split peas
2 T. barley
2 T. lentils
¾ c. coarsely chopped onion
¾ c. coarsely chopped carrot
¾ c. coarsely chopped celery
one 14.5 oz. can whole tomatoes
1 t. dried basil
pinch dried thyme
pinch red pepper flakes
1 bay leaf
salt

Put navy, kidney and black beans, black-eyed peas, green and yellow split peas, barley and lentils in a large bowl. Cover with an ample amount of water and let stand at room temperature for eight hours or overnight. Drain.

Put in soup pot with onion, carrot, celery and 12 c. water. Coarsely chop tomatoes and add with their juice. Add basil, thyme, pepper flakes, and bay leaf. Bring to boil, turn heat to low and simmer for almost three hours. Add water as necessary to maintain soupy consistency. Add salt.

Corn Chowder
serves eight

5 slices thick cut bacon, cut in ¼″ pieces
2 T. butter
2 c. coarsely chopped onion
1½ c. coarsely chopped green pepper
¾ c. coarsely chopped celery
2 T. flour
4 c. milk
3 c. chicken broth
1 bay leaf
pinch dried thyme leaves
½ t. salt
pinch white pepper
2 c. potatoes, peeled and cut in ⅓″ dice
6 ears corn, husked and cooked (or 1½ c. drained canned corn)

In soup pot over medium low heat, cook bacon until medium brown, stirring from time to time. Discard as much bacon fat as possible. Add butter, onion, pepper, and celery to bacon in pan and cook a few minutes, stirring from time to time. Add flour and mix in well. Add milk gradually, stirring well between additions. Add chicken broth, bay leaf, thyme, salt and pepper. When mixture simmers, add potatoes. Cook about fifteen minutes until potatoes are tender.

Cut corn kernels off cobs and add kernels to soup or add canned corn. Heat until piping hot.

Adjust seasoning.

This can be made as a vegetarian soup without the ham and with water instead of chicken broth.

Split Pea Soup
serves eight

3 T. butter
½ c. ham, cut in small cubes
2 c. coarsely chopped onion
1½ c. coarsely chopped carrot
¾ c. coarsely chopped celery
2 t. minced garlic
1 lb. split peas
12 c. chicken broth
1 bay leaf
pinch dried thyme leaves
1 heaping t. salt
good grinding black pepper
½ c. croutons (p. 328)
2 T. minced parsley

In soup pot over medium heat, cook butter, ham, onion, carrot and celery, stirring from time to time, until vegetables are soft. Stir in garlic and cook a minute longer. Add split peas, broth, bay leaf, thyme, salt and pepper. Simmer until split peas are very tender, at least an hour.

Cool slightly. Put a ladleful of soup into blender. Puree. Return to pot. Repeat so some of soup is pureed but most is still chunky.

Heat until piping hot, adding water if necessary to thin. Adjust seasoning.

Serve topped with croutons and minced parsley.

If you have a milk foamer, make this soup even more special with a layer of froth and a small grating of nutmeg atop each portion.

Wild Mushroom Soup
serves six

½ c. dried cepes, otherwise called porcini mushrooms
3 T. butter
1 c. finely chopped onion
20 oz. mushrooms, wiped clean and sliced
3 T. uncooked white rice
3 c. chicken broth
few sprigs fresh thyme or ¼ t. dried thyme leaves
salt
pinch white pepper
1 c. cream
¼ c. cooked wild rice
1 T. sherry

Soak cepes in 2 c. hot water for thirty minutes. Lift from water, rinse in several changes of water to remove all traces of sand, squeeze dry and chop coarsely. Filter soaking liquid through coffee filter or paper towel lined strainer. Reserve.

Put butter and onion in soup pot and over medium heat saute onion until soft, stirring occasionally. Add sliced mushrooms. Raise heat to high and cook stirring often until mushrooms are golden brown. Remove ⅔ c. of mushrooms and reserve. Add cepes, filtered soaking liquid, white rice, broth, thyme, salt and pepper. Cook slowly until rice is tender, about thirty minutes.

Cool slightly. Puree in blender until smooth. Pass through a fine sieve. Add cream, wild rice, and reserved mushroom slices. Heat until piping hot. Adjust seasoning. Off heat, add sherry.

This is yet another recipe that derives from Marcella Hazan. From her book, I learned that seriously long cooking is the secret to perfect minestrone.

Minestrone
serves eight

2 T. olive oil
1 c. coarsely chopped onion
½ c. coarsely chopped carrot
½ c. coarsely chopped celery
1 c. zucchini, cut in ½″ cubes
4 c. coarsely chopped cabbage
2 t. minced garlic
½ c. shelled fresh cranberry beans, if available
1 c. green beans, cut in ½″ lengths
1 c. potato, peeled and cut in ½″ cubes
1 c. peeled, seeded and coarsely chopped tomato or 1 c.
   canned tomato, coarsely chopped
8 c. beef broth or (for vegetarians) water
1 t. salt
good grinding black pepper
1 c. freshly grated Parmesan cheese

In soup pot over medium heat, put olive oil and onion. Cook, stirring from time to time, adding carrots, celery, zucchini, cabbage and garlic as you get them ready. Cook these vegetables all together, stirring occasionally, for five minutes. Add cranberry beans, green beans, potato, tomato, broth, salt and pepper. Cover, turn heat to low and simmer for two hours, stirring once or twice. Adjust seasoning. Serve in hot bowls, offering cheese on the side.

This summer variation also a la Marcella is amazing.

Cold Minestrone with Pesto
serves six

8 c. minestrone
½ c. Arborio rice
½ t. salt
good grinding black pepper
¼ c. pesto (p. 254)

In soup pot over medium heat, bring minestrone, 3 c. water, salt and pepper to boil. Stir in rice, turn heat to low, and simmer for fifteen minutes. Turn off heat and whisk in pesto. Adjust seasoning.

Cool to room temperature. Garnish with minced parsley.

A perfect easy recipe for the summer garden classic.

Gazpacho
serves six or more

6 c. tomato juice (1 large can)
1 c. coarsely chopped onion and 1 c. finely chopped onion
⅓ c. coarsely chopped green pepper and 1 c. finely chopped green pepper
½ c. coarsely chopped, peeled cucumber and ½ c. finely chopped, peeled cucumber
1½ c. coarsely chopped tomato and 1½ c. finely chopped tomato
2 t. minced garlic
¼ c. extra virgin olive oil
¼ c. red wine vinegar
salt
good grinding black pepper

In blender jar combine 1 c. tomato juice, the coarsely chopped onion, pepper, cucumber, tomato, garlic, oil and vinegar. Blend until well pureed. Mix in rest of juice.

At serving time stir in finely chopped vegetables. Season to taste with salt and pepper.

My own favorite recipes include a large number of dishes for cold buffet, some of which I originated and some of which are just excellent renditions of classics. My favorite way to entertain is by setting out a huge array of dishes for room temperature eating. I love to decorate platters with all manner of garden garnishes, and nothing makes me happier than seeing people go back to the buffet again and again to reload their plates.

Other dishes in this book that are great for buffets are roast beef with black peppercorns and sea salt, lentil salad, stuffed red peppers, caponata, marinated shrimp, Barry's seafood salad, fried chicken, curry chicken salad . . .

I devised this as a zippier, easier to serve buffet alternative to poached salmon, and everyone seems to love it. Just make sure you eat it all because left-over salmon gets rubbery in the refrigerator.

Barbecued Salmon
serves ten

ten 6 oz. salmon steaks, all of the same thickness and overall dimensions
1 recipe maple barbecue sauce (following recipe)
1 recipe dill sauce (p. 312)

Marinate salmon steaks in barbecue sauce for one hour at room temperature, flipping midway.

If oven is separate from broiler, preheat oven to 400 degrees and preheat broiler. If oven and broiler are one unit, preheat broiler.

Cover broiler tray with aluminum foil and put salmon steaks on tray. Brush tops with barbecue sauce. Broil 1″ from heat source until well browned, about five minutes. Transfer salmon to oven, or (for combined unit) put salmon on middle rack and turn oven to 400 degrees. Bake until just done, about five minutes longer. To test for doneness, cut into a steak near the center bone with a small paring knife. The flesh should separate into a flake and no longer look translucent. Remove salmon and let cool to room temperature.

Cut in halves, so pieces look like apostrophes. Remove bones.

Serve with dill sauce.

Maple Barbecue Sauce
makes one and a half cups

½ c. maple syrup
½ c. beef broth
⅓ c. Dijon mustard
¼ c. apple cider vinegar or balsamic vinegar
1 T. soy sauce
1 T. minced garlic
1 T. minced ginger
¼ t. salt
good grinding black pepper

In medium saucepan over medium heat bring maple syrup, broth, and mustard to boil, whisking from time to time. Lower heat and simmer for five minutes. Turn off stove and add vinegar, soy sauce, garlic, ginger, salt and pepper.

Dill Sauce
makes one cup

2 T. minced shallot
2 T. white wine vinegar
1 c. homemade (or Hellman's) mayonnaise
½ t. lime juice
pinch white pepper
2 T. chopped dill
salt

Put shallot, vinegar and 1 T. water in a small skillet. Cook over low heat stirring occasionally until all but a few drops of liquid evaporates. Let cool. Fold into mayonnaise along with remaining ingredients. Add salt to taste. Let stand in refrigerator for ½ hour or more.

Chinese Eggplant (adapted from *The Chinese Cookbook* by Craig Claiborne and Virginia Lee)

serves ten or more

4 medium eggplants
½ c. soy sauce
¼ c. red wine vinegar
¼ c. sherry
¼ c. sesame oil
2 T. sugar
¼ c. vegetable oil
¼ c. minced ginger
2 T. minced garlic
¼ c. sesame seeds, preferably hulled
¼ c. chopped coriander leaves

Steam whole eggplants until tender. Cool in colander so liquid can drain away.

Combine soy sauce, vinegar, sherry, sesame oil and sugar.

Heat oil in small skillet over medium high heat. Add ginger and garlic. Cook for fifteen seconds or so, just to release aroma. Add soy sauce mixture. Turn off heat. Let cool.

Remove tops from eggplant and discard, but leave peel on. With fingers pull eggplant into narrow strips. Pour sauce over eggplant, toss to mix thoroughly.

Let stand for half an hour or so. Garnish with sesame seeds and chopped coriander.

The red cabbage is a pretty addition to cole slaw that you'll be serving within the day, but if you need to hold slaw longer, omit red cabbage and use twice as much green.

Cole Slaw
serves ten or more

6 c. shredded green cabbage
6 c. shredded red cabbage
¼ c. cider vinegar
½ c. grated carrot
¼ c. grated radish
¼ c. finely chopped green pepper
2 T. minced shallot
2 T. minced parsley
½ c. homemade (or Hellman's) mayonnaise
2 T. sour cream
½ t. Dijon mustard
¾ t. sugar
½ t. salt
large pinch white pepper

Toss cabbage with vinegar. Let stand one hour. Add other ingredients and mix well. Let stand in refrigerator for several hours before serving.

Potato Salad
serves ten or more

3 lb. scrubbed new potatoes
salt
2 T. sherry vinegar
2 T. white wine
large pinch white pepper
¾ c. finely chopped, blanched celery
½ c. finely chopped red onion
½ c. minced parsley
2 T. chopped chives
¾ c. homemade (or Hellman's) mayonnaise
1 heaping T. Dijon mustard

Put potatoes and 2 t. salt in large pot. Cover amply with cold water. Bring to boil then simmer until potatoes are tender.

Cut into small pieces while warm. Dress with vinegar and white wine while warm. Season with salt and pepper. When cool add celery, red onion, parsley, chives, mayonnaise and mustard. Mix well.

Let stand at least one hour in refrigerator. Adjust seasoning.

Marinated Red Peppers
serves six or more

6 medium red peppers
extra virgin olive oil
6 cloves garlic, peeled and cut into thin slices
¼ t. salt
good grinding black pepper

Preheat broiler. Line a baking sheet with foil and lay peppers on their sides on sheet. Place baking sheet about 2″ from broiler. Broil until peppers are blackened on side nearest heat. Turn peppers and continue broiling and turning until all sides are blackened. Peppers should be soft but not limp. If they become blackened before they are soft, place baking sheet in 350 degree oven for ten minutes or so.

Let cool slightly, then pull out tops, peel and discard seeds, keeping peppers as intact as possible. Put on a plate and set the plate on top of a table knife so that the plate is at a slant. Let sit for half an hour to allow liquid to drain from peppers.

Use a small bowl or crock to marinate peppers. Put a bit of olive oil, garlic, salt and pepper at bottom of bowl, then place a layer of peppers. Continue layering, ending with a covering of oil, garlic, salt and pepper. Let marinate several hours before serving. Peppers can be stored in the refrigerator for several days, but should be brought to room temperature before serving.

with anchovies:

6 small whole anchovies, preserved in salt
extra virgin olive oil

Using a paring knife, scrape skin from anchovies. Cut top filet from bone. Remove bone and discard. Trim away any bits of bone or skin remaining on filets. Put in small bowl and cover with olive oil. Anchovies will keep for a week in the refrigerator.

This salad is a treat in late summer when cranberry beans, green and yellow beans, and peppers are at their peaks. In the winter you can always increase the amount of dried beans and green beans since you won't find cranberry or yellow beans in the store.

Five Bean Salad
serves twelve or more

1 c. dried chick peas
1 c. dried red beans
1 lb. cranberry beans
1 lb. green beans, ends snipped off, broken into 1″ pieces
1 lb. yellow beans, ends snipped off, broken into 1″ pieces
1 marinated red pepper (preceding recipe), cut in ½″ dice
⅓ c. Kalamata olives, pitted, cut in halves
½ c. scallions, sliced thin
¼ c. minced red onion
¼ c. extra virgin olive oil
3 T. red wine vinegar
2 T. balsamic vinegar
2 T. minced parsley
1 t. chopped fresh oregano or ¼ t. dried oregano
1 t. minced garlic
1 t. salt
generous grinding black pepper

Soak chick peas and red beans separately overnight. Drain, place in separate saucepans with water to cover amply and simmer over medium low heat until tender. Drain and combine in a large bowl.

Wash shelling beans before shelling so that shelled beans will be free of sand. Steam beans until tender and refresh under cold running water. In separate batches, do the same with green and yellow beans. Add to other beans in bowl.

Add peppers and all remaining ingredients to beans. Mix well and let stand at room temperature for at least an hour before serving.

Ratatouille

serves ten or more

1 large eggplant
salt
vegetable oil as needed
4 c. zucchini, scrubbed and cut in 1″ pieces
4 c. green peppers, cored, seeded and cut in 1″ squares
6 c. tomatoes, peeled, seeded and cut in ¾″ pieces
2 T. olive oil
4 c. onions, cut in 1″ pieces
1 T. minced garlic
good grinding black pepper
1 t. fresh thyme or ½ t. dried thyme
2 bay leaves
1 T. chopped fresh basil

Rinse eggplant, cut and discard top and "zebra" peel, leaving alternating stripes of peel. Cut in 1″ chunks. Toss with salt and leave to drain in colander an hour or so while you prepare other ingredients.

Put enough vegetable oil in saute pan to cover the bottom generously. Heat until smoking. Add zucchini and cook over medium heat stirring frequently until zucchini are nicely browned. Remove with slotted spoon to a dinner plate. Set the dinner plate at an incline on top of an upside down spoon so that remaining oil will drain away. Return this oil to the saute pan and put the zucchini in the baking dish. While the zucchini drains, continue to cook and drain the peppers in the same way. Put the tomatoes directly in the baking dish.

Rinse and towel dry the eggplant. Replenish the oil in the saute pan, heat well and cook and drain the eggplant in he same way as the zucchini and pepper.

(continued) ☞

Add the olive oil to the saute pan. Add onions and cook over medium heat until golden brown, stirring from time to time. Stir in garlic and cook one minute longer.

Add onions to baking dish.

Add salt, pepper, thyme and bay leaves to vegetables in baking dish. Mix well. Bake at 350 degrees for 30 minutes, until piping hot throughout.

Let cool slightly and fold in basil. Serve hot or room temperature or cold.

Saffron Rice Salad
serves ten or more

⅔ c. wild rice
1½ t. salt
⅔ c. dry white wine
½ t. saffron threads
1½ c. rice
⅔ c. dried currants
1 c. extra virgin olive oil
½ c. orange juice, preferably freshly squeezed
¼ c. lemon juice
1½ t. minced ginger
1 t. grated orange rind
1 t. grated lemon rind
¼ t. freshly grated nutmeg
large pinch white pepper
⅔ c. sliced almonds
⅔ c. finely chopped scallions

Put 5 c. water and ½ t. salt in medium saucepan. Bring to boil. Stir in wild rice. Turn heat to medium low and simmer, stirring occasionally until rice splits open and is tender, about one hour. Drain.

Meanwhile bring 2½ c. water, white wine, and ½ t. salt to boil in another medium saucepan. Add saffron, turn off heat, cover and let steep for thirty minutes. Bring liquid back to boil, stir in rice and simmer covered over low heat until tender, about eighteen minutes.

Turn off heat, fluff with fork and let stand covered for ten minutes. Add currants to warm rice.

Combine olive oil, orange and lemon juice, ginger, orange and lemon rind, remaining ½ t. salt, nutmeg and pepper in blender. Pour over warm rice and currants. Let stand for an

(continued) ☞

hour at room temperature or for several hours in the refrigerator.

Preheat oven to 350 degrees. Spread almonds on baking sheet. Bake until golden brown, about ten minutes, stirring often. Cool.

Garnish rice salad with toasted almonds and scallions.

Southwestern Rice Salad

serves ten or more

1 ¼ c. white wine
1 t. salt
1 ½ c. white rice
5 ears of corn, as fresh as possible
1 red pepper
½ c. finely chopped scallion
¼ c. olive oil
2 T. sherry vinegar
½ t. salt
large pinch white pepper
1 ripe avocado

In a medium saucepan, bring 1 ½ c. water, the white wine and salt to a boil. Stir in rice, cover and simmer over low heat until tender, about eighteen minutes. Cool.

Bring a large pot of water to boil. Husk corn and put ears in pot for two minutes. Drain. Cut kernels off husk and put cut corn in a large bowl with rice.

Preheat broiler. Char pepper on all sides under broiler. When cool enough to handle, peel away blackened skin. Remove top and seeds and discard. Cut pepper into ¼″ dice. Add to bowl with scallion, oil, vinegar, salt and pepper. Mix well. Let stand one hour.

Just before serving time, cut avocado into ¼″ dice. Fold into rice salad. Adjust seasoning.

Although they are wonderful as hors d'oeuvres, I'd never be sorry to see hummus, tabbouleh, or stuffed grape leaves on a cold buffet either.

Hummus
makes three cups

½ lb. dried chick peas
1 T. minced garlic, or more to taste
½ c. tahini
½ c. lemon juice
1 heaping t. salt
pinch of paprika
¼ t. olive oil
12 small whole wheat pitas

Cover chickpeas with an ample amount of water and let stand at room temperature for eight hours or overnight. Drain. Put chickpeas in a large saucepan with water to cover amply. Bring to boil and simmer until tender, about an hour. Drain, reserving ¾ c. cooking liquid.

Combine all the ingredients including ½ c. of the cooking liquid in the bowl of a food processor or blender. Process until mixture is smooth and fluffy. Add more cooking liquid if necessary. Put in a serving bowl, sprinkle with paprika and drizzle oil on top of paprika.

Toast pitas in 400 degree oven or toaster until slightly dry. Cut into wedges.

Serve hummus with a basket of pita wedges on the side.

Tabbouleh

serves eight or more

1⅔ c. fine bulgur
⅔ c. minced onion
⅔ c. scallions, sliced thin
⅓ c. cucumber, peeled, seeded and cut in ¼″ dice
1 c. tomato, peeled, seeded and cut in ¼″ dice
1⅓ c. chopped parsley
3 T. chopped mint
½ c. olive oil
⅓ c. lemon juice
½ t. salt
good grinding pepper
8 large romaine lettuce leaves
12 small whole wheat pitas

Soak bulgur in 5 c. hot water for fifteen minutes. Drain and wring dry in cheesecloth.

Add remaining ingredients. Mix well let stand for thirty minutes.

Wash and dry romaine thoroughly.

Toast pitas in 400 degree oven or toaster until slightly dry. Cut into wedges.

Serve tabbouleh on a bed of romaine lettuce leaves with a basket of pita wedges on the side.

Middle Eastern recipes often call for grated onion. Grating seems to bruise the fibers and create a bitter taste which offsets the sweet tastes of sugar, currants and dill. So don't be tempted to mince the onion instead.

Stuffed Grape Leaves
makes about eighty pieces

100 large tender grape leaves
4 c. grated onion
1 c. uncooked white rice
¼ c. pine nuts
¼ c. currants
¼ c. minced parley
¼ c. snipped dill
⅔ c. olive oil
5 T. lemon juice
salt
pinch white pepper
pinch sugar
2 lemons, cut in wedges

Pick fresh unsprayed grape leaves in early June when they reach a good size but are still light green and tender. Blanch in batches in a large pot of boiling water. Refresh under cold running water. Drain well. Make piles all facing shiny side up. Roll in bundles of a dozen and freeze a year's supply in freezer bags or containers. Defrost as needed. Or buy grape leaves preserved in brine and rinse well.

Mix onion, rice, pine nuts, currants, parsley, dill, olive oil, 2 T. of the lemon juice, salt, pepper and sugar.

Set leaves shiny sides down on counter. Put a heaping tablespoon of filling on base of leaf. Bring in sides and fold into a compact cylinder about 2½″ long. Leave a tiny bit of room so that rice can expand.

Cover bottom of medium size non-reactive pot with a dozen leaves. Place filled grape leaves on top, seam sides down.

(continued) ☞

Arrange stuffed grape leaves close together, making several rows as needed. Mix remaining 3 T. lemon juice with 1 c. water and salt to taste. Pour over grape leaves. Top with remaining unstuffed leaves. Weigh down with a heat proof plate, and simmer over low heat for fifty minutes. Cool in pan and refrigerate. Put stuffed grape leaves on serving platter and garnish with lemon wedges.

This recipe omits the almost raw egg that traditionally holds Caesar salad dressing together, so the look isn't as pretty, but the taste is still great. Add mashed anchovies to the dressing if you like. Serve over small pieces of romaine hearts with lots of croutons.

Caesar Salad

serves eight

20 c. Romaine lettuce hearts, washed, broken into small
    pieces, and dried
1 recipe Caesar salad dressing (following recipe)
1 recipe croutons (p. 328)

Chill lettuce. At serving time, blend dressing well. Use as needed to generously coat greens. There may be some left over. Mix in a third of the croutons and use another third to top salad. Use remaining croutons in another salad or in soup.

Caesar Salad Dressing

makes one cup

⅓ c. finely grated Parmesan cheese
1 t. Dijon mustard
1 t. minced shallot
1 t. minced garlic
¼ t. salt
good grinding black pepper
¾ c. extra virgin olive oil
2 T. lemon juice
1 T. red wine vinegar

In blender, combine cheese, mustard, shallot, garlic, salt and pepper. Blend together.

Add oil in a thin stream while blender is running. Blend in lemon juice and vinegar. Adjust seasoning.

Croutons
about eight cups

¼ c. olive oil
1 T. butter
8 c. slightly stale French bread cut into ½" cubes
2 T. minced garlic

Preheat oven to 325 degrees.

In small skillet cook garlic and olive oil together over low heat stirring often. Turn off heat before garlic colors. Add butter. Pour garlic and oil over bread cubes and mix well.

Place croutons on baking sheet in shallow layer. Bake until golden brown, about half an hour, stirring every five minutes or so to ensure even browning. Pay close attention as croutons can quickly become too dark.

Offering this salad is one of the most satisfactory ways to conclude a dinner party. In spite of any rules about wine and salads clashing, it harmonizes well with red wine, so the wine can keep flowing. Later in the evening, you can bring on the dessert. My all time favorite dinner party dessert, by the way, is Trudy and Joe's marinated citrus.

Romaine Lettuce Salad with Blue Cheese and Walnuts

serves eight

5 T. extra virgin olive oil
1 T. red wine vinegar
¼ t. salt
good grinding black pepper
4 oz. Danish blue cheese, crumbled
12 c. Romaine lettuce hearts, washed, broken into small
  pieces, and dried
½ c. walnut halves, crushed by hand

Put olive oil, vinegar, salt, pepper and half the blue cheese in a large bowl. Mash cheese to make a smooth dressing. Mix in lettuce, coating well.

Divide lettuce on salad plates. Sprinkle each portion with remaining blue cheese and walnuts.

This is an adaptation of the sauteed bay scallop dish (p. 144) I adore but can't usually justify making because of the exorbitant price of scallops. Here the scallops go four times as far in a salad that tastes fabulous in its own right.

Wilted Spinach Salad with Peconic Bay Scallops

serves eight as a first course or four as a main course

1 lb. spinach leaves, preferably very young and tender
1½ lb. Peconic Bay scallops
6 T. olive oil
flour
2 T. minced shallot
½ t. minced garlic
1 T. sherry
2 T. sherry vinegar
salt
good grinding black pepper

Wash and dry spinach thoroughly.

Dry scallops by spreading on paper towels.

Over high heat, heat oil in large skillet until very hot but not smoking. Lightly flour scallops and slip into oil. Flip pan to brown quickly on all sides. Remove from pan with slotted spoon.

Add shallots and garlic to oil, turn heat to low and cook stirring often just to soften. Add sherry and cook a few seconds. Turn off heat and add vinegar, salt and pepper. Mix well. Return scallops to pan, toss in dressing and pour entire contents over spinach, mixing well.

Serve immediately on warm plates.

Ribs are a great stand alone main course needing little as accompaniment, perhaps just some steamed corn.

Barbecued Spareribs
serves four

four racks of baby back pork ribs
1 recipe Hoisin barbecue sauce (following recipe)

Put ribs in a large pot. Add cold water to cover ribs completely. Bring to a boil. Simmer over low heat for twenty minutes. Turn off heat and let ribs stand until cool. Drain well.

Brush ribs with barbecue sauce. Let marinate for an hour or so, reapplying sauce from time to time. Grill ribs over medium heat, brushing with barbecue sauce and turning several times.

Cut into small sections or individual ribs.

Hoisin Barbecue Sauce
makes one and a half cups

1 c. Hoisin sauce
1 c. soy sauce

Mix together.

Moussaka (adapted from Paula Wolfert's *Mediterranean Cooking*)
serves eight

2½ lb. eggplant
salt
½ c. olive oil
1½ lb. lean ground beef
1 medium onion, coarsely grated
1 c. canned tomatoes, coarsely chopped
¼ t. cinnamon
salt
good grinding black pepper
2 c. low fat plain yogurt
3 eggs, well beaten
¾ c. grated Parmesan cheese
3 T. minced parsley
¼ t. freshly grated nutmeg
2 T. melted butter

Peel eggplant and slice into ½″ rounds. Sprinkle generously with salt and leave to stand in colander in sink or over bowl for several hours to discharge liquid. Rinse and dry by spreading on dish or paper towels for a half hour.

Preheat oven to 375 degrees. Line baking sheets with aluminum foil.

Brush eggplant on both sides with a very light coating of olive oil. Reserve remaining oil. Set eggplant slices on baking sheets and put in oven. Cook for ten minutes, turn slices and bake until golden brown, about fifteen minutes longer.

Put meat, reserved olive oil and onion in large heavy bottomed skillet. Cook over medium heat until meat is nicely browned, stirring often. Add tomato, cinnamon, salt, and pepper. Cook to evaporate almost all the liquid, stirring often. Cool.

(continued) ☞

Whisk yogurt in large bowl until smooth. Whisk in eggs, cheese, parsley, salt, pepper and nutmeg.

In greased shallow oven dish with ten cup capacity, arrange half the eggplant slices, overlapping slightly. Spread half the meat on top. Make another layer of eggplant and a final layer of meat. Pour yogurt mixture over all and drizzle with melted butter.

Bake until puffed and golden brown, about forty-five minutes.

This is one of my all time favorite accompaniments, great with fish and seafood, chicken and duck . . . practically anything except an entree with a lemon sauce.

Lemon Pecan Wild Rice (adapted from *Gourmet* magazine)

serves six

1 lemon
4 c. chicken broth
1 T. butter
½ t. salt
1¾ c. wild rice
⅔ c. pecans
3 T. sliced scallions
2 T. minced parsley

Remove the zest from the lemon using a peeler and a light touch. Cut zest into fine julienne. Squeeze the lemon. Put zest, juice, broth, butter, and salt in a medium saucepan and bring to a boil. Stir in the wild rice, cover and simmer gently until cooked, about an hour. The rice should be tender but not mushy.

While rice cooks, preheat oven to 325 degrees. Put pecans on a baking sheet and bake until fragrant, about seven minutes. Chop coarsely. When rice is done, fold in pecans, scallions and parsley.

I love to serve cornbread with practically anything, too.

Cornbread
serves twelve

2 c. flour
1 c. cornmeal
½ c. sugar
2 T. baking powder
¾ t. salt
1½ c. milk
6 T. melted butter
1 egg

Preheat oven to 400 degrees.

Put a large cast iron skillet in oven until hot. Grease bottom generously.

Into large bowl, sift together flour, cornmeal, sugar, baking powder and salt. In another bowl, beat together milk, butter and egg. Add to dry ingredients. Mix just until well combined. Pour into hot pan.

Bake until golden brown and dry at center when tested with a cake tester, about thirty minutes.

Because I don't really like to bake, this is my favorite dessert to whip up on short notice. I often make triple batches of cobbler topping and store it in baggies in the freezer. When someone shows up for dinner, I sweeten, spice and thicken whatever seasonal fruit is on hand, sprinkle with frozen topping, drizzle with melted butter and bake. Instant delicious dessert.

Apple Cobbler
serves eight

3 lb. tart apples
3 T. sugar, or more to taste
1 T. flour
½ t. cinnamon
1 recipe cobbler topping (following recipe)
2 T. melted butter

Put oven rack in top third of oven. Preheat oven to 400 degrees.

Peel and core apples. Cut into thin slices. Mix with sugar, flour and cinnamon. Put fruit in shallow baking pan with an eight cup capacity.

Make cobbler topping and sprinkle over fruit, leaving no bare spots.

Put cobbler in oven and bake until topping is golden brown and fruit is tender when pierced with a cake tester, about forty minutes. Serve warm.

Cobbler Topping
1 c. flour
⅔ c. sugar
1 t. baking powder
½ t. salt
1 egg

Mix dry ingredients in food processor. Mix in egg just long enough to create crumbly mixture.

Margaret Brown, a friend who is super-active in our community, gave me this recipe for the cake she brings to the ten million community events she attends. The cake is always greeted with acclaim. I have made it on several occasions with cooked spaghetti squash substituted for the carrots. Phoebe loves this, but as I've never been able to give it a decent presentation—it's quite a pale cake—I consider it a work in progress. The carrot cake, on the other hand, is definitive.

Another dessert that's more for cooks than bakers.

Carrot Cake
serves twelve to sixteen

2 c. sifted cake flour
2 t. baking soda
2 t. cinnamon
1 t. salt
4 large eggs
1½ c. vegetable oil or melted butter
1⅔ c. sugar
3 c. finely grated carrots
1 recipe cream cheese frosting (following recipe)

Preheat oven to 350 degrees.

Oil and flour a 9″ × 13″ pan.

Sift together cake flour, baking soda, cinnamon and salt.

Beat eggs and oil together until well mixed. Add sugar and mix well. Fold in flour mixture and carrots.

Pour into prepared pan. Bake until cake tests dry with a cake tester, about fifty minutes. Let cake cool in pan. Cover with icing.

Cream Cheese Frosting
makes two cups

12 oz. cream cheese, at room temperature
4 oz. butter, at room temperature
½ lb., or more or less to taste, sifted confectioner's sugar
2 t. vanilla extract

Beat cream cheese, butter, confectioner's sugar and vanilla together until well combined and smooth and light.

You need to own a propane torch if you want to make creme brulee. The little gourmet store ones won't work; you need the type from the hardware store capable of soldering and burning the place down. It may be a worthwhile investment if you really love this dessert.

Crème Brulée
serves six or more

1 qt. heavy cream
1 vanilla bean, split lengthwise
8 egg yolks
scant ¼ c. sugar, plus additional sugar as needed
kettle of boiling water
sugar as needed

Put rack in center of oven and preheat to 325 degrees.

In a heavy-bottomed saucepan over low heat, bring cream and vanilla bean to simmer. Let cream stand 15 minutes. Heat to simmer again.

While cream is reheating, combine yolks and sugar in electric mixer beating well until light lemon colored. Add hot cream, beating only until combined.

Strain cream and discard the vanilla bean. Pour cream into individual shallow custard dishes. Set dishes in baking pan and pour boiling water into baking pan until it reaches halfway up the sides of custard dishes.

Put in oven and bake until almost set. A knife put in center should come out practically clean. This will take about half an hour.

Take from oven, cool slightly and take custard cups from water. Cool on rack. Wrap with plastic wrap and refrigerate for at least six hours.

At serving time, distribute a thin layer of sugar over custards and using plastic wrap press lightly on sugar to compact.

Use blow torch to caramelize. Serve right away.

If you really don't want to make any dessert at all, serve good ice cream with this fantastic sauce.

Hot Fudge Sauce (adapted from Craig Claiborne's *New York Times Cookbook*)
makes two cups

½ c. unsweetened cocoa
1 c. light corn syrup
⅔ c. sugar
½ c. cream
2 T. butter
pinch salt
1 T. brandy
1 t. vanilla extract

Combine cocoa, corn syrup, sugar, cream, butter and salt in small heavy bottomed saucepan. Cook over medium heat, stirring constantly until mixture comes to a full rolling boil. Boil briskly for three minutes, stirring occasionally. Remove from heat, cool slightly, and stir in brandy and vanilla.

No Secrets to Success

For six years Jim and I ran Local Talent as a many purpose food business in rural Cutchogue, NY. We catered, operated a prepared foods store, and, little though I like to bake (although I actually do enjoy bread baking), wholesaled bread and baked goods to one or two local stores and farm stands. Our bread was modeled on a recipe for David Liederman's bread that had been run in the NY Times and had become my home baking standard. The recipe must have come from a commercial formula down sized for the article then up sized by us for our business and again down sized for this book. So the recipe has even more elasticity than the bread and that is saying something!

What I love about the bread is that it's so wet that it bakes with lots of holes, and it's got plenty of fight under the tooth. Local Talent used King Arthur flour in all its breads, and I consider that the indispensable ingredient. King Arthur flour has a wonderful taste, rather than an absence of flavor like most white flour. It's now pretty readily available. If you can't get it or something equally special, don't bother making the bread.

French Bread
makes three loaves

5 c. King Arthur flour
2 packages dry yeast
1 scant T. salt

In a large standing mixer with a flat beater or in a large bowl and using a wooden spoon, mix yeast, flour and salt. Pour in about 2 c. water while mixing until the dough is thoroughly moistened and quite tacky. If using a mixer, switch to a dough hook and knead at medium speed for eight minutes. Otherwise, put dough on a lightly floured counter and knead for about ten minutes. As the gluten in the dough is developed by kneading, the dough will stop looking like "cellulite" and begin to show long strands when the dough is gently pulled apart. At this point stop kneading. Put dough in a large bowl, cover with a dishtowel and let stand in a cool place.

In about three hours, the dough will have risen to its capacity. To test for this, dip several fingers in flour and keeping them together, plunge them about 1" into the dough. If the dough springs back, it needs more time; if it stays still or starts to sink down it is ready to be "rounded." Letting the dough rise too long is worse than not letting it go for long enough.

(*continued*) ☞

Cut the dough with a kitchen knife into three equal pieces. Knead each piece on the floured counter just long enough to remove air pockets, and gather it into a ball.

Set each ball a few inches apart on the counter and cover with dishtowels.

Do the same finger test as before to see if the dough has risen sufficiently after second rising. The second rising will take about half the time of the first.

When the dough has risen fully, heat oven to its highest setting. Form loaves on the lightly floured counter by patting each round into an 8″ circle. Fold in half and pinch edges to seal semi-circle. Fold in half again and pinch into a cigar shape. Placing hands in the center of the "cigar" roll the dough with light pressure while sliding hands towards ends. Breads should be about 12″ long. Cover with the dishtowels and let rest for ten minutes. Stretch bread by holding ends, pulling gently and letting middle sag down. Breads should be stretched a few inches longer than the trays on which they will bake because they will contract a bit when set down. Use the longest bakery trays that will fit in the oven or specially designed French bread pans which will give the bread a rounded shape. If pans are not well seasoned, oil them a bit. Lay the breads straight on the pans with a few inches between breads.

Slash the tops of the breads at an angle with a sharp serrated knife, cutting only ½″ into the surface. Make four or five cuts per bread.

Put breads in the oven and add some water to the oven at the same time. Do this by giving a good blast with a plant mister or using a bulb baster to splash the oven bottom. Repeat every other minute for the first six minutes of baking, then turn oven down to 425 degrees and bake until golden brown. Put on a cooling rack right away.

Ficelle
makes five breads

1 recipe French bread dough (preceding recipe)

When dividing dough, cut into 5 pieces. Otherwise, follow recipe exactly. When divided dough has risen completely, shape as for French bread. After dough relaxes, stretch as for French bread. Ficelle should be almost as long as the French bread and considerably thinner. Bake as for French bread. Baking time will be somewhat less.

Focaccia

makes three breads

2 packages dry yeast
5 c. King Arthur flour
1 scant T. salt
½ c. olive oil
cornmeal as needed

In a large standing mixer with a flat beater or in a large bowl and using a wooden spoon, mix yeast and ½ c. warm water. Let stand ten minutes. Add flour, salt and olive oil. Pour in about 1½ c. cold water while mixing until the dough is thoroughly moistened and quite tacky. If using a mixer, switch to a dough hook and knead at medium speed for eight minutes. Otherwise, put dough on a lightly floured counter and knead for about ten minutes. As the gluten in the dough is developed by kneading, the dough will begin to show long strands when it is gently pulled apart. At that point stop kneading. Put dough in a large bowl, cover with a damp dish towel and let stand in a cool place.

In about three hours, the dough will have risen to its capacity. To test for this, dip several fingers in flour and keeping them together, plunge them about 1″ into the dough. If the dough springs back, it needs more time; if it stays still or starts to sink down it is ready to be "rounded."

Cut the dough with a kitchen knife into three equal pieces. Knead each piece on the floured counter for a few seconds just to remove air pockets, and gather into a ball.

Set each ball a few inches apart on the counter, cover with dish towels and let rise again. The second rising will take about half the time of the first. Do the same finger test as before to see if the dough has risen sufficiently.

(continued) ☞

When the dough has risen fully, set a 10″ cast iron skillet in oven and turn oven to its highest setting. Form loaves on the lightly floured counter by patting each round into a 9″ circle.

Topping:

2 heaping c. sliced onion
3 T. olive oil
1 t. dried thyme
¼ t. salt

Mix topping ingredients.

Take hot skillet out of oven and sprinkle with corn meal. Lay a circle of dough in skillet and spread one third of topping mixture leaving a ½″ border. Put skillet in oven and bake until golden brown, about ten minutes. Remove focaccia to wire rack, wipe out skillet. Repeat with other pieces of dough.

Pizza
makes three small pizzas

1 recipe focaccia, dough only (preceding recipe)
2 c. marinara sauce (p. 39)
½ lb. grated mozzarella
1 c. red pepper, cut in fine julienne
1 T. minced garlic
1 t. fresh oregano
1 T. olive oil

Follow focaccia recipe exactly. Top each 9″ circle with one third of the sauce and one third of the cheese. Toss the pepper, garlic and oregano in the olive oil and sprinkle one third of the pepper mixture over the pizza. Bake as for focaccia until crust is golden brown. Repeat with other two pieces of dough.

Bread Sticks
makes about 100 pieces

1 recipe focaccia, dough only (p. 346)
½ c. sesame seeds

Preheat oven to 300 degrees.

On well floured board, place a piece of twice risen dough and sprinkle with one third of the sesame seeds. Press seeds into dough with rolling pin and roll out to ¼″ thickness. Use pizza cutter or sharp knife to cut in ¼″ wide strips. Place strips on lightly oiled baking sheet with at least ¼″ space between them. Bake until golden brown and thoroughly dry. Cool on a rack. Repeat with other pieces of dough.

Country Bread
makes four loaves

Starter:

1 c. whole wheat flour
1 c. King Arthur flour
1 package dry yeast
¼ onion, held together with wood or metal skewer

Beat together all ingredients except onion with 1 c. cold water until well mixed. Bury onion in mixture. Let stand at room temperature for twenty-four hours. Remove onion.

Feeding starter:

½ c. whole wheat flour
½ c. King Arthur flour

Every two days, refresh starter by mixing in whole wheat flour, bread flour and ½ c. cold water. Let stand at room temperature for an hour or so, then put away in refrigerator.

Making bread:

4 c. King Arthur flour
2 heaping cups starter
1 package dry yeast
scant T. salt
cornmeal, water and flour as needed

One week or more after beginning starter, follow instructions for mixing and rising of French bread exactly using above ingredients and 1 c. cold water, or a bit more or less. Rising times will be longer. When dividing dough, cut into four pieces.

When divided and rounded pieces of dough have risen fully, set a large baking sheet in oven and turn oven to its highest setting. When oven and baking sheet are hot, take out sheet and sprinkle it with cornmeal. Gently set two bread rounds

(*continued*) ☞

on tray. Splash tops of loaves with water, sprinkle with a bit of flour and use a sharp knife to slash top to form "X."

Put in oven and bake as for French bread, misting frequently until loaves begin to brown. Stop misting, bake until well browned. Remove loaves to cooling rack, wipe off sheet and repeat with other two loaves.

NOTE: If oven is large, it is ideal to bake all four loaves at once. but as they rise considerably, there must be sufficient clearance.

Health food stores sell products that mix a number of kinds of flour as six, seven or eight grain mixes. Any fresh mix that contains only grains and seeds should give a good result. Since the white flour here plays a very minor role, I can authorize using any type.

Six Grain Bread
makes two loaves

2 packages dry yeast
2⅔ c. flour
5 c. six grain flour
2 t. salt

Mix yeast with ½ c. warm water and let stand for five minutes.

In a large standing mixer with a dough hook or in a large bowl and using a wooden spoon, mix flour, six grain flour, and salt until well combined. Add yeast and about ½ c. additional warm water, enough to create a dough which is quite tacky. Beat with the dough hook using medium speed or knead by hand for ten minutes. As the gluten in the dough is developed by kneading, the dough will begin to show long strands when it is gently pulled apart, At this point stop kneading.

Put dough in a bowl, cover with a dishcloth, and set aside in a warm spot until doubled in size, two hours or so.

Punch down. Knead back into a ball and cut into two equal pieces. Shape into loaves by forming into rectangles which you let rest a few minutes. Roll up rectangles and pull ends underneath. Put into greased loaf pans. Cover with dishcloths and let rise until above pan top and light looking.

When dough has almost fully risen, put oven racks in the middle of the oven and preheat oven to 425 degrees.

Bake risen dough for fifteen minutes, then turn heat down to 325 degrees. Continue baking for twenty-five minutes longer. Turn hot bread out of pan and return to oven for ten minutes more.

Cool before slicing.

Among Local Talent's specialties were handmade croissants, pains au choco-
late, and especially morning buns. Their popularity overtook our ability to roll
dough, so we decided to invest in a device for rolling dough mechanically,
called a sheeter. Before going to test machines, I made up a large quantity of
dough for testing. Eleven year old Phoebe stood next to me as I waged battle
with a huge rolling pin against a large and intractable piece of dough. After
some time, she said, "You know how some people want their children to take
over their business? You don't feel that way do you?" Certainly not, but if
anyone wants to take over knowing how to make croissants, that would be
great!

These croissants and variants can be made up and stored in the freezer for a
week or two. When needed, set on baking tray, thaw, and allow to rise
according to directions for unfrozen dough.

Croissants
makes about thirty croissants

Dough:

2 c. warm milk
2 packages dry yeast
5¼ c. King Arthur flour, plus extra for rolling
scant ½ c. sugar
2 t. salt

Dissolve yeast in milk. Put flour, sugar and salt in mixer bowl.
Add milk and yeast and mix with a wooden spoon or paddle
until just mixed. Cover with plastic wrap and refrigerate
overnight.

Butter layer:

14 oz. cold butter
scant ½ c. flour

Work flour into butter by using a rolling pin and pastry
scraper. Don't use your hands in order to keep butter cool.

Take dough from refrigerator and roll into a 10″ × 18″ rectangle with long side running top to bottom. Put butter on in

(continued) ☞

small pieces to cover lower two thirds of dough, going not quite to the edges.

Fold down unbuttered top third and enclose with remaining third. Rotate dough 90 degrees.

Lightly flour counter or board and surface of dough. Roll out to same 10″ × 18″ size and fold in thirds again, starting from top. Rotate 90 degrees and repeat. Wrap dough in plastic wrap and let rest two hours.

Take out dough and repeat twice more. Wrap and return to refrigerator and let rest two hours.

Lightly flour counter or board and surface of dough. Roll dough into a sheet about 18″ wide and 24″ long.

Cut into strips 6″ wide, cutting lengthwise. Cut strips into rectangles about 7″ wide on longest side and 5″ on short sides. Roll from long side and put on baking sheets, curving ends in as you set them down leaving a good inch between pieces. Let rise until light looking, about forty minutes.

Preheat oven to 400 degrees toward the end of the rising period.

Egg wash:

2 eggs
3 T. milk

Make egg wash by beating together eggs and milk. Brush over risen croissants gently, using a pastry brush. Bake croissants until golden brown, about thirty minutes. Cool on rack.

Pains au Chocolate
makes about thirty pieces

1 recipe croissant dough (preceding recipe), rolled out as for croissants
1 lb. best quality semi sweet chocolate, cut in ¼" pieces

Cut dough into 6" squares. Just below center, put a line of chocolate, leaving a tiny bit of space on edge. Roll. Set flap sides down on baking sheet. Let rise until light looking, brush with egg wash and bake as above.

Morning Buns
makes about three dozen pieces

1 recipe croissant dough (p. 353), rolled out as for croissants
1 c. lightly packed dark brown sugar
2½ c. pecan halves or pieces

Spread sugar over dough, leaving ½" border all around. Roll up lengthwise to form a long cylinder. Stretch cylinder slightly so dough is a bit less than 2" in diameter.

Grease muffin pans. Drop a heaping tablespoon of pecans in each cup.

Slice dough into 1" pieces. Put a piece in each cup.

Let rise until light looking, brush with egg wash and bake as above.

Let cool for ten minutes in muffin pans. Remove buns with a dinner knife and invert on cooling rack.

Anyone who can make croissant dough can make puff pastry. And then use it for cheese straws or sausage straws or in place of pie dough especially where it's used as a top crust.

Puff Pastry

makes two pounds, enough for several projects

Dough:

4 c. flour
1 c. cake flour
1 T. salt
2 sticks cold butter, cut in ¼″ pieces

Mix flours and salt in food processor. Cut in butter well. And 2 c. cold water and pulse to just barely mix. Wrap dough in plastic wrap and refrigerate.

Butter layer:

6 sticks slightly soft butter
½ c. flour

Work flour into butter by using a rolling pin and pastry scraper. Don't use your hands in order to keep butter cool. Form dough into 5″ square. Wrap in plastic wrap and refrigerate an hour or so.

After butter is cold, remove dough and butter from refrigerator. Roll dough into 9″ round. Place butter square on top and enclose in dough.

Lightly flour board or counter and roll dough into 12″ × 20″ rectangle with long side running top to bottom. Fold down top third. Then fold up bottom third. Rotate 90 degrees and repeat.

Wrap dough in plastic and refrigerate one hour.

Repeat.

Repeat a second time for a total of six rolling and foldings. Dough is now ready to use or can be cut into two pieces, well wrapped and frozen for a month or two. Thaw before using, but roll while still cold.

We got into mail order baking with "Brownies on Tour" in order to bring our resort based business onto a more year round schedule. We soon found that mail order desserts had their own seasonal insanity, at least with products that have no shelf life. The lunacy of Christmas/Chanukuh season varied slightly depending on where the Hebrew calendar set Chanukah down. When it fell early, we had carte blanche to ship corporate orders sooner, and when it fell on top of Christmas, the season compressed into ten brutal days.

This was nothing, however, compared to Valentine's Day, the most sacred day on the chocoholic calendar. Deliveries on February 13th or 15th were not going to cut it. I'll always remember the sob filled phone call of the paramour whose beau's brownies duly delivered by us, languished undelivered in his office mail room.

The week before one particularly memorable Valentine's Day we got an absolutely splendid and unexpected write up in the NY Times food section. The avalanche of orders had me working around the clock for several days, with tears streaming down my face through the last of them. When I finally saw my home and children again on Valentine's Day, Jim, my funny valentine, had left a gift—a competitor's brownies!

Our commercial brownies were made as small bars in specially made pans to ensure the perfect crust to center ratio. However, without the pans this is about as good as it gets. The only trick is making sure not to over bake. Remove brownies while the center still tests quite wet, although not an absolute liquid.

Brownies
makes one dozen large brownies

2 sticks unsalted butter
8 oz. unsweetened chocolate, chopped into ¼″ chunks
6 eggs
3½ c. sugar
2 T. vanilla
2 T. instant espresso
½ t. salt
1½ c. all purpose flour
1 c. walnut halves (optional)

Preheat oven to 425 degrees.

Butter an 8″ × 12″ pan and line the bottom with baker's parchment or wax paper and butter the paper.

(continued) ☞

In a medium saucepan, heat butter until melted and bubbling hot. Turn off heat and add chocolate. Stir together well until chocolate has melted and mixture is smooth.

Put eggs, sugar, vanilla, espresso and salt together in a large bowl. Beat with an electric mixer at high speed for ten minutes. Add chocolate and butter mixture and beat at low speed until thoroughly combined. Add flour and mix at low speed until flour disappears. Add walnuts if desired. Pour batter into prepared pan. Level batter using a metal spatula or knife.

Bake for 20 minutes. Lower oven heat to 350 degrees and continue baking for twenty minutes more. Do not bake until a cake tester tests dry. These brownies are intended to be very moist.

Cool brownies in pan and then cut around with a knife to loosen edges. Unmold brownies onto a cutting board, remove paper, and then turn right side up. Cut into twelve 3″ squares.

We developed several unique variations on the basic brownie, starting with a Black Forest brownie with dried cherries in Kirsch. The Antwerp cookie is its cookie incarnation, also from our mail order line.

Antwerp Cookies
makes about six dozen

1½ c. dried cherries
1 T. Kirsch
4 T. butter
24 oz. semi-sweet chocolate chips
6 oz. unsweetened chocolate
4 eggs
2¼ c. sugar
½ t. instant espresso
½ t. vanilla extract
¼ t. almond extract
½ c. flour
½ t. baking powder
½ t. baking soda
12 oz. chocolate chips

Several days before making cookies, coarsely chop cherries. Mix with Kirsch and let stand covered, stirring from time to time.

Melt butter, half the chocolate chips and all the unsweetened chocolate in double boiler or microwave. Stir until smooth and cool slightly.

In electric mixer beat eggs with sugar for a minute or so. Add melted chocolate mixture, espresso, vanilla and almond extracts. Mix flour with baking powder and baking soda. Fold flour mixture, remaining chocolate chips and chopped cherries into mixture and stir to combine.

Drop rounded tablespoons of dough onto well greased baking sheets leaving a bit of space between cookies.

Preheat oven to 350 degrees.

Brush cookies with water. Bake until just firm, about ten minutes.

Istanbul Cookies
makes about six dozen

½ lb. soft butter
1⅔ c. sugar
2 eggs
¾ t. vanilla extract
¾ t. almond extract
4 c. shelled, unsalted pistachios
1½ c. flour

Mix butter and sugar together well. Beat eggs in thoroughly. Add vanilla and almond extracts. Fold in pistachios and flour. Form cylinders, wrap and freeze.

To bake, thaw dough slightly and cut with heavy sharp knife into slices ¼″ thick. Lay on cookie sheet.

Preheat oven to 375 degrees,

Bake until light golden brown, about ten minutes.

While not able to survive the rigors of mail order, these bars are great, too.

Lemon Bars
makes one half sheet pan, approximately 48 bars

Base:

3¾ c. flour
1 packed c. brown sugar
¾ t. salt
2 sticks and 2 T. softened butter

Preheat oven to 350 degrees.

Grease a 12″ × 18″ sheet pan, cover with baker's parchment or wax paper, and butter parchment or paper.

In a food processor fitted with metal blade, combine flour, brown sugar and salt. Add butter. Process until dough looks like cornmeal.

Spread base in pan. Press down.

Bake base for fifteen minutes, rotating pan half-way through baking.

Make topping.

Topping:

3 c. sugar
1 c. lemon juice
¼ c. grated lemon rind or rind of 4 lemons
6 eggs
⅔ c. flour
¾ t. baking powder

In food processor, combine all filling ingredients. Pour mixture over partially baked crust. Bake for about twenty minutes, rotating pan halfway through baking until lightly browned and set.

Cool and slice into small squares. Sprinkle on confectioner's sugar using a small sieve.

Pecan Bars
makes one half sheet pan, approximately 48 bars

Base:

1 c. confectioner's sugar
4 c. flour
1 lb. softened butter

Preheat oven to 350 degrees.

Grease a 12″ × 18″ sheet pan, cover with baker's parchment or wax paper, butter parchment or paper.

In a food processor fitted with metal blade, combine confectioner's sugar and flour.

Add butter. Process until dough looks like cornmeal. Spread base in pan.

Bake for twenty-five minutes, rotating pan half-way through baking.

Make topping.

Topping:

2 sticks plus 6 T. butter
1 packed c. dark brown sugar
1 c. honey
¾ c. cream
½ t. salt
7 c. pecan halves

In large saucepan over low heat, melt butter. Add brown sugar and honey. Stir to dissolve. Off heat stir in cream and salt. Add pecans and mix in well. Pour mixture over partially baked base.

Bake for twenty minutes rotating pan halfway through baking.

Cool completely before cutting.

Two Tone Bars
makes one half sheet pan, approximately 48 bars

Base:

3 c. flour
1⅓ packed c. dark brown sugar
3 sticks softened butter
4 egg yolks
1½ t. vanilla

Preheat oven to 350 degrees.

Grease a 12″ × 18″ sheet pan, cover with baker's parchment or wax paper, butter parchment or paper.

In a food processor fitted with metal blade, combine flour and brown sugar. Add butter. Process until dough looks like cornmeal. Add yolks and vanilla with a few quick pulses. Spread mixture in pan. Press down.

Bake for twenty-five minutes until lightly browned, rotating pan half-way through baking.

Make topping.

Topping:

1 lb. best quality semisweet or bittersweet chocolate, cut
    into small pieces
2 c. walnuts or lightly toasted pecans, coarsely chopped

Spread chocolate over baked base. Return pan to oven for three minutes to melt chocolate. Spread with metal spatula. Sprinkle nuts over hot chocolate.

Cool completely before cutting.

Lorette Patzwald, the talented baker who worked for Local Talent, developed this great recipe for the lightest cheesecake and together we came up with these many variations.

Plain Cheesecake
serves twelve or more

9 T. melted butter
2¼ c. graham cracker crumbs
2 lbs. cream cheese at room temperature
1 c. sugar
2 eggs
1 T. cornstarch
1 t. vanilla extract
½ t. almond extract
1 c. sour cream

Preheat oven to 450 degrees.

Mix butter and crumbs and evenly line the bottom and sides of a 9″ spring form pan, being careful not to leave a thicker layer where sides and bottom meet.

Beat cream cheese until soft. Add sugar and beat until light and fluffy. Add eggs one at a time, beating well after each. Add cornstarch, extracts, and sour cream to batter and mix thoroughly.

Put batter in pan. Level with spatula and tap pan gently a few times to remove air pockets.

Bake for 15 minutes. Turn oven to 200 degrees and bake twenty minutes or so longer until cakes puff up. Turn off oven, open door and let stand twenty minutes before removing to rack.

Cool and refrigerate.

Hazelnut Cheesecake
serves twelve

1 recipe plain cheesecake (preceding recipe)
¼ c. hazelnut paste
3 T. Frangelico (hazelnut liqueur)

After adding eggs, add hazelnut paste and Frangelico.

Raspberry Cheesecake
serves twelve

1 recipe plain cheesecake (p. 364)
⅓ c. best quality raspberry preserves

Spoon preserves on top of unbaked cake in six places. Swirl with knife to marbleize.

Peach Praline Cheesecake
serves twelve

2 large ripe peaches
1 t. lemon juice
1 recipe plain cheesecake (p. 364) made with 1½ t. almond
  extract instead of vanilla extract and with 2 T. cornstarch
¼ c. praline powder (p. 13)

Bring a small saucepan of water to boil. Boil peaches for fifteen seconds. Drain and run under cold water to chill. Slip off skins.

Slice peaches into food processor. Add lemon juice and puree. Measure 1 c. and use remaining puree for something else.

Add 1 c. peach puree to cheesecake batter after eggs are well incorporated. Sprinkle cake top with praline powder before baking.

Pumpkin Cheesecake

serves twelve

1 recipe plain cheesecake (p. 364) made without vanilla and
   almond extracts and with 2 T. cornstarch
1 t. cinnamon
¼ t. ground ginger
¼ t. ground cloves
¼ t. freshly grated nutmeg
1½ c. pumpkin puree
¼ c. praline powder (p. 13)

Beat cinnamon, ginger, cloves and nutmeg in with cream
cheese when adding sugar. Mix cornstarch with pumpkin
puree and add after last egg is incorporated. Sprinkle cake
top with praline powder before baking.

Chocolate Cheesecake

serves twelve

9 T. melted butter
2¼ c. chocolate wafer cookie crumbs
12 oz. semi sweet chocolate, cut into small pieces, or use
   chocolate chips
½ c. strong hot coffee
1 lb. cream cheese at room temperature
1⅓ c. sugar
4 eggs
1½ t. vanilla extract

Preheat oven to 450 degrees.

Mix butter and crumbs and evenly line the bottom and sides
of a 9″ spring form pan, being careful not to leave a thicker
layer where sides and bottom meet.

Combine chocolate and coffee. Stir from time to time until
chocolate is completely melted and smooth.

(continued) ☞

Beat cream cheese until soft. Add sugar and beat until light and fluffy. Add eggs one at a time, beating well after each. Beat in the cooled chocolate and vanilla.

Put batter in pan. Level with spatula and tap pan gently a few times to remove air pockets.

Bake for 15 minutes. Turn oven to 200 degrees and bake twenty minutes or so longer until cakes puff up. Turn off oven, open door and let stand twenty minutes before removing to rack. Cool and refrigerate.

This recipe puts blackberries to their best possible use.

Chocolate Raspberry or Blackberry Cheesecake
serves twelve

1 recipe chocolate cheesecake (preceding recipe) with 1 T.
   cassis substituted for vanilla
1½ c. raspberries or blackberries, slightly mashed

After chocolate is well incorporated, fold berries into batter.

This simple pound cake and the orange poppy variation are the sort of understated finale I like, so I will exit with them.

Lemon Cake
serves twelve

2 lemons
3 c. flour
2 t. baking powder
½ t. salt
2 sticks butter
2¼ c. sugar
4 eggs
1 c. milk

Preheat oven to 400 degrees.

Butter and flour a 9″ tube pan.

Grate lemon rind and juice lemons.

Sift together flour, baking powder and salt. Cream butter until soft. Add 1¾ c. sugar and beat until light and fluffy looking. Add eggs one at a time beating well after each. Add lemon rind. Add half the flour mixture, beating slowly just to incorporate. Add half the milk and beat until just mixed in. Repeat with remaining half of flour and milk.

Pour batter into pan. Level with spatula and tap pan gently a few times to remove air pockets.

Put in oven. After ten minutes, lower heat to 350 degrees. Bake until light brown and cooked through. A cake tester will just come out dry after about one hour. Cool ten minutes on wire rack. Invert and remove pan.

Mix ⅓ c. lemon juice with remaining ¾ c. sugar and brush this glaze all over warm cake.

Orange Poppy Cake
serves twelve

1 orange
1 lemon
3 c. flour
2 t. baking powder
½ t. salt
3 T. poppy seeds
2 sticks butter
2¼ c. sugar
4 eggs
1 c. milk

Preheat oven to 400 degrees.

Butter and flour a 9″ tube pan.

Grate orange rind and juice orange and lemon separately.

Sift together flour, baking powder and salt. Add poppy seeds.

Cream butter until soft. Add 1¾ c. sugar and beat until light and fluffy looking. Add eggs one at a time beating well after each. Add orange rind. Add half the flour mixture, beating slowly just to incorporate. Add half the milk and beat until just mixed in. Repeat with remaining half of flour and milk.

Pour batter into pan. Level with spatula and tap pan gently a few times to remove air pockets.

Put in oven. After ten minutes, lower heat to 350 degrees. Bake until light brown and cooked through. A cake tester will just come out dry after about one hour. Cool ten minutes on wire rack. Invert and remove pan.

Mix 3 T. orange juice and 2 T. lemon juice with remaining ¾ c. sugar and brush this glaze all over warm cake.

INDEX

Notes

Notes